CLOCK AND WATCH ESCAPEMENTS

CLOCK AND WATCH ESCAPEMENTS

W. J. GAZELEY, F.B.H.I.

ROBERT HALE · LONDON

© *W. J. Gazeley 1956*
First published in Great Britain 1956
Reprinted 1973, 1975, 1977, 1980 and 1992

ISBN 0-7090-4738-X

Robert Hale Limited
Clerkenwell House
Clerkenwell Green
London EC1R 0HT

Printed in Great Britain by
St Edmundsbury Press Limited, Bury St Edmunds, Suffolk.
Bound by WBC Bookbinders Limited.

CONTENTS

PREFACE

THE AUTHOR'S BOOK *Watch and Clock Making and Repairing* was written to meet a demand by readers of *The Watchmaker, Jeweller and Silversmith,* and it has since been felt that the subject of escapements for both clocks and watches could be treated in more detail because of its special importance. The treatment is again based on practical experience as the author specialised for a time in escapement making. Some escapements described are no longer fitted in new clocks and watches, but many examples are still in use and will require repair from time to time, and as there is very little literature available on the subject this book seeks to provide the necessary information. It is also hoped that the reader's interest will be aroused by the detailed descriptions of these old escapements as well as of their likely failings. Again, as the mass-produced watch is cheaper there is no longer a large demand for hand-made escapements, but those in use will require repair for many years to come and replacements may be called for. Complete information for making all types of escapements and for the location and correction of faults in both modern mass-produced and hand-finished watches is therefore provided.

Polishing is another subject in which many readers show great interest. The tools described and illustrated have all been made by the author although not necessarily to his own design. With practice their use can give high finishes in the minimum of time.

To avoid unnecessary repetition reference is at times made to *Watch and Clock Making and Repairing*.

The author hopes that the book will be a real help to the younger members of the craft and will encourage them to maintain the high-quality craftsmanship for which English watchmakers have always been noted.

W. J. GAZELEY

vii

PART I
CLOCK ESCAPEMENTS

THE VERGE OR CROWN WHEEL ESCAPEMENT

THE VERGE ESCAPEMENT IS the earliest form of escapement known. There is ample evidence to show that it was invented prior to the thirteenth century, but neither the exact date nor the name of the inventor is known. It is, of course, now obsolete, but there are still many verge clocks requiring attention.

The verge escapement consisted of a crown wheel, *i.e.* a wheel with its teeth set at right angles to the plane of the wheel, and the verge itself, which was an arbor pivoted at both ends and having two pallets protruding from the sides, one at each end and set at a little more than a right angle to each other.

The verge was set at right angles to the wheel, and as the wheel revolved, the teeth engaged the pallets alternately, one side of the wheel engaging one pallet and the opposite side engaging the other pallet. Thus the verge was first pushed one way and then the other continuously as the wheel revolved.

Mounted on the verge arbor was either (1) a foliot, (2) a balance or (3) a pendulum, whose function was to steady the action and to control the speed of the backward-and-forward motion of the verge. This motion is sometimes termed oscillation, but is more commonly known as vibration.

(1) *The Foliot*—This was a bar fitted to the verge, notched progressively from the centre to the outside to carry weights which were hung on to the bar as a means of controlling its speed or of regulating the time taken for each vibration, the farther the weight from the centre, the slower the vibration, and vice versa.

(2) *The Balance*—This was simply a rim of metal joined by a single arm to its centre, which was again mounted on the verge. There was no means of regulating the balance type except through the motive power, which was increased to make the clock faster and reduced to slow the clock down. The verge escapement is very susceptible to changes in motive power.

(3) *The Pendulum*—This was a big improvement on the other types, as it gave greater control of the clock. At first the pendulum was fitted directly on the verge, and the back pivot was formed into a knife edge and was supported in a V-bed to lessen the friction caused by the weight of the pendulum rod and its bob. In the later pendulum clocks with verge escapements a crutch was fitted to the

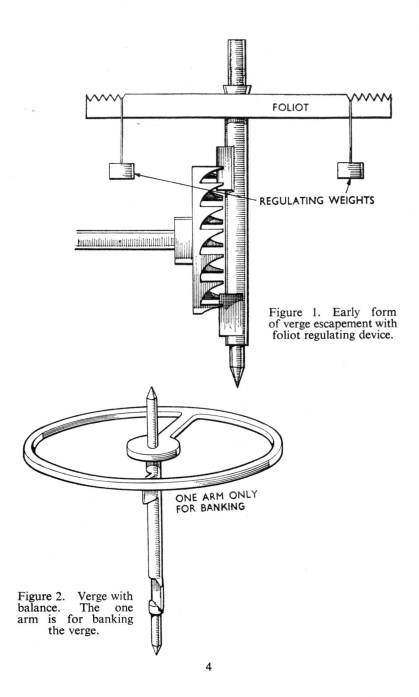

FOLIOT

REGULATING WEIGHTS

Figure 1. Early form of verge escapement with foliot regulating device.

ONE ARM ONLY FOR BANKING

Figure 2. Verge with balance. The one arm is for banking the verge.

4

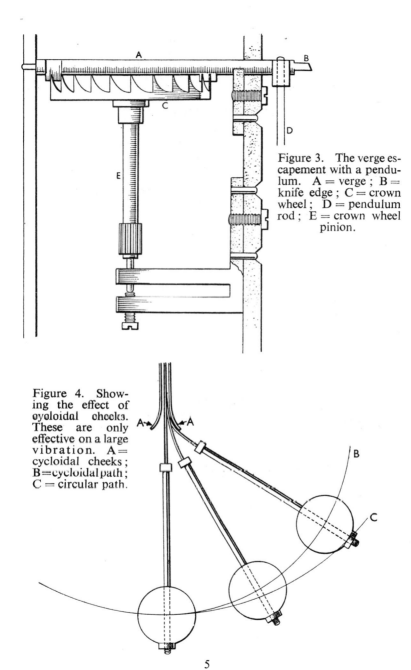

Figure 3. The verge escapement with a pendulum. A = verge ; B = knife edge ; C = crown wheel ; D = pendulum rod ; E = crown wheel pinion.

Figure 4. Showing the effect of cycloidal checks. These are only effective on a large vibration. A = cycloidal cheeks ; B = cycloidal path ; C = circular path.

verge and the pendulum had a separate suspension. This was a further advance in timekeeping. The older type, however, was still used until a much later date, as it was cheaper. The verge escapement gave an arc to a pendulum of about 90° to 100°. This was considered to be unsatisfactory because the pendulum did not traverse a cycloidal path, and as a result the time of vibration was not constant. The pendulum was therefore supported on lines and what are called cycloid cheeks were added, these cheeks forcing the pendulum on to a cycloidal path.

EXAMINING THE ESCAPEMENT

The verge is a recoil escapement, *i.e.* the wheel recoils as soon as the vibration exceeds the arc required to allow the wheel to escape. When commencing the examination it is necessary to see that the crown wheel pinion pivots are a close fit in their holes and that the holes are not oval or elongated by wear.

The action of the escapement is examined with a small amount of power on the train. The crutch or pendulum should be led first one way until the crown wheel tooth only just drops off the pallet, and the exact amount the tooth moves until it is arrested by the other pallet should be noted, then the direction is reversed until the tooth from the other pallet is released, and again the amount of tooth movement should be noted. The movement should be exactly the same in each direction.

Drop

This tooth movement is called drop, and as it is all loss, it must always be kept to a minimum. If the drop on each side is unequal it is obvious that there must be excessive drop, otherwise the wheel tooth will not be free on the side with least drop when at correct depth.

Unequal drop can be caused by two factors, namely the verge not being planted truly central across the crown wheel or the verge not being parallel to the wheel teeth. Sometimes when an old clock is being examined it is found that the drop is equal on one part of the wheel, but as the wheel revolves the drop becomes unequal. This is caused by the wheel being either out of truth, out of flat or unequally divided; whatever the cause, this inequality of drop must be rectified.

Worn Pallets

The pads or pallets must be in good condition. Before examining these it is important first to wedge up the train so that the crown wheel cannot run. (This is imperative because the crown wheel teeth are easily damaged.) When the wheel is wedged the back cock is taken off and then the verge is removed. If one did not wedge the train, the taking out of the verge would release the wheel, which

6

would start to run at increasing speed until the teeth struck one of the pallets, and the wheel would probably be ruined, or at least damaged.

The front pivot is now examined to see that it is smooth and quite round. These pivots often wear on the top side and become oval, in which case they must be repaired.

The pads are the next part to be examined. They will probably have wear marks on them, and deeper wear-like pits; if either of these faults is present the pads must be smoothed up.

If the movement has a knife-edged pivot this is now scrutinised.

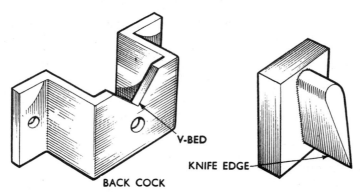

Figure 5. Knife-edged pivot and V-bed which supports it. This method is only used when the pendulum is mounted directly on the verge arbor.

Some movements have a pivot where there is a crutch, but where the pendulum is attached to the verge arbor there is, or should be, a knife-edged pivot. This knife edge should be dead centre with the arbor, but if it is much worn the arbor becomes too low and thus out of truth, and the escapement will not function. If there is only a small amount of wear the sides can be repaired and the edge brought up sharp again, but if the wear is too great the only thing to do is to fit a new knife edge.

The Third or Contrate Wheel

The next step is to examine the depth or gearing between the third wheel, which is a contrate wheel, and the crown wheel pinion. This pinion must not be proportionately small in relation to the third wheel because the escapement is a recoil and the action is thus two-fold: when the wheel is giving impulse or pushing the pallet the third wheel is a driver; when the crown wheel is recoiling the pinion acts as a driver and pushes the third wheel backwards. If the pinion is small there is every chance of the leaf butting on top of the tooth

7

of the third wheel. The size of the crown wheel pinion should therefore be correct. (Further details of gearing will be found in *Watch and Clock Making and Repairing.*)

In some of the very old clocks where the wheels are hand cut it is often difficult, but one can compromise and at the same time guard against this butting fault. The endshake of the contrate pinion should never be excessive. It must have endshake, but the less the better.

To Repair the Crown Wheel

Where the wheel teeth are only slightly damaged the wheel and pinion should be placed in the lathe between female dead centres and the top of the teeth carefully turned with a graver until the tops are all of equal height. The wheel teeth are then filed up by hand to leave a flat top of about 1° on each tooth. It is important that the straight front of the teeth is not touched under any circumstances, all the touching up being done from the back of the tooth only. This is the only way to keep the division, *i.e.* the space between the teeth, equal.

If the wheel is out of flat the arms or the pinion arbor may be bent. If, on the other hand, the wheel is out of truth it must be trued.

LEAVE COLLET
FULL TILL LAST

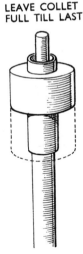

Figure 6. Recolleting the pinion to raise the wheel. The collet is placed high, the back being finished off last.

This is done by dismounting the wheel from the pinion and mounting it in the lathe perfectly true, and with a cutter in the cross slide or slide rest turning the hole perfectly true. The best way to be sure of the wheel being true is to turn a sink in a wood chuck into which the wheel will fit precisely.

It will be necessary to recollet the pinion because it will not fit the new hole in the wheel. When recolleting it is always as well to mount the wheel high on the pinion, as the correct adjustment of the escapement depth can be made with the adjusting endpiece screw fully low. This screw is situated at the bottom of the pottance or the cock supporting the bottom pivot of the crown wheel pinion.

If when the wheel is trued the drop is not constant it means the wheel is unequally divided.

Equalling the Divisions—The wheel can be put up in the wheel-cutting engine and the front of the teeth recut with a very sharp single-blade cutter until all the fronts of the teeth have been cut with the cutter.

It is as well to set the machine so that the cutter will cut the most forward tooth and then gradually let the blade in until all the teeth are touched. It is useless to try to recut the teeth from the backs.

When the wheel has been recut and trued, *etc.*, it seems there is some irregularity when the clock is running. This is often due to the variations in the motive power, so one should not be deceived by the sound. As previously stated the third wheel is often the offender.

Equalling the Drops—When the wheel teeth have been repaired and the wheel trued, *etc.*, the drops may be constant but still unequal. This is due to the verge being out of position. The verge should lie dead central over the top crown wheel pivot. It requires only a small deviation from dead central to make the drops unequal, so testing the escapement is the only check.

Looking squarely at the verge and crown wheel with the front plate as the nearest point, the wheel should be visualised as a clock dial with the back-plate side of the wheel as XII o'clock, the verge passing through XII and VI.

If there is too much drop from the pallet at XII this means the verge lays towards XI, *i.e.* providing the crown wheel turns clockwise, C, Figure 7. To correct this the verge must be moved clockwise or towards the I o'clock, A, Figure 7, the reason being that the wheel tooth will be released later and also the drop on to the pallet will be relatively earlier. If the extra drop is say 0·01 in. the verge must be moved half the distance, *i.e.* 0·005 in., because the drop on to the pallet will also be altered by the same amount. In nearly all escapements any alteration on one pallet also alters the other pallet. This alteration can be carried out by moving the back cock over, but it may be necessary to elongate the screw holes to allow the cock to move.

After the holes have been treated the back cock is lightly screwed in place, and a piece of boxwood, which will not bruise brass, is put against the side of the cock and used as a punch. A sharp blow with a hammer on the punch will force the steady pins in the cock, and the

9

cock will move over. It is important to make sure the cock will still go back to a constant position afterwards. Sometimes the steady

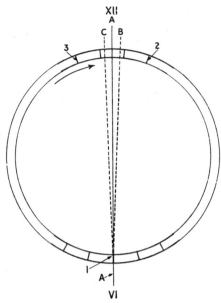

Figure 7. Correcting the drop. (1) Denotes VI o'clock. (2) Denotes I o'clock. (3) Denotes XI o'clock. A = centre line across wheel; if the verge lies towards B the drop will be too little; if it lies towards C the drop will be too great.

pins in the cock will be sheared off, but usually the amount of alteration is too small and the pins will readily give that amount.

The Knife Edge

This is a very important part of the verge, and is formed from the back pivot in order to reduce the friction when the pendulum is fitted directly on to the verge.

The knife edge is often worn, or as a result of various repairs is out of centre, and as a result the back-verge pallet is deeper into the crown wheel than its opposite number. This gives a false impression with regard to drop and makes the action of the escapement uncertain because the verge will not be running true.

If the knife edge is only slightly worn it can, of course, be repaired and smoothed, but if, on the other hand, it is badly worn and off centre a new knife edge must be fitted.

10

To do this the pendulum rod, which is riveted into the verge block and which will easily punch out, is removed, then the verge block must be softened without softening the back pallet of the verge. If

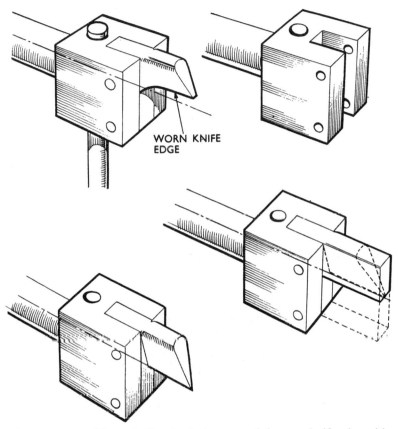

WORN KNIFE EDGE

Figure 8. Repairing a knife-edged pivot: *top left*, worn knife edge with outline of the repair; *top right*, knife edge cut away and block slotted to take plate steel; *bottom right*, plate steel fitted and rivets in place; *bottom left*, the complete job with the knife edge fixed in place and polished.

this pallet is held in a large pair of pliers whilst the block is being heated the heat will not reach it and it will remain hard.

Next the old knife edge is filed away, but the block must not be reduced, then a slot is filed in the place where the knife edge is to be. This slot should be quite straight so that a piece of suitable flat steel can be closely fitted into it.

A piece of flat steel is chosen which can be hardened, and this is

11

fitted into the slot which has been made. Two holes are now drilled in the block and through the piece of steel which is to form the new knife edge, these being lightly broached so that steel pins can be closely fitted. The knife edge to-be is now pinned in place with temporary pins and the end filed up into a male centre. The verge is now put in female centres and the knife-edge centre drawn whichever way required until the verge arbor runs true. The centre remaining will be the position of the active part of the knife edge.

An equal amount is filed off each side, checking this by putting the verge in the clock and seeing that the sides of the knife edge, which should be about 20° to each other, are the same distance from the sides of the V-bed as each tooth is dropped. When the knife edge is almost finished it is removed from the verge block and hardened. After hardening it is cleaned up and put back in place in the block.

Two almost straight pins are now filed up to fit the two holes previously drilled, and are pushed in. After making sure that the knife edge is firmly held in place, the pins are given a tap with a hammer to give extra tightness; this must be done with care, as the knife edge is hard.

The pins are shortened until the smaller ends stand proud by about 0·003 in., and the other ends are almost flush with the block. The pins are now lightly riveted over until flush with the block. The knife edge should be checked in the clock to see that it has not altered in the process.

Polishing the Knife Edge—The knife edge now has to be smoothed and polished. This is carried out by laying the edge on a piece of cork or willow wood and rubbing the flats of the edge quite smooth with a piece of flat steel of suitable width, which after having been filed smooth and flat has had a mixture of powdered oilstone and oil smeared on the filed face. The flat steel or polisher as it is called is filed up again to make it quite clean and is then smeared with a mixture of diamantine and oil, after which the sides of the knife edge are rubbed with this until quite bright. The edge is not a razor edge but is slightly rounded and about 0·001 in. wide. The total length is now shortened until it is just free of the endplate, which is screwed to the back cock.

The top of the knife edge must be just free of the banking block, which is fitted to the endplate. The object of this block is to prevent the verge from rising up and out of action with the crown wheel, and the endplate is to keep the endshake of the verge close. The end of the knife edge that touches the endplate must be filed back at an angle so that only a small part is in contact, thus keeping the friction to a minimum.

The V-Bed

The V-bed must be clean with no root in the base, and the sides must be at an angle of about 140° from each other, otherwise if the vibration of the pendulum is long the sides of the knife edge may bounce on the sides of the V-bed. The usual vibration of a verge pendulum with a knife edge is about 90° to 100° and the angle of the knife edge is 20°, so this leaves very little. If left more than 140° the knife edge will tend to come out of the bottom of the V-bed and run up the sides, with serious loss of impulse.

Making a New Verge

Sometimes the general condition of the verge makes a complete new verge necessary. For this a piece of flat steel which can be hardened and tempered is chosen. For the usual size a piece $\frac{3}{16}$ in. by $\frac{1}{8}$ in. is suitable. One side is left untouched, but the other side is filed to suit the clock.

The crown wheel and the back cock are put in place and the steel is laid across the plates where it will be fitted. First the front pivot

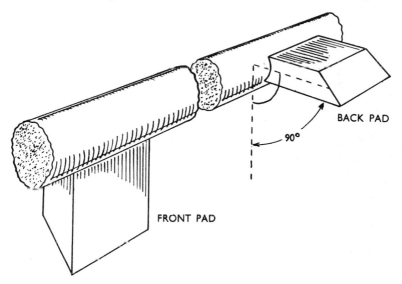

Figure 9. Showing correct angle of pads to each other; 90° is the best angle.

is marked off, then in turn the front pallet, the back pallet, the pendulum block and the knife edge. The metal not required is next filed away, leaving the pads standing up and the pendulum block, *etc.*

Enough metal is now filed away to leave the remaining steel of square section, which is again filed until it is approximately round. The steel is now twisted until the pads or pallets-to-be are at 90° to each other. This is done by gripping each pad in a pair of strong pliers and heating the steel in between to red heat, and at the same

13

time twisting the pallets until the correct angle is reached. The back pad is then held and what will be the pendulum block and knife edge twisted so that it lies evenly between the two pallet pads.

It is necessary to make sure that the crown wheel turns clockwise, because the direction of the wheel controls the direction in which the verge is twisted. Providing the crown turns clockwise the pallet must be twisted in the same direction, *i.e.* looking at the verge from

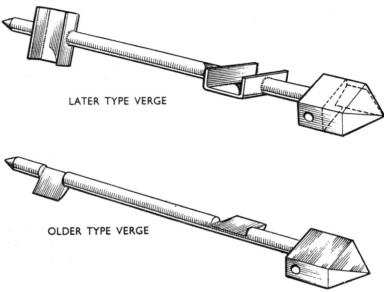

Figure 10. Verges under construction: *top*, the later type of verge pads extended both sides of the arbor; *bottom*, the older type where pads do not extend beyond the centre of the arbor. Both verges are ready for final fitting or ' turning in '.

the knife edge the far pallet will be twisted anti-clockwise or to the right. It is easy for the verge to become bent in the twisting, and it must be examined to make sure that it is straight.

Next the pallets are filed to half their thickness, making certain that the filing is done on their acting faces and that the metal is left quite·smooth and flat, as this will save a lot of work when the verge is hardened.

The hole for the pendulum rod is now drilled in the block and the knife edge roughly filed. If the verge has a crutch there will be a pivot instead of a knife edge, but it will still have the block.

Hardening the Verge—To harden and temper the verge it is covered in iron binding wire and heated over the gas until it is a rich cherry red in daylight but slightly less in artificial light. As soon as the whole verge has reached the required colour it is plunged endwise in cold water, then the binding wire is taken off and the verge is tested with a file to make sure it is hard all over. It is then tempered by putting it in a pan with brass filings and completely covering it, after which a piece of bright clean steel is placed on the top and quite visible and heated until the bright steel turns a deep blue. The verge is then quickly removed and allowed to cool in the air. It must not be plunged in water.

When almost cold it is placed in oil to cool completely. This will tend to stave off rust.

Now the verge is put between centres to see if it is still true or if it has bent or warped in the hardening, in which case it must be paned true. This is done by stretching the hollow part with a hard steel hammer, but on no account must it be hammered on the high part, as if this is done it is certain to break. When true the arbor is turned and the work generally cleaned up, the front pivot is turned and either the knife edge or pivot made.

The pallets should be the correct length, *i.e.* one-third the distance between two teeth from the centre to the end. The back of each pad should be filed back about 45° so that the acting part of the pallet is thin at the end, to give the maximum amount of engagement. The faces of the pallets are now polished and left quite bright.

Adjusting the Escapement

The verge is now put in place, the knife edge shortened to correct endshake and also clear of the banking block. The drop is tested and if excessive is reduced to a minimum; if it is excessive the pallets

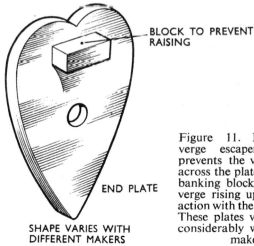

BLOCK TO PREVENT
RAISING

END PLATE

SHAPE VARIES WITH
DIFFERENT MAKERS

Figure 11. Endplate of verge escapement. This prevents the verge moving across the plates, whilst the banking block prevents the verge rising up and out of action with the crown wheel. These plates vary in shape considerably with different makers.

get badly pitted, and apart from that it is all loss of impulse. Sometimes, however, the drop cannot be reduced because the crown wheel teeth have been repaired many times and are as a result shorter. In these circumstances either the crown wheel must be recolleted to raise it, a new crown wheel must be made with longer teeth or the wheel must be higher. Sometimes the wheel cannot be raised because it already touches the bottom of the top cock, and in this case there is no alternative but a new wheel with taller or longer teeth.

The Pallet Pads

The length of the pallet pads is usually treated very lightly, but it is most important to have them the correct length. With English clocks the length of the pad from the centre of the arbor to the extreme dropping-off corner should be one-third the distance between two teeth, and if less there must be excessive losses and if more

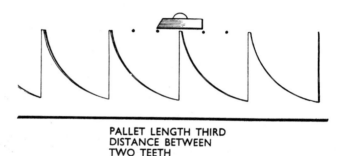

PALLET LENGTH THIRD
DISTANCE BETWEEN
TWO TEETH

 LATER VERGE   EARLY VERGE

Figure 12. Showing the correct length of the pallet pads in relation to the teeth of the wheel to give the best results: *bottom left* shows the length of pads of the later verge; *bottom right* shows the early type of verge pads.

the action will be very bad. If the pads are too long, the action will be similar to that of a proportionately too large pinion in a train of wheels. In other words, the two pads will be too far apart at the ends and the incoming tooth will butt on the pad it is about to engage or, in extreme cases, will get round the back of the pad and become locked.

To clear the teeth by making the pad shallower will only create excessive drop and will not put the action right. Therefore, the pallet must be shortened.

In some of the Continental clocks the verge pads are very long, and this is overcome by having far fewer teeth and thus a greater distance between them on the same size wheel. The distance apart of the verge and crown wheel is, of course, greater and the path of

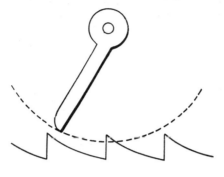

Figure 13. Showing how the teeth must be wider apart (or less teeth in the wheel) if longer pads are used. The dotted line shows the path of the pad.

the verge pads describes a larger circle, and thus the intersection into the wheel is proportionately less.

This type of clock, of course, requires appreciably more motive power and the arc of vibration is less, but is much more easily upset. There were apparently only a few of these made, but they are best left as in the original, as any alteration is a lengthy and thus costly business.

A point to be remembered regarding pallet pads is that the angle between the pads does not affect the equality of the drop. At first glance it would seem that if one increases the angle it must affect the outside freedom as against the inside, but it alters the action of both in the same manner, and the wider the angle, the shorter the pallets must be. Any angle between the two pads above 100° is detrimental because the friction increases very greatly in proportion to this.

Using Round Rod Steel Instead of Flat—As flat rod steel is very difficult to obtain these days $\frac{3}{16}$ in. round rod silver steel has to be substituted, and this can be worked in various ways to get the same results.

The round portions can be turned and the blocks left standing and then filed flat to the correct thickness, or a slightly smaller rod can be used, the round parts turned and the other part hammered flat while in a red-hot condition. When using this method care must be taken to see that the steel does not crack or fracture; this being the one objection to hammering into shape.

17

Making a New Crown Wheel

A verge crown wheel always has an odd number of teeth; if this were not so the wheel could not pass. While one tooth is engaged on the one pallet, the other pallet lies between two teeth or in the space between two teeth. It is always as large as the clock will take, the limiting factor being other parts of the clock.

When making a wheel a blank disc is obtained very near to the finished size or diameter. This is flattened on one side, fitted to a wax chuck and the outside turned to the correct size and perfectly true. The middle is now turned, leaving the part on which the teeth are to be cut standing. This is turned to leave the bottom as thin as is consistent with the necessary strength, then a hole is drilled as true as possible through the blank and the hole opened to the required size with a cutter in the slide rest. The hole and the blank must be dead true and also dead flat.

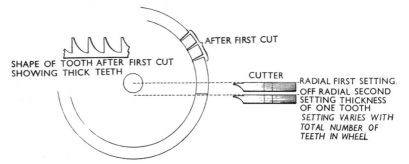

Figure 14. Method of cutting crown wheel to ensure the top of the teeth being straight from back to front, and not thinner on the inside. The cutter is shown in its two different settings.

The wheel blank is next set up in the wheel-cutting machine, which must have a narrower cutter than the space between two teeth so that more than one cut is required to complete the tooth profile. This is cut with at least two settings, the first setting being made with the cutter radial, whilst the second setting is made with the cutter set off the radial. When the first cut has been taken it will be noticed that the teeth are thick on the outside and thin on the inside, but this is bound to be the case where the cutter is set to cut radial because the inside circumference is smaller, and as the cutter takes the same amount from the inside as the outside there must be less metal left on the smaller circumference. Therefore when the first cut is taken the inside is left about the correct thickness and a second cut is taken at a lower setting of the cutter and metal is taken only from the outside circumference. Thus the slight flat left on the top of the tooth is of equal width.

The amount the cutter is set lower depends, of course, on the number of teeth in the wheel, and this can be found out only by trial, as is often the case when one is cutting individual wheels. If the cutter is nicely polished there will be no necessity to touch the teeth, but if the teeth are rough they can be smoothed with powdered Water of Ayr stone and oil on a piece of boxwood of suitable shape.

After the teeth are cut the crossings are filed out, or, as is usually said, the wheel is crossed out, *i.e.* the centre of the wheel is filed out to leave the usual 4 arms. The idea is to make the wheel lighter in weight as well as making it look nice. The wheel must be as light as possible but of the necessary strength. If too thin it will be a nuisance to handle, and if the arms should get broken it will mean a new wheel.

Mounting the Wheel—Before mounting the wheel the lower endpiece or adjusting screw on the pottance supporting the lower pivot of the crown wheel pinion is unscrewed until it holds the shoulder of the pivot just clear of the pivot hole. The wheel is now mounted on the pinion and the collet turned back until the wheel teeth are just free of the verge arbor. Then it is tried to see if the teeth will just pass freely. If they will not the wheel is lowered on the collet until it does pass. The wheel is then firmly riveted on to the collet and is checked to see that it runs flat and true. If it does not it should be dismounted and the pinion recolleted and turned on the pinion with the pivots running in female dead centres. It is essential that the wheel should be flat and true.

Antique Verges

It is very difficult to make antique verge clocks perfectly correct without extensive replacements which would often lower their market value. If this chapter is understood, however, one will be able to improvise and put the escapement in working order without resorting to new parts.

It is always important to notice in which direction the wheel of an old clock revolves, and to take particular notice of the type of verge, as some have the pallets extended on both sides of the arbor whilst others have the pallets on one side only. Again particularly amongst Continental clocks the pallets are appreciably longer and the crown wheel and verge are pitched farther apart; it is unwise to alter the construction, because although the principle may be wrong, these clocks have been going and will do so again.

Conversions

It is always unwise to convert a verge clock by fitting a modern escapement, the reason being that whilst a verge clock in good order will give a good performance if converted it may not give a modern performance. Another reason for not converting is the fact that in their original condition these clocks will probably have a good market value, but if converted they are worthless. There is, however, one way of converting them without destroying their original pieces, this being done by substituting the verge only and keeping the rest of the clock in its original form. A plain arbor with a type of dead-beat pallets mounted on it takes the place of the verge, the pallets consisting of a piece of plate steel of a thickness equal to half

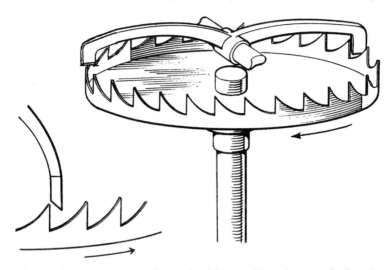

Figure 15. Verge conversion to dead-beat. The advantage is that the clock can be very easily put back as it was originally. The pallets are shown in position *right*, and the impulse plane and locking face of the pallet pad are shown *left*.

the distance between two teeth of the crown wheel. This is planted where the verge was, and filed away to clear the centre and make lighter, leaving only pads to engage the crown wheel teeth. Impulse planes are filed on these pads, and are then hardened and polished flat. Only the pallets need be hardened. The V-bed is filled in and a hole drilled for the back pivot of the arbor. The endplate is still required to take the thrust when the pallets are given impulse, and one is also necessary at the front to take the reverse thrust. The suspension for the pendulum can be added to the existing back cock.

A conversion of this nature can easily be made and the clock still be all but in its original form.

2

THE RECOIL ESCAPEMENT

IT WAS SHOWN IN the previous chapter that the verge escapement had a large arc of vibration, and after the seconds or Royal pendulum came into being the clockmakers realised that another type of escapement was necessary. Therefore about 1675 the recoil escapement was invented. It is difficult to prove who was the actual inventor, but it is usually ascribed to Dr. Hooke, whilst William Clement was the maker.

With a verge escapement the arc of vibration was about 100°, whereas with this new recoil escapement the arc of vibration was reduced to between 5° and 10°, with the result that the long pendulum could be used in place of the short bob pendulum in the long-case, narrow-waisted clocks then popular. Clement used a pendulum beating 1¼ seconds, but the seconds pendulum became the most popular.

There are really two types of recoil escapement: the anchor escapement and what is called the ordinary recoil. The anchor was first used with the long pendulum, and the ordinary recoil with short pendulums in house clocks and bracket clocks. The anchor escapement gives a smaller arc than the ordinary recoil.

The escapement was called ' the recoil' because after the 'scape wheel had dropped or escaped the extra movement of the pallets caused the wheel to recoil or go backwards. The idea behind this was what is called isochronism, which means that whatever the extent of the arc of vibration, the time of vibration remains constant. With a moderate recoil this is largely achieved, but with extensive recoil the time of vibration slows as the arc increases. By experiment it has been found that an impulse plane of 3° gives the best result.

If through indifferent gearing or other causes the motive power increased or decreased the effect on the timekeeping was not apparent in ordinary clocks, so the recoil became the ideal for cheaper clocks, and also one of the most popular escapements.

LAYOUT OF THE RECOIL ESCAPEMENT

As already stated, the pallets or verge of the verge escapement were set at right angles to the plane of the crown or 'scape wheel. With the recoil both pallets and 'scape wheel are in the same plane, and this makes construction easier. The escapement consists of a 'scape wheel (trade term for escapement wheel), a pair of pallets and pallet arbor. The number of teeth in the 'scape wheel varies from 30 to 40 and even more in particular cases according to the train of wheels driving it and the length of the pendulum controlling it, but in any case a short pendulum means a larger number of teeth in the 'scape wheel.

The 'scape wheel and pallets are set at a certain distance apart, or, more accurately, a certain distance of centres apart. This distance of centres means the distance apart of the pallet-arbor bearing and the 'scape wheel pinion-arbor bearing. This is the radius of the 'scape wheel multiplied by 1·4, and this will give the best results with a recoil escapement.

The pallets are made from flat plate steel which can be made quite hard, and consist of two nibs joined by a curved arm and mounted centrally on an arbor pivoted in the clock frame. The one engaged first by the wheel is the entrance pallet and the one engaged later is the exit pallet. The term nibs of the pallets means the complete acting unit which contains the impulse planes, *etc.*, and the necessary metal supporting them. These nibs should always be quite hard, but the body and arms of the pallets should be quite soft.

Fitted to the pallet arbor is the crutch, which can be of any suitable type because its function is to convey the power from the escapement to the pendulum, thus keeping the pendulum vibrating.

The pallets span a quarter of the wheel teeth, so that with a wheel of 30 teeth the pallets span $7\frac{1}{2}$ teeth and it is said that there are $7\frac{1}{2}$ teeth inside. The pallets are spanned by 1 tooth more or $8\frac{1}{2}$ teeth of the 'scape wheel, and it is said that there are $8\frac{1}{2}$ teeth outside.

As in all mechanism, there must be freedom, so there has to be drop in a recoil escapement. Thus, when the wheel tooth has finished its impulse it drops off and the seventh tooth farther round the wheel drops on to the other pallet. When the drop is from the entrance pallet it is termed inside drop, when it is from the exit pallet it is termed outside drop. With a recoil escapement this drop is the same as the shake or freedom, so the terms inside and outside shake are used.

This shake, freedom or drop must be equal and always at a minimum because it is all loss but very necessary loss, as unequal or unnecessary drop causes serious wear on the impulse planes of the pallets.

PLANNING THE ESCAPEMENT

When planning the escapement a drawing or sketch of it is necessary, and in order to get a good idea of the procedure a 'scape wheel of 30 teeth is taken as an example, and the method of drawing this is shown in Figure 16.

First a circle is scribed representing the circumference of the wheel, then the diameter is drawn and extended beyond the circumference, A. There are two ways of arriving at the correct distance of centres. One way is by setting the compasses at the radius of wheel multiplied by 1·4 and marking this on the line forming the diameter plus, which will be called the centre line. The other way is to mark off two lines with a protractor, one on each side of the centre line and both lines at 45° to the centre line C_1 and C_2.

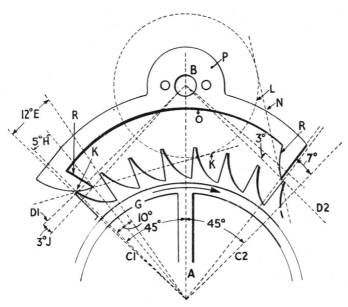

Figure 16. Theoretical drawing of a recoil escapement. The wheel is of 30 teeth whilst the pallets span 7 teeth and are spanned by 8.

Tangents are drawn at the points where these lines join up on the extended centre line, and if these lines have been carefully drawn they should cross the centre line at the same point, which will be the pallet-arbor centre B. These last four lines will form a perfect square.

The 'scape wheel has 30 teeth, and as a circle is 360° there must be 12° between each tooth, E. There must, however, be some metal at the tips of the teeth, so 1° is allowed for each tooth, which leaves 11°. There must also be a 1° drop, which leaves 10°, G, and as this is divided between the two pallets the maximum thickness of each pallet is 5°, H.

To proceed, the position of the teeth is marked off and only the necessary number drawn; there is no need to draw them all. The teeth are radial at the back and concave at the front or acting side.

Next 1° is marked off on the outside of the left-hand 45° line, C_1, and then every subsequent 12° until eight teeth radials have been

23

marked, then starting at the same 45° line 12° is marked off for each subsequent tooth front. This will decide the correct position of the teeth E.

The Impulse Planes

Again using the 45° from the wheel centre which marks the front of the first tooth, 5° must be marked off for the length of the actual impulse plane, H. (By this is meant 5° towards the centre or clockwise.)

Now from the tangent joining the pallet-arbor hole 3° is marked off towards the wheel, J; this line will cross the 5° line which gives the width of the impulse plane. Where these lines cross, a line is drawn joining this line to the point where the front of the first tooth is marked, K. These points are now joined and the line extended to the centre line of the drawing, A. A circle is now scribed to which this line is a tangent, L.*

Going now to the opposite side, a line is drawn from the impulse plane of the exit pallet, C_2. 1°, which is the drop, is marked off anti-clockwise from the 45° line from the wheel centre, then 5° for the tooth and impulse. This will give the dropping of corner of the exit pallet and the impulse plane. To a certain degree the rest can be drawn to suit personal preferences.

The front must be drawn to form the belly of the pallets, i.e. a curve, to give the teeth clearance and to leave solid around the centre of the pallets or the pallet-arbor hole, O. A boss is left to enable the pallets to be fixed to the arbor, P. The inactive part of the nib is filed back sufficiently to allow the pallet to run into the teeth without bending the tips, R.

If one is making the escapement this drawing can be stuck on to suitable plate steel and the steel filed to the drawing. If space is limited the 3° angle of lift or impulse can always be reduced, but it is inadvisable to increase it because the addition in friction is so great that it may prove too much for the clock to lift.

The impulse planes illustrated in Figure 16 are straight, but it is considered advisable to ease the recoil which would be consistent with this, so the face is curved back from the impulse plane proper or the angle is raised. This tends to retard the swing of the pendulum, which is, of course, the object of the curve.

Making the Pallets

A piece of plate steel about four or five times the thickness of the 'scape wheel is chosen, and it is important to select a piece that can be hardened, i.e. not mild steel, which can only be case hardened. The drawing is stuck to the steel with a good adhesive, and holes are then drilled all round and just clear of the pattern, but almost touching each other. The hole for the pallet arbor must be very care-

---

* A tangent is a line which meets a circle without cutting it, and if the radius was drawn to meet at the contact point it would form a right angle to the tangent.

fully drilled, as it is essential that this should be as accurate as possible. When all the holes are drilled they are joined by using a piercing saw until the rough pallets are cut clear, when they should be filed near to the pattern in order to leave as little metal as possible to remove in the finishing.

The rough pallets are now mounted on their arbor and the 'scape wheel, which is also mounted on its pinion or on a true arbor, is put

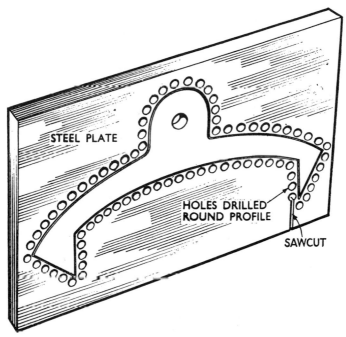

STEEL PLATE

HOLES DRILLED
ROUND PROFILE

SAWCUT

Figure 17. Method of making pallets from plate steel. The drawing is stuck to the metal and holes are drilled all round. They are then joined by sawing.

in the depth tool. The pair are tested together and the depth tool adjusted to see if the inside and outside shakes are equal, and, if they are, the distance of centres is marked in the frame and the hole drilled.

The nibs of the pallets are now hardened, and it is most essential that they should be quite hard. A heavy pair of tongs is used for this operation, first gripping one nib and hardening the other and then reversing the process by holding the hardened nib with the tongs, which will prevent the heat from softening it.

The pallets are now cleaned up generally and polished or at least made very smooth on the acting faces or impulse planes; the smoother these planes, the better the action and, of course, the less wear on the wheel teeth.

When assembled it is necessary to make sure that the shakes or drops are equal; if the outside shake is excessive the escapement is too shallow or the bearings are too far apart; if the outside is tight the reverse is the case. The inside shake is almost unaffected by the depth in the recoil escapement, and this point will be dealt with later.

Making Recoil Pallets to Depth

Owing to wear or other reasons an old clock often requires a new pair of pallets. It is sometimes advisable to make the pallets to depth rather than to alter the layout. This means making a pair of pallets to suit existing bearings or holes, as they are called.

Again, a drawing is made on a piece of stiff paper or thin brass plate.

The circle of the wheel is marked by making a hole in the paper just large enough to fit the 'scape-pinion arbor, then the distance

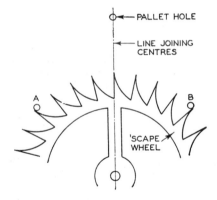

Figure 18. Making a pair of recoil pallets to depth for a 30-tooth 'scape wheel. The illustration shows the holes marked out for the point where the entrance pallet is first engaged and also the dropping-off line of the exit pallet.

between the 'scape hole and pallet-arbor hole is measured and marked on the paper, after which the hole and the mark are joined by a line extended beyond. The wheel is now put in place on the paper with the front of the tooth resting on this line. Now a dot is made where the fourth tooth in a clockwise direction on the 'scape wheel lies. In like manner a dot is made where the fourth tooth in an anti-clockwise direction lies.

These will denote the position of the impulse plane of the entrance pallet and the drop-off corner of the exit pallet. The wheel is now moved round half a tooth and dots made where the fourth tooth in a clockwise direction lies.

There are now two dots on each side. If a line is drawn from the first dot on the entrance to pass midway between the two dots on the

26

exit side this will give the impulse plane for the entrance pallet. A circle is drawn to which this line is a tangent, then a tangent to this circle is drawn which will pass through the last dot on the exit side. This will give the impulse angle for the exit pallet.

Figure 19. Method of obtaining impulse planes when making recoil pallets to depth. A = first engagement, entrance pallet. B = dropping-off line, exit pallet. C = dropping-off line, entrance pallet. D = first engagement, exit pallet. E = circle scribed to line joining point Λ to point midway between D and B. F = line joining A to point between D and B. G1, G2 = radial lines passing through C and B respectively.

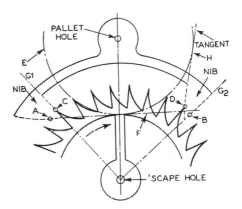

All that remains to be done is to finish up the drawing as before, making sure to drill the pallet-arbor hole very carefully, and also making certain that the drawing is fixed firmly to the steel, because if it comes off half-way through the job it will make further working very difficult and may even mean starting afresh.

Polishing the Pallets—If it is desired to make a first-class job the impulse planes can be polished by the following method: First they are examined to see if there are any file marks present, and if there are these must be removed. To do this a piece of flat steel about $\frac{3}{16}$ in. wide, 5 in. long and $\frac{1}{16}$ in. thick is required. The flat side of this is roughened with a file and a mixture of powdered oilstone and oil is smeared on to it, making sure that the mixture is really oily so that it will work quickly. The pallets are rested on a piece of cork held in the vice with the impulse faces uppermost and the faces rubbed with the polisher and oil, taking care to preserve the angle, until all marks are removed, when the pallets are cleaned in benzine, leaving no trace of oilstone.

The faces now have to be polished with a zinc polisher, making sure that the zinc is sufficiently thick to withstand undue bending under pressure. A piece of zinc with a $\frac{3}{16}$-in.-square section and of the same length as the steel polisher is most suitable, and after being roughened this is smeared with clean, well-beaten diamantine. The pallet faces are then rubbed hard with this polisher with a circular motion until suitably polished. The diamantine polishes as it dries and with a final bloom when quite dry, but if it is rubbed too long when dry the polished face will become foxy and the process has to be started again.

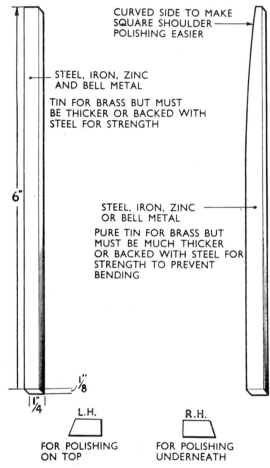

CURVED SIDE TO MAKE
SQUARE SHOULDER
POLISHING EASIER

STEEL, IRON, ZINC
AND BELL METAL

TIN FOR BRASS BUT MUST
BE THICKER OR BACKED WITH
STEEL FOR STRENGTH

6"

STEEL, IRON, ZINC
OR BELL METAL

PURE TIN FOR BRASS BUT
MUST BE MUCH THICKER
OR BACKED WITH STEEL FOR
STRENGTH TO PREVENT
BENDING

$\frac{1}{8}$"

$\frac{1}{4}$"

L.H.

R.H.

FOR POLISHING
ON TOP

FOR POLISHING
UNDERNEATH

Figure 20. General purpose polishers. These are used for polishing pallet faces, arbors, *etc*. They can be used in a lathe, throw or overhand, and when smeared with diamantine can give a very high polish.

Diamantine is purchased ready for use at the material dealers and is beaten up with oil to the consistency of putty. It cuts when wettish and polishes when dry.

Repairing the Escapement

As in all escapements, the pivots of the 'scape pinion and pallet arbor must be in good condition. The pallet-arbor pivots wear

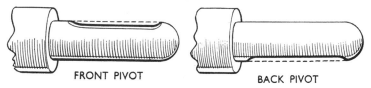

FRONT PIVOT   BACK PIVOT

Figure 21. Showing how pallet arbor pivots wear: *left*, front pivot (dial end) wears on top; *right*, back pivot wears underneath through weight of crutch.

differently from the pivot of a pinion, the front pivot wearing on the top and the back pivot wearing at the bottom owing to the weight of the crutch. If worn these pivots must be made round and the holes renewed to fit closely but freely to the pivots.

RECOIL ESCAPEMENT

To repair the pallet-arbor pivots the crutch must be removed in most cases, as if it is not taken off it will foul the lathe bed.

Where the crutch is screwed to the brass collet on the pallet arbor it can be easily taken off, but in quite a number of clocks, particularly the long-case variety, the crutch is riveted to the arbor. If the crutch is riveted to the brass collet it can be driven off by using a punch with a hole in it large enough to pass over the arbor and rest on the brass collet. For this operation the boss of the crutch is supported on either a slotted or split stake and the punch given a sharp blow which will be sufficient to dislodge the crutch.

With the long-case pallets the crutch is fitted through a hole drilled in the steel boss of the pallet arbor. Some of these appear solid, but by careful examination the riveting will be found. Again a split stake is used, the crutch itself being placed in a hole just larger than the arbor with the boss resting on the closed stake. A punch just a little smaller than the crutch is used, and one with a short, stubby end for strength is most suitable. A sharp blow on the punch should dislodge the crutch first time.

Sometimes the crutch ends in a flat head, which is fitted into a filed slot in the pallet arbor. This must always be looked out for, as it entails the use of a different procedure. The best way to deal with this is to pass the crutch between the partially closed jaws of a vice with the boss resting on the jaws and to use a punch as before.

After the pivots are repaired it may not be easy to rivet the crutch again. It is always as well to chamfer the hole where the crutch is riveted so that it will rivet up better, because the crutch and pallets must be as though in one solid piece.

The holes wear in a similar manner and become oval. These must be replaced, taking care to leave them in their original state (see *Watch and Clock Making and Repairing*, page 366).

Repairing the Pallets

After the escapement has been in use for some time the pallet faces, although glass hard, become worn. If there is room the pallets can be moved on their arbor to bring a fresh part of the face

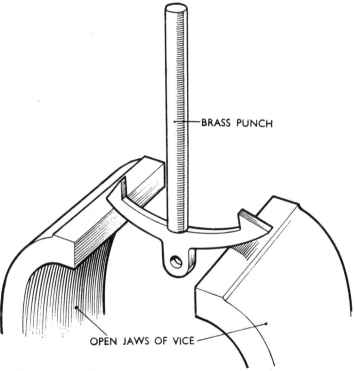

BRASS PUNCH

OPEN JAWS OF VICE

Figure 22a. Method of closing recoil pallets in a vice, the jaws of which should be brass lined; a blow struck with a brass punch will close the pallets. They can be opened by turning them up the other way in the vice and again striking them with a punch, but in this case great care must be taken to see that the pads do not rest on the vice jaws.

to bear, but if this has been done before they must be repaired. They should be treated in the same way as for new pallets, all signs of wear must be removed. It also pays to polish them.

Obviously when the pallets are repaired there is more drop because metal has been taken off, and if this is not attended to the pallets wear much more quickly and deep pits are made where the wheel

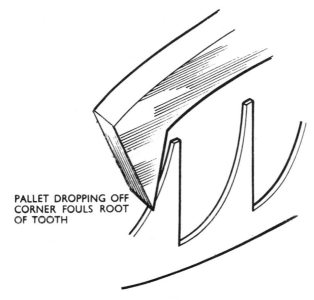

PALLET DROPPING OFF
CORNER FOULS ROOT
OF TOOTH

Figure 22*b*. Effect of closing the pallets if they are high angled. The dropping-off corner of the exit pallet may rake the wheel tooth and the point of the tooth will not act as it should.

Figure 22*c*. The best type of recoil pallet in which the impulse angles are low.

drops. This excessive drop is corrected by closing the pallets to take up the excessive inside shake and then deepening the intersection to close the outside shake.

Before closing the pallets it must be made sure that the body is quite soft, otherwise the pallets will break. If the body is soft the pallets should be laid nibs up on the open jaws of a vice, and with a brass punch resting on the centre. A blow on the punch will bring the nibs closer together, but they must not be closed too much, as it is awkward to open them again.

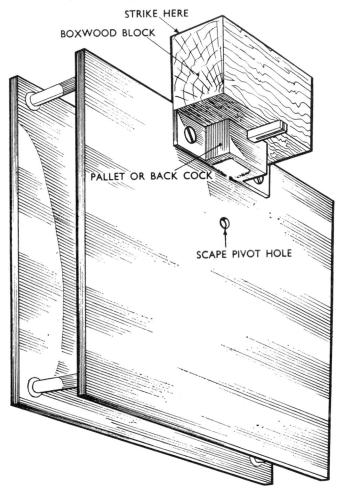

Figure 23. Method of moving back cock, showing how it can be lowered without any bruising with the aid of a boxwood block. The back cock can be moved sideways by a blow on the side.

When the inside shake is close the outside shake will be doubly excessive. The back pivot of the pallet arbor is usually in a back cock. To take up the outside shake the back cock is put in place, making sure the screw-threads do not fit the holes in the back cock closely. If they do, the holes should be filed oval at the top so that the cock can move downwards.

When in order the cock is lightly screwed in place, a block of box-wood is put across and given a sharp blow with a hammer. This should not be done with the pallets in place, as otherwise there would be the danger of a pivot breaking off the pallet arbor.

The steady pins in the cock will give and the pallets will be closer to the wheel through the cock moving downwards. Where a great deal of alteration is required it may also be necessary to lower the arbor from the front by drawing the hole downwards. Some clocks are provided with a turntable to allow this adjustment, but as a rule these are of Continental manufacture.

It is not advisable to soft solder pieces of mainspring to the pallet faces, as is the habit of a number of workmen. This is bad practice, and is very often useless. It causes considerable wear to the 'scape-wheel teeth, and as it is soft the top surface is worn off very quickly, so that any advantage there may have been is rapidly lost, and the pallets are in a worse state than before they were altered.

Repairing the Wheel Teeth

In time the wheel teeth of a recoil 'scape wheel become worn, *i.e.* the acting corners of the tips of the teeth become rounded. This increases the acting surface and also increases the friction to a considerable extent and affects the timekeeping.

If this wear is very serious a new wheel is the only remedy. When only ordinary wear is present the teeth are repaired by putting the wheel and pinion up in female dead centres in the lathe and lightly filing the tops of the teeth with an exceptionally fine-cutting file. The lathe must revolve fast, and the file end must be rested either on the T-rest or on some other firm part and moved near to the wheel very carefully, otherwise the teeth will be damaged. Above all, the file must not bump in and out of the teeth.

When all the teeth have been touched it is advisable to finish with a piece of Water of Ayr stone with oil on it in place of the file. This operation will thicken the teeth, and if they should be thickened too much they can be thinned again. There are two ways of doing this, the best, of course, being by the use of the wheel-cutting engine, but failing this the acting side of the tooth can be thinned with a file conforming to the shape of the teeth. In no circumstances should the radial backs of the teeth be filed, because the correct divisions are likely to be lost and the wheel will be spoiled.

If full control can be maintained with a graver the tops of the wheel teeth can be turned using a very sharp graver instead of filing, but very great care must be exercised. These operations should always be carried out in dead centres.

No lathe collet yet made is true enough for this kind of work, and if it were true enough the pinion arbor would probably not be true.

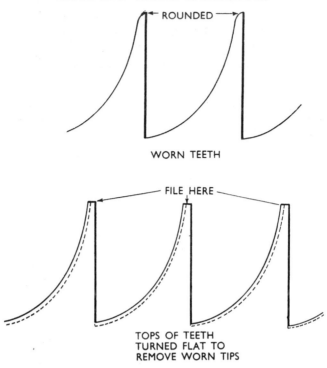

Figure 24. Repairing worn teeth. The tops are turned flat and the sloping side of each tooth is filed up, making sure that the radial side is not touched. Verge crown wheel teeth are repaired in the same way.

It should always be remembered that the wheel will be smaller after repair, and thus the inside shake will be noticeably increased.

THE ANCHOR RECOIL ESCAPEMENT

Although the principle is the same with all recoil escapements, there are variations in the way that the principle is applied. The recoil already surveyed is for short pendulums, *i.e.* pendulums of about 6 in. or less in length. If this were used on a long seconds pendulum which is 39·14 in. in length the pendulum would hit the sides of the case.

When discussing escapements it is convenient to give the arc of the pendulum movement in degrees, but it must be borne in mind that a degree will have a longer or shorter arc depending upon the size of the circle from which it is taken. Whatever the size of a circle, it must still contain 360°, and therefore whilst a degree in a circle with a diameter of 0·01 in. would be only 0·00087 in., with a 10-in. diameter the arc for 1° would be 0·087 in., whilst for the arc to be 1 in. the diameter would have to be 114·59 in. In the case of a seconds pendulum although the centre of oscillation is 39·14 in. the total length is usually about 46 in. Therefore with a 2° arc the movement of the pendulum at the end would be 0·8 in. each side, or a total of 1·6 in. Because all actions are in a circular path it is very easy to use degrees and to work out the dimensions or measurements from them after the calculations are made.

The early long-case clocks were narrow waisted, so the anchor escapement was often used; the distance of centres of the anchor

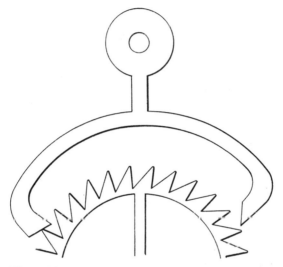

Figure 25. Anchor recoil escapement. The angles of impulse appear to be high but the distance of centres is greater. The shape of the pallet arms varies considerably in different movements.

varied considerably, but usually this distance was the diameter of the 'scape wheel. The objection, of course, was the length of the impulse planes and the increased friction, more so because the pallets embraced more teeth than with the ordinary recoil, the number so embraced varying with different makers. The later clocks had the usual recoil with low-angled pallets. The difference in the two types can be noticed by careful study of the drawings Figures 16 and 25.

The objection to long impulse planes is, of course, the changing of the oil due to changes in temperature. Thus the longer the pallet arms and the greater the distance of centres, the longer the impulse planes, although in degrees they are the same or maybe less.

The Crutch

As already stated, the impulse is passed to the pendulum through the crutch. This is an arm of brass or steel which is fixed to the pallet arbor and engages with the pendulum rod, giving it a periodic push, so keeping it vibrating or making up for the losses due to friction at the suspension and the resistance of the air.

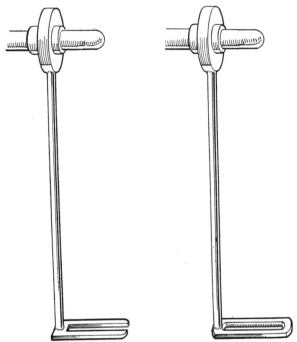

Figure 26. Types of crutch in long-case clocks: *left*, open-ended crutch; *right*, crutch with closed end. The crutch with the closed end is stronger but not so convenient.

It is necessary to have the crutch of a correct length, and this is controlled by the weight and length of the pendulum, a long, heavy pendulum requiring a long crutch. The pendulum must take control. With a short crutch there is always the tendency for the suspension spring to give way as the impulse is given, the top of the pendulum getting the impulse whilst the pendulum proper, which is the bob, gets very little. With a very weak suspension spring this is

36

even more apparent. A 6-in. pendulum needs the crutch to be about $2\frac{1}{2}$ in. long, but with a seconds pendulum the crutch should be about 4 in. or even as much as 5 in. in length.

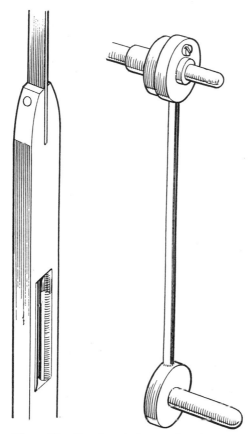

Figure 27. Bracket clock crutch and pendulum rod: *left*, pendulum rod showing connection of suspension spring and impulse notch or slot; *right*, crutch with impulse post, joined to the pallet arbor collet by one or sometimes two screws.

It is interesting to observe a long pendulum with a short crutch. At each impulse one will see the top of the pendulum quiver. An important point is to make sure that the crutch fits the pendulum rod closely but not tightly, as any freedom is loss, although there must be definite freedom.

As the pendulum swings it takes a circular path and thus, being longer than the crutch and the two centres not being coincident, the sides of the crutch rub up and down, so they must be rounded and not flat. If the crutch ends in a steel post, then the slot in the pendulum rod must be well rounded and nicely burnished or polished.

Another point is to see that the pendulum hangs square with the crutch so that there is no binding through the pendulum being on the twist. Also if the pendulum rod is steel the crutch should be brass, whilst if the pendulum has a brass block for the crutch to work on the crutch must be steel, or, as is often the case, iron or mild steel.

The pendulum suspension is very important. The suspension spring must be firmly fitted on the pendulum rod and must be firmly anchored on the back cock, and there must be no movement in its anchorage. Where there is an adjustment the moving cheeks of the movable arm must embrace the suspension spring without any discernible freedom. It must not bind' on the suspension spring, however, because of the risk of buckling the spring.

OTHER TYPES OF RECOIL ESCAPEMENTS

There are many types or adaptations of the recoil escapement. The French clocks have escapements where the wheel has as many as 40 teeth, and there are others where the pallets span but a few teeth, whilst one particular type called the drum escapement has only one tooth embraced by the pallets. Also in this particular type all of the impulse and all of the recoil are on one pallet, the other pallet being part of a circle scribed from the pallet hole and only holding the wheel tooth until the reverse vibration, when it just drops the tooth on to the impulse plane of the other pallet; this is referred to as the dumb or dummy vibration.

This escapement was used with a very short pivoted pendulum in small, round clocks in the shape of a drum, hence the drum escapement. With most of these the impulse angle was too high and resulted in failure, therefore some clockmakers altered the dummy pallet and put in an impulse plane, but this was not the answer. By lowering the impulse angle the arc was reduced and required less power to keep going. This, of course, meant new pallets.

Making a Recoil 'Scape Wheel

Good hard brass blanks are required for 'scape wheels, and sometimes one is able to obtain stampings of a good-quality brass which only require finishing up. With 4-arm crossings this saves a lot of work because the crossings are partly done, but in the case of 3-arm crossings which are sometimes required one must obtain a disc of near size and thickness.

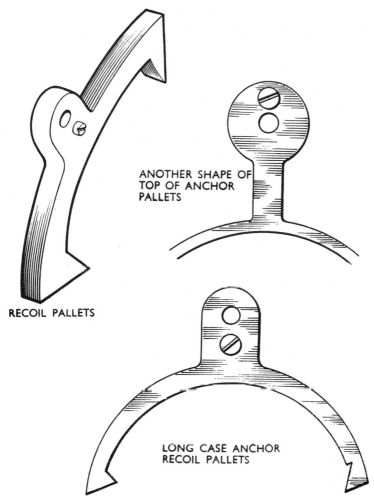

ANOTHER SHAPE OF
TOP OF ANCHOR
PALLETS

RECOIL PALLETS

LONG CASE ANCHOR
RECOIL PALLETS

Figure 28. English recoil pallets: *top left*, typical type of short pendulum recoil pallets; *top right*, alternative shape of pallet arm for anchor pallets; *bottom*, alternative shape of anchor pallets.

A 'scape wheel functions much better when it is light in weight, but at the same time it must not be ridiculously delicate, as some wheels are. The first operation is to cut the teeth, and this is carried out by the use of one or two cutters. The objection to one cutter is that it is likely to leave a burr in the bottom of the tooth, or as it is termed the root of the tooth, which can be cleared only with a file.

When using two cutters the first cutter follows the profile of the tooth except that it is thinner, thus after the first cut a thick tooth remains. The acting front of the tooth is cut first, after which a cutter slightly longer in the blade but shaped at the point to overlap the cut of the first cutter is used. The last cuts should be slight, because otherwise the fact of cutting will bend the tip of the tooth over. A single blade or fly cutter is used and in the first place must be made by hand, but these cutters can be used many times and for several sizes of wheels.

When using a single cutter the front is cut first in just the same way as when using two, but when the second cut is taken the dividing head must be advanced and the cutter also advanced to take a deeper cut; if one is very careful a good wheel can be cut in this way. The second cut is, of course, the radial face or the back of the tooth.

With the ordinary French 8-day clock the teeth vary. Some are similar to the English type, and some are straight back and front. The backs are radial, but the fronts are about 12° back cut. Also as a rule the teeth in the French 'scape wheels are thinner and more delicate, and as a result have to be handled with great care in order that they should not be bent. When once damaged they are difficult to put exactly right.

French Clock Pallets

The same faults as previously described exist with the French recoil escapements, the pallets becoming worn and having to be polished in the same way as the heavier English type.

When the pallets are much worn, and have been moved to different parts so that all the width of the pallet face is worn, the pallets are difficult to rectify, as one cannot close up the inside drop owing to the construction, and a new pair of pallets is the only remedy.

Sometimes a pair can be obtained from the material dealers, but if not the procedure is the same as described earlier. It must always be remembered that the number of teeth in the wheels varies and the pallets vary accordingly.

Often the pallets have a square hole which is fitted on to the pallet arbor, which is also squared. If it is desired to move the pallets to bring them into a different position in relation to the wheel the pallets should not be driven farther up the arbor because they may break, instead the sides of the square should be smoothed on the pallet arbor and the pallets then firmly pushed on so that they are tight enough not to work off in action. A very light tap may be given to ensure that they are firmly on, but great care must be taken.

VARIOUS TYPES OF FRENCH RECOIL ESCAPEMENTS

There are many types of recoil escapement, and the most varied are of French origin. Some pallets span as few as 3 teeth, and the drum escapement mentioned earlier embraced only 1 tooth; with this the impulse pallet had all the impulse and all the recoil, the other pallet simply providing a lot of friction but no impulse, the object being, of course, to reduce the arc of vibration. Where only a few teeth are spanned by the pallets the arc of vibration tends to be large or excessive.

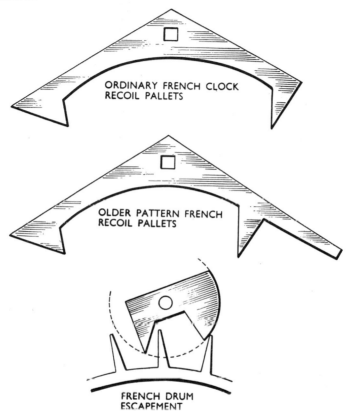

ORDINARY FRENCH CLOCK
RECOIL PALLETS

OLDER PATTERN FRENCH
RECOIL PALLETS

FRENCH DRUM
ESCAPEMENT

Figure 29. French and continental types of recoil pallets: *top*, the most usual type; *centre*, mostly found on older French clocks; *bottom*, French ' drum ' escapement.

Most of these types had the pendulum suspended on a thin silk cord, which had some advantages, but more disadvantages, at least as far as the repairer was concerned, and they are not made now.

These French escapements give better results if the impulse angles are low, but the angles are often high, and any sort of disturbance tends to stop them. If trouble is encountered with these the best thing to do is to reduce the impulse angles, even if the pallets have to be repitched, and if much worn a new pair with lower angles must be put on. Where the impulse angles are high the recoil is often excessive and trouble is experienced with the gearing between the fourth wheel and 'scape pinion. It must always be ensured that the 'scape pinion is the correct size.

TOMPION'S TIC-TAC

Thomas Tompion invented a type of recoil referred to as a tic-tac, and in this the pallets and pallet arbor were usually made from one piece of metal. The pallets spanned 3 teeth, and it was in some ways similar to the French drum escapement, the difference being that the tic-tac was pitched closer to the wheel teeth and left no room for a separate arbor, whereas the drum escapement had a pallet arbor.

The one pallet was circular on an arc from the pallet centre, and as a result was just a rest whilst the other pallet had all the impulse and recoil. Obviously the pendulum had a large vibration.

THE MODERN TYPE OF RECOIL ESCAPEMENT

The mass-produced clock of today, although using the principle of the recoil escapement, entails a different principle of manufacture.

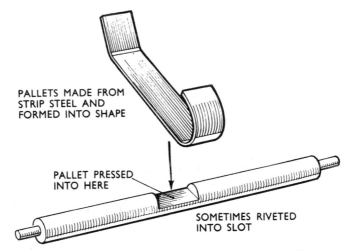

PALLETS MADE FROM
STRIP STEEL AND
FORMED INTO SHAPE

PALLET PRESSED
INTO HERE

SOMETIMES RIVETED
INTO SLOT

Figure 30. Modern type of mass-produced recoil pallets and pallet arbor. In some of these the pallet is pressed into position, whilst in others a rivet secures the pallets to the arbor.

Instead of solid pallets strip metal is bent round a specially made former and makes the impulse planes. These are easily repaired and when badly worn can also often be replaced from stock by either the manufacturers or the material dealers.

These impulse planes are either fitted to the pallet arbor by a rivet through the belly of the pallets and the pallet arbor or are fitted into a recess in the pallet arbor and the top of the recess forced over to hold the pallets in place. These pallets can be closed where the inside shake is excessive, whilst if the outside shake is too great the depth

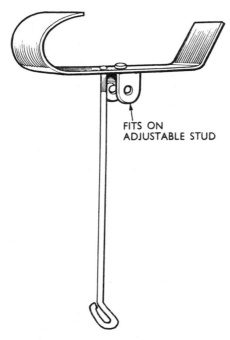

FITS ON
ADJUSTABLE STUD

Figure 31. Typical American recoil pallets which move on a stud on an adjustable cock instead of the pallet arbor.

can be deepened in the same manner as with the better-quality pallets. If the inside shake is close the inside edge of the entrance pallet can be reduced to correct this.

In most of these clocks the pallet-arbor holes are on separate cocks and there is considerable scope for adjustment. They must not be indiscriminately moved, however, but altered only after very careful thought.

The American type of recoil had the pallets mounted on a brass plate which was bent round and holes drilled in it to form bearings, the pallets being planted on a stud which again was planted on a movable cock riveted to the frame, and this cock provided adjustment. The crutch was a bent piece of brass wire riveted to the pallets.

Provided the wheel is sound, these clocks cause very little trouble. If the wheel is unsound it can be touched up, but the radial back of the tooth must be left alone. As before, the wheel is trued in the round. If the wheel is true it is a very great help.

3

THE DEAD-BEAT ESCAPEMENT

THE DEAD-BEAT ESCAPEMENT WAS invented by George Graham about 1730, and under certain conditions is undoubtedly the best clock escapement. It is useless in a small clock, but with a seconds pendulum it will give a remarkable performance. To give its best the motive power must be a constant factor, and as the escapement in a weight-driven regulator its performance leaves little to be desired.

It is an escapement which has to be very carefully made. The pivot holes or bearings have to be a close fit to the pivots, and in the best regulators the 'scape and pallet-arbor pivot holes are jewelled.

The acting faces of the pallets are also often jewelled, the reasons being that there is some easing of friction because a jewel will give a higher polish, and also that when they become worn the stones can be replaced and the pallets are as new again. Where they are not jewelled and become worn the act of repairing or repolishing the faces spoils the escapement, because the drop is increased. It often pays to have the pallets jewelled, or if this is difficult to carry out the pallets can be slotted and steel pads let in and polished flush with the original faces.

The escapement is called dead-beat because when the wheel tooth drops on to the locking face, however far the pallets move, the wheel remains unmoved, as distinct from the recoil, which moves backwards or recoils.

Layout of the Escapement

The best dead-beat escapement consists of a 'scape wheel of 30 teeth. The pallets span 8, 10 or even 14 teeth. The distance of

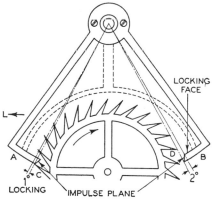

Figure 32. Old pattern Graham dead-beat escapement in which the pallets span 14 teeth of a 'scape wheel of 30 teeth, giving dead seconds. The dotted lines show how the pallets are sometimes shaped. A = entrance pallet. B = exit pallet. The tooth C rests on locking of entrance pallet A. As the pallets move to the left C reaches the impulse plane and pushes the pallet towards L. As C reaches the end of the impulse plane tooth D drops on to the locking face of exit pallet B.

45

centres is usually as in the recoil, the radius of the wheel multiplied by 1·4. This, of course, varies with different escapements, depending on the number of teeth of the wheel and the number of teeth spanned by the pallets.

In quite a number of Continental clocks of high quality and usually in astronomical clocks which have a seconds hand and a half-seconds pendulum there is a dead-beat escapement with a 'scape wheel of 60 teeth. Often these have pallets which span 20 or even more teeth.

It is not often one meets a clock with a seconds pendulum where the pallets span 14 teeth of a wheel of 30, but they have been made; the performance, however, cannot be compared with an escapement where only 8 or 10 teeth are spanned.

To Draw the Escapement

There are various ways of drawing the dead-beat escapement, and an attempt will be made to describe it in such a way that its actions can be easily understood (Figure 33).

First a circle is scribed representing the full diameter of the wheel A_1. The diameter is drawn through the centre and extended by a little more than the radius beyond the circle A_2. On this line is planted the pallet centre or what would be the pallet-arbor hole B. For convenience the wheel will have 30 teeth; whilst the pallets will span 8 teeth and be spanned by 9 teeth, *i.e.* 9 teeth outside the pallets and 8 teeth inside. The centre of the pallet faces will be on a line 45° from the centre line.

These two lines are now drawn one on each side of the centre line and long enough to cross the circumference C_1 and C_2. The point where these lines meet the circumference will be the centre of the pallet faces D_1, D_2. Tangents are now drawn from these points to pass through the centre line E_1, E_2, and if correctly drawn the two tangents will meet at precisely the same point B, which will be the pallet-arbor hole and pallet centre.

There is a 12° space between 2 teeth which is the total width of the two pallet faces plus drop and the thickness of the tip of each tooth. This means $\frac{1}{2}$° drop, which on an inch-diameter wheel is 0·004 in., with the same amount for the tip of the tooth. These figures are for a very accurate wheel and pallets, but for the ordinary dead-beat and for the purpose of the drawing 1° is allowed for each. This will leave 10° for the total thickness of both pallets or 5° each, which is, of course, the width of the impulse planes.

$2\frac{1}{2}$° is now marked off each side of the 45° line on the left side F_1, C_2.

The impulse in a dead-beat is usually 2°, but it is not imperative from a practical point of view; however, if a really close rate is wanted 2° has been proved to be the best, so 3° is marked off below line E_1. This includes 1° locking or rest as well as the 2° impulse. The locking face of the entrance or first pallet G_1 is found by joining

46

up the line on the far left, *i.e.* the line $2\frac{1}{2}°$ F_1 anti-clockwise of the 45° line, to the pallet centre.

A circle is drawn using the pallet centre as centre and the locking face as the point in the circumference. This will give both the locking face of the entrance pallet and the outside circle of the exit pallet

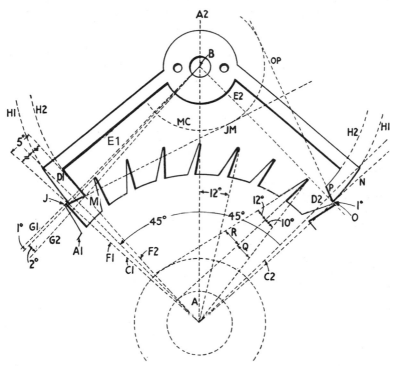

Figure 33. Theoretical drawing of Graham dead-beat escapement in which the pallets span 8 teeth and are spanned by 9. This is the recognised standard type.

or dropping-off corner H_1. 1° is now marked off from the pallet centre on line G_1 towards the wheel and a line drawn crossing the circumference and meeting the circle of the pallet faces. This represents 1° locking or rest, G_2. In a very accurate escapement this can be reduced $\frac{1}{2}°$. This point is where the impulse plane commences, J.

2° is marked off from line G_1 again towards the wheel and a line drawn to cut the circumference of the wheel. This is the angle of impulse or the amount the pallet moves or is lifted.

47

From the centre of the wheel a line is drawn which is 5° to line G_1 and which will cross the circumference   This line gives the width of the pallet face, and where it meets G_1 is the dropping-off corner, M.   The points J and M are now joined and extended to the centre JM.   The compasses are set at the pallet-arbor centre and opened to meet point M, and a circle is scribed which will give the inside faces of both pallets or nibs, M_2.   Another circle is scribed to which the line JM is a tangent.   This will decide the impulse plane of the exit pallet, MC.

On the opposite side at C_2 a line N is drawn which is $2\frac{1}{2}$° outside C_2 and where N is met by the circle will give the dropping-off corner of the exit pallet H_1O.   A tangent is drawn from point O to the circle to which JM is a tangent, and where this line meets the two circles denoting the inside and outside faces is the impulse plane of the exit pallet, P.   This is shown as line OP.

The wheel teeth are not radial on the front or acting faces, but are under cut usually about 10° so that only the tip of the tooth is in action Q, this ensuring the minimum amount of friction.   The back of the tooth is usually 12° to the front, but for strength it is sometimes more, R.   The wheel is usually crossed out to make it as light as possible, but it must be quite strong, and although sometimes only 4 arms are left, the best quality often have 6 arms.

The wheel is usually screwed on to the collet of the 'scape-pinion arbor, thus guarding against the distortion which often occurs if the wheel is not riveted to its collet very carefully.   It should be unnecessary to add that the wheel must be perfectly flat and dead true if any rate is to be obtained, for any lack of truth means extra freedoms and losses.

When setting out the escapement in cases where the pallets are designed to span 10 teeth the distance of centres is equal to the diameter of the wheel.   The pallets are spanned by 11 teeth.   Therefore point B on Figure 34 does not apply, neither do lines C_1 or C_2, as these last two would be replaced by lines at an angle of 57° to the central line, but otherwise the set-out is the same.   Thus the distance of centre and lines C_1 and C_2 varies according to the number of teeth spanning the pallets.

It will be noticed how the angles of impulse are raised as the number of teeth spanned are increased, although the amount of lift is the same.   The arms of the pallets are also increased in length, and one naturally assumes that less power is required to move the pallets as the arms lengthen; this is so, but as the length of the impulse planes is longer, the friction is increased.

The changing oil, due to temperature changes, affects the rate of the dead-beat escapement to a great extent, and thus one has to consider the amount of time that the impulse planes are engaged, although the engagement takes only a second in each case.   To put it plainly, the speed of the tooth is greater where the impulse plane is longer and is more easily affected by changing oil.

Oil, which is, of course, essential, becomes thinner in a higher temperature and thicker in a lower temperature, whilst there is also the adhesive friction, which is more exaggerated the longer the parts are in action. The aim therefore must be to reduce the extent to

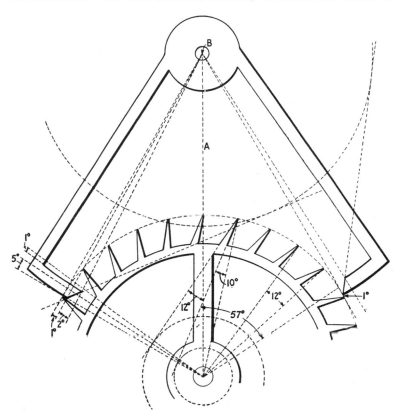

Figure 34. Dead-beat escapement. In this the distance of centres is greater and there are higher impulse angles. The pallets span 9 teeth and are spanned by 10.

which surfaces are in action, and this is the reason why the escapements with pallets spanning or embracing 8 teeth are preferable to ones spanning a higher number.

Inside and Outside Shake or Freedoms

All escapements suffer more or less from wear and have to be repaired, holes or bearings which support the pivots of the pallets and 'scape pinion becoming worn and having to be renewed. When replacing holes great care must be taken to avoid drifting from the original position, for if any drift does take place the inside and outside shake suffer or the drops become unequal, and one or the other may become too close, with the result that the 'scape wheel cannot pass.

With all dead-beat escapements the golden rule is that if the outside shake is tight the 'scape and pallet depth or the distance of centres is too close. This must be corrected by drawing the pallet hole or bearing an appropriate amount away from the 'scape hole, or the distance between the two holes must be increased, but if the inside shake is close, then the holes must be brought nearer to each other. The amount of movement is, of course, only half of what it appears to be.

All double-beat escapements, *i.e.* those where there is impulse to each vibration, have one definite factor, and this is that all alterations act in two ways. Thus if one pallet is altered say 1° the opposite pallet is also altered 1°, making a total of 2°, so if there is a total drop of 2° and it is all on one pallet, if 1° is taken off one it will also make 1° difference to the other, and will bring the two pallets equal.

The Locking or Rest

As previously stated, in a first-class dead-beat escapement $\frac{1}{2}$° locking is ample, but it must be remembered that the wheel tooth must unquestionably lock, or the escapement will fail and the clock will stop.

When wear has taken place and the pallets have been repaired it may be found that as the wheel tooth is released from one pallet it drops on to the impulse plane of the other pallet instead of on the locking face, and if this occurs it is said that the escapement mislocks. With a dead-beat escapement the only way to alter this is to close the pallets or to bend the two arms closer together. Unless, of course, the 'scape wheel and pallets have been very badly planted, and this is most unlikely, the fact of altering the depth will not affect the locking, but as stated earlier will only alter the drops.

Unequal Lockings—Sometimes pallets are badly treated or repaired, and it may be that the wheel tooth locks on one pallet and mislocks on the other. This means that the impulse planes are at different angles or that one is shorter than the other.

If the former is the case the only way to correct it is to make the impulse planes the same. This would mean that they would then both mislock, and it would also entail closing the arms to make the locking correct. If, on the other hand, the latter is the case it may mean that a new pair of pallets will be needed. If, however, only one pallet is bad and the other is in good order a new pallet can be put on the faulty side.

Fitting a New Pallet—This is done by cutting away the pallet and part of the arm, and filing the arm to half its thickness for a short

50

distance, sufficient to be quite sound. A piece of steel is fitted to this and filed so that the new piece and the remaining half of the arm combined equal the thickness of the original. The two pieces are fitted together and two suitable holes drilled through both of them while they are clamped in this position. They are then riveted firmly together as though solid. Next the new pallet-to-be is marked off with a pair of dividers, using the other pad as a guide.

The width of the impulse planes can easily be marked off with the

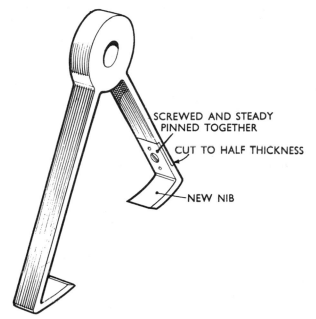

SCREWED AND STEADY
PINNED TOGETHER

CUT TO HALF THICKNESS

NEW NIB

Figure 35. Fitting a new nib or part of a pallet and arm is often quicker than making a new pair complete.

dividers, but the angle of impulse is not quite so simple, and in a repair job this can be arrived at only by trial. First, a flat face is filed as near to the angle as possible and then the pallets are put in the frame with the 'scape wheel and the angle altered until the locking is equal on both pallets. If when the lockings are equal they are too deep the impulse plane can be filed back, carefully preserving the angle until the lockings are correct, but it must not be forgotten that the amount which is filed away is only half of what might be expected.

Continental clocks are often provided with a turntable on the front plate, the turntable having the pallet-arbor pivot hole planted eccentrically in the table. Thus the depth of the escapement is easily adjusted and the inside and outside shake made perfect, but as previously stated this will not correct the locking.

Polishing the Pallets—Dead-beat pallet faces are best polished on a lap so that they can be kept perfectly flat.   For this purpose a polishing lap made from zinc or from vegetable ivory can be used, the latter being the hardened or dried kernel of the coconut, and it is better than elephant ivory for polishing.   The ivory gives a better polish than zinc and is also quicker, but it must revolve at high speed, and the work must be kept moving, otherwise the surface becomes ridgy. Diamantine, which is purchased mixed with oil at the material dealers, is used on the lap, but the mixture must be more oily than when used for other polishing.   It must be well beaten in mixing, otherwise it will scratch.

Diamantine cuts or grinds when wettish, but polishes as it dries, and when a high-speed lap is being used this must be stopped just before the diamantine dries.

Polishing Laps, *etc.*

The lap is fitted to an arbor and held in a split collet in the lathe, and it must run true and flat.   It is worth while to make a special holder

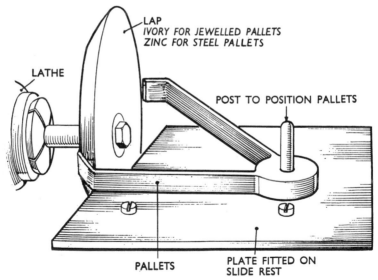

Figure 36.   Polishing dead-beat pallets using a lap in the lathe.   The shaped back of the lap is shown polishing the inside of the pallets.

to fit in the lathe so that laps can be changed over and still run flat and true.

A flat plate is fitted to the slide rest or the cross slide as it is some-times termed, and on this plate is a post which fits the pallet-arbor hole. The pallets are placed on this plate with the hole on the post, and the lead screw is eased off so that it is inoperative. The slide rest is adjusted so that the impulse face is coincident with the face of the lap, and this face is smeared with diamantine, then the lap is set in motion. Light pressure is maintained on the pallets, both to keep them flat on the plate and also to press the pallet faces against the lap, and the slide rest is pushed backwards and forwards rapidly. Care must be taken to keep the face of the pallets on the lap and not to run off the edge, for if this does happen the lap and pallets may be ruined.

The curved locking face and the reverse curved side of the exit dropping-off edge are polished in the same way because these curves can be followed. The inside dropping-off face of the entrance pallet and the locking face of the exit pallet are polished on the back face of the lap, which must be shaped to suit.

Diamantine is only suitable for solid steel pallets, and if the pallets are jewelled diamond powder must be used instead of diamantine. Diamond powder can now be purchased in different grades ready for mixture and use; it is mixed with oil and smeared on the lap in just the same way as diamantine. It must be emphasised that there is no connection between diamantine and diamond powder.

Fitting Pallet Stones

Jewelled pallets are made in steel in exactly the same manner as steel pallets but when they are finished the faces are slotted for about one-third and suitable stones ground to fit. The stones are fixed in position with shellac, and care must be taken to see that they are securely fixed, otherwise they may move in the process of polishing. After fixing, the stones are ground down until flush with the steel.

The grinding is carried out in the same way as the polishing, except that a grinding lap is used. This is a copper lap into which coarser diamond powder is rolled, and as such remains permanent, unlike the polishing lap, which has to be cleaned and recharged every time it is used. Water is used on the grinding lap and not oil, but although it must be kept wet, if too much water is used it will be thrown off by the lap and everything smothered with water, including the operator.

Quite a number of pallets are jewelled with agate, but the best quality are jewelled with sapphire, which never needs repolishing or renewing except when damaged by rough handling or accidents.

The 'Scape Wheel

The 'scape wheel must be light but of course of a necessary strength, and is made from good-quality hard-rolled brass.

The teeth are cut using two cutters, one to cut the front or acting side and the other the back. They can be cut by using only one cutter, but it would have to be a very well-made one. The first cutter

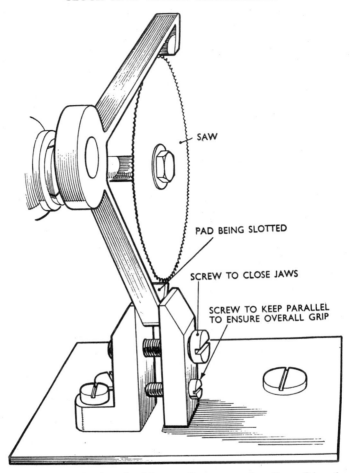

SAW

PAD BEING SLOTTED

SCREW TO CLOSE JAWS

SCREW TO KEEP PARALLEL
TO ENSURE OVERALL GRIP

Figure 37. Slotting dead-beat pallets to receive slips of jewel.
The pallets are clamped firmly in jaws fitted to the slide rest of
the lathe.

will cut the acting face, and must be set off radial by 10°. The easiest
way to set this cutter correctly is to put it dead radial at first, put the
wheel blank in position and adjust the depth of the cutter to just make
a line on the blank. Then using either the 360-division or the 90-
division plate the blank is moved 10 divisions on the 360 plate or $2\frac{1}{2}$
divisions on the 90 plate. It is quite easy to judge the $\frac{1}{2}$ division.

The position of the cutter is altered to correspond to the original
line, which has moved with the dividing plate, and will then cut a

tooth with a 10° undercut. The 30 spaces can now be cut, the first cut taking away about half the required space.

The second cutter is next put in position and the procedure repeated, and at the first setting this should cut about two-thirds of

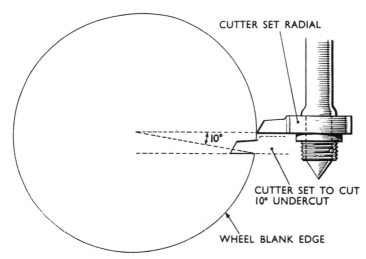

CUTTER SET RADIAL

10°

CUTTER SET TO CUT
10° UNDERCUT

WHEEL BLANK EDGE

Figure 38. Method of cutting teeth where the acting face is undercut (dotted lines show first setting). The cutter is then set 10° higher to give correct setting for cutting. A single blade or flying cutter is used.

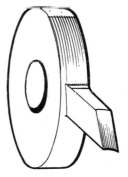

Figure 39. Single blade or flying cutter. The end is shaped to form the band of the wheel while cutting the sides

the remaining metal. If too much metal is removed the top of the tooth will bend over, so it is far better to take a little off each cut, even if it does mean extra time is spent doing the job.

The cutters should be highly polished so that after cutting the teeth need no further attention.

The Pendulum and Suspension

A good escapement cannot give of its best without a good pendulum and coupled with this a good suspension. Dead-beat escapements require heavy pendulums, and a heavy pendulum needs a very strong and firm suspension; the case must also be strong and firmly

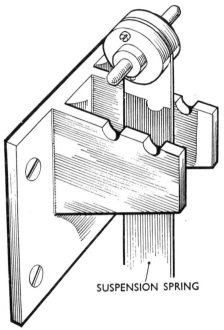

SUSPENSION SPRING

Figure 40. Bracket to support pendulum. The bracket is screwed to the back of the case and the pendulum is free of the movement except at the crutch. This gives greater rigidity and the back cock is not under strain.

anchored. Often the pendulum is hung on a strong cast-iron bracket to which the movement is also fixed, but the movement need not be fixed to the same bracket, and as long as the pendulum support is very firm and solid the escapement will give good results.

There must be the minimum amount of freedom between the crutch and the pendulum rod, as any shake here means loss of impulse and deviation in the extent of the arc of vibration of the pendulum.

The reason why the case must be a firm fixture is that a heavy pendulum will cause the case to move each time it swings or, as it is said, will cause the case to oscillate. Any serious oscillation of the case will cause minutes of variation if it does not stop the clock altogether.

The suspension spring must be as weak as possible yet strong enough to support the weight of the pendulum plus the extra strength required to prevent the pendulum rolling or wobbling during its vibration. The point of suspension should be as near as possible coincident with the pallet-arbor pivot hole in the back cock; the reason for this being that the crutch and the pendulum rod will be

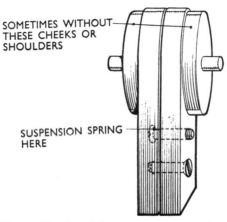

SOMETIMES WITHOUT THESE CHEEKS OR SHOULDERS

SUSPENSION SPRING HERE

Figure 41. Pendulum suspension spring block. This fits in a bracket fitted to the back of the case. The block is in two halves and the suspension spring is clamped between them.

working in the same circular path and there will be no up-and-down motion between the two, and thus no extra friction.

The suspension spring must be firmly anchored to the pendulum rod without any possibility of give. In most regulators the suspension spring is firmly clamped between steel cheeks which are screwed together and the clamp is also screwed to the pendulum rod. The top end of the suspension spring is also clamped to steel cheeks which are pivoted with appropriate pivots. These pivots rest in half holes in the pendulum bracket, with the pivot shoulders resting against the sides of the bracket, and there is no question of movement.

The Crutch of a Dead-beat Regulator

In most regulators the crutch is adjustable for beat. Thus instead of putting in beat by bending the crutch, as often has to be done in the cheaper clocks, the crutch can be set by screws or nuts.

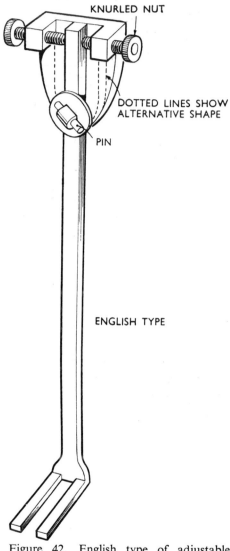

KNURLED NUT

DOTTED LINES SHOW
ALTERNATIVE SHAPE

PIN

ENGLISH TYPE

Figure 42. English type of adjustable crutch. In this very convenient way of putting the regulator in beat the main table is fitted to the pallet arbor, whilst the crutch is pinned friction tight to the table and is moved as required by the thumb screws before finally fixing it in place.

The principle is that the collet on the pallet arbor is as usual, but has screwed to it a brass plate on which are mounted blocks through which screws are fitted, and these screws, one on each side, have small thumb-nuts fitted to them.

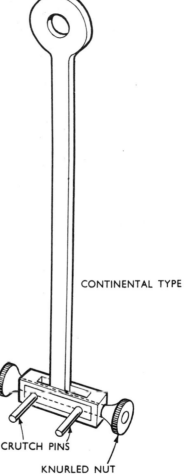

CONTINENTAL TYPE

CRUTCH PINS

KNURLED NUT

Figure 43. Continental type of adjustable crutch. In this type the impulse notch is adjustable, but it is not so popular as the English type because it is not so rigid.

The crutch itself fits closely on the pallet arbor and is kept in place by a brass washer with a pin through the arbor, thus holding the collet firmly but not tightly against the boss of the crutch. The upper part of the crutch is extended at the top and passes between the two screws. The regulator is put in beat by screwing one screw in and the other out, thus moving the crutch. When in beat the two screws hold the crutch quite tightly, and there are no losses. This is a typically English method of construction.

Another method which is favoured by Continental makers has the adjustment at the bottom of the crutch, and in this case the crutch consists of two pins spaced to embrace the pendulum rod. The pins are fitted into a brass plate which is tapped with a screw-thread and which has a screw passing through, usually with a small thumb-nut fitted to each end. This screw is pivoted at each end into the crutch proper and holds the crutch pins and plate firmly against the crutch. To put in beat the screw is turned the required amount and the crutch pins are moved over. This action is similar to the slide rest of a lathe with the screw acting as the lead screw.

THE BROCOT PIN-PALLET DEAD-BEAT ESCAPEMENT

The Graham dead-beat escapement has been dealt with at some length because so much that applies to it is also applicable to other escapements, but there is a French dead-beat escapement which has many favourable features, and this will now be described. In the Graham escapement the pallets were solid pieces, but in the Brocot the pads are fitted into the pallet arms. These pads, which are the pallets proper, are round rods of steel cut exactly in half, and the wheel teeth work on the half-round section and not on the flat sides. In quite a number of these escapements, especially where they are visible or showing on the dial, the pallet pads are made in the cheaper variety of semi-precious stone, such as cornelian. The only thing in their favour is their appearance, because they are a deep red in colour and thus attractive. Some very good escapements of this type have been made in which the pads were of sapphire; these were used for regulators with a seconds pendulum, but their performance was not equal to that of a Graham escapement.

The Brocot escapement is really very simple to construct and repair, and yet almost all those of this type which come to hand for repair are in a deplorable condition. It cannot be thought that they were constructed incorrectly, so it can only be imagined that they have suffered at the hands of repairers. One difficulty with this escapement is keeping the pallets lubricated, but if the wheel is planted close to the pallet arms this difficulty is largely overcome.

The escapement consists of a wheel with a varying number of teeth to suit the length of pendulum used, the lower the number of teeth, so the greater the angle of impulse or lift. The pallets consist of two arms which have holes drilled at the base, whilst the pallet pads, which are fitted closely into the drilled holes, stand out at right angles. The wheel teeth are radial on the acting faces, but in some the teeth are cut back like a Graham 'scape wheel to impart slight recoil should the vibration become excessive. The pallet pads should be slightly less in diameter than the space between two teeth

60

to allow for drop and the necessary freedoms. The best way to understand the escapement is by making a practical drawing, and instructions for the preparation of this will now be given.

Drawing the Escapement

A 'scape wheel of 30 teeth will be taken as an example because this would be the type used with a long seconds pendulum, also it is easier to draw.

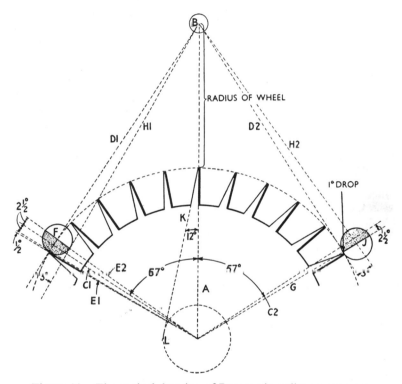

Figure 44. Theoretical drawing of Brocot pin-pallet escapement. This is suitable for shorter pendulum movements.

As in the Graham escapement, the pallets will span 10 teeth and they will be spanned by 11 teeth.

The circle representing the path of the wheel teeth is scribed as usual and the centre line A drawn and extended as before. The distance of centres will be the diameter of the wheel, so this can be measured and point B marked. Again this can be checked by drawing the lines left and right of the centre line. These lines are 57°

from the centre line and are extended for convenience beyond the circumference C_1 and C_2. These will give the centre of the pallet pads, pins or rollers, whichever term may be preferred. Pads is really the best term and is most understood.

Where these lines meet the circle of the path of the wheel, tangents are drawn to meet the centre line A. These tangents will meet at point B, which as already measured makes the distance of centres equal the diameter of the 'scape wheel. These lines are D_1 and D_2. The thickness of the pads will be 5°, thus allowing $\frac{1}{2}$° drop and $\frac{1}{2}$° for the thickness of the tooth. $2\frac{1}{2}$° is now marked off on each side of line C_1 and lines E_1 and E_2 are drawn. Another line is now drawn $\frac{1}{2}$° below E_1. This will be the thickness of the wheel tooth, and where line E_2 meets the circumference of the circle will be the centre of the pallet pad F.

A circle is scribed using point F as the centre and the point where E_1 meets the circumference as the radius; this gives the full size of the pad. Only half of the circle is used, so line E_2 forms the flat side of the pad or in practice the clearance flat. If a line is now drawn from point B to meet the inside of the pad it will show 3°, which is the impulse angle or angle of life H_1. Another line is marked off from point B and 3° outside line D_2. This will give the centre of the outside pad, H_2.

A line is now marked off $2\frac{1}{2}$° below line C_2 from the centre of the wheel and continued beyond the circle of the wheel to cross line H_2 at J, then with J as the centre and where line G meets the circle of the wheel a circle is scribed for the exit pad, with line G forming the flat side of the pad.

The teeth are now drawn, and as the fronts of these are radial, all that has to be done is to draw the radial lines 12° apart, starting from line E_1 and then marking off $\frac{1}{2}$° for tooth thickness, then proceeding to draw the backs. The backs are 12° from the point of the tooth, so a line is marked 12° and long enough to pass the wheel centre. A circle K is drawn to which this line is a tangent, all of the backs of the teeth being tangential to this circle.

The Pallet Pads

As stated previously, and as one will observe from the drawing Figure 45, the full diameter or size of the pallet pads is very critical. Sometimes pallet pads are found which have been cut to less than half with the idea of clearance. This is a bad mistake, because if the full diameter is too large it is impossible to get them free and at the same time to safely lock the wheel teeth. If, on the other hand, the pads are too small there is serious loss of impulse and, of course, increased drop and subsequent wear. A clock will keep going on small pads but not on large pads.

Another point is that the clock will not perform satisfactorily if the flat side is engaged by the wheel, at whatever angle it is placed, because the pallet pads will not clear.

NECESSARY FREEDOM

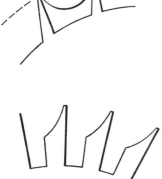

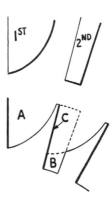

Figure 45a. The upper diagram shows the correct size of pallet pads for a Brocot pin-pallet escapement; often the pads have to be smaller should the wheel be inaccurate. The lower diagram shows the alternative shape of dead-beat wheel teeth.

Figure 45b. Method of cutting wheel teeth using two cutters.

Sometimes the holes drilled in the pallet arms to take the pads are too large and one is deceived into thinking the holes denote the size of the pads. It is always advisable to check these holes for size.

Making New Steel Pallet Pads

To make correct pads a piece of round silver steel rod or steel which can be hardened is chosen. The rod is tried between two teeth to make sure that it can be inserted between them to a depth a little more than half its diameter. Checking with a micrometer, exactly half of the rod is filed away, leaving it quite flat and straight. There must be no tapering, because the endshake of the pallet arbor and 'scape pinion will bring different parts of the pads into action.

When filed up, the rod is partly cut through at the correct length and then hardened in water. While still joined to the rod the rounded side is polished to a high polish. When finishing the flat side it need not be polished, but the rounded side should be laid on a groove in a filing block. This helps to keep it flat, because as one presses, so the rounded side gives, and the result is an almost dead flat surface.

Where the Holes in the Arms Are too Large—The holes to take the pads, if too large, can be treated in two ways. First, they can be bushed and then opened up to the correct size, but care must be taken not to drift, or secondly, and the better way, is to make what can be described as pivoted pads.

A piece of steel rod which nicely fits the holes is chosen and turned down in the lathe to the correct length and size to suit the wheel.

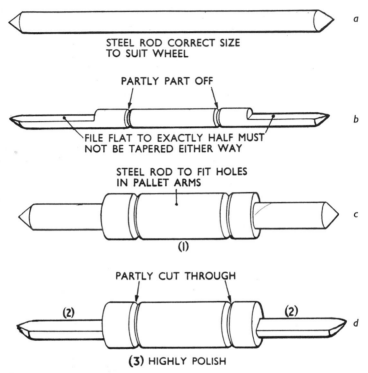

STEEL ROD CORRECT SIZE
TO SUIT WHEEL

a

PARTLY PART OFF

FILE FLAT TO EXACTLY HALF MUST
NOT BE TAPERED EITHER WAY

b

STEEL ROD TO FIT HOLES
IN PALLET ARMS

(1)

c

PARTLY CUT THROUGH

(2)   (2)

(3) HIGHLY POLISH

d

Figure 46. Method of making pallet pads for Brocot escapement: *a* and *b* are used when the holes in the pallet arms are the correct size; *c* and *d* pivoted pads are used when the holes are too large. The pivots are turned on rod to size and length (1) filed flat to exact half (2) and (3) hardened and polished while on the rod. When finished they are broken off at the parting.

The pad proper will be like a pivot on the section which fits the hole in the arm. There is no need to·shellac steel pads into the arms, as would be done with jewel pads, and they can be fitted so that they require just a light tap with a punch to drive them home to be quite secure. They must, however, always be placed in the correct position before being driven home.

The pads are placed with the round side active, and should be so positioned that a perpendicular line to the flat face would be a tangent to the path of the wheel. This will ensure the maximum freedom and the maximum impulse, and the wheel will lock dead central on the pad.

THE BROCOT PIN-PALLET AS A RECOIL

The Brocot pin-pallet is sometimes adopted as a recoil, but whether intentionally or otherwise is a matter of opinion. In one case the wheel is mounted the reverse way and the sloping backs of the teeth against the pads provide recoil, whilst in the other case, which is the lesser of two evils, the wheel teeth, instead of being radial, are cut back like a Graham and tend to draw the pallet pad into the wheel, thus a resistance to unlocking is provided and the effects of a large vibration nullified because the vibration is reduced almost at once. The idea behind this is to reduce the vibration of the pendulum by adding its worst enemy, friction.

The Brocot pin-pallet gives its best performance as a dead-beat, and if the vibrations are excessive the obvious and sensible course is to reduce the motive power, *i.e.* put in a weaker mainspring or lighten the weight driving it.

The Locking and Drops

Like the Graham dead-beat, the drops are equalised by altering the distance of centres. Thus if there is no outside shake or freedom

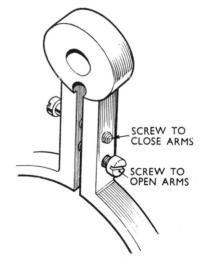

Figure 47. The adjustable arms on a Brocot pin-pallet or similar escapement enable the depth of locking to be adjusted.

SCREW TO CLOSE ARMS

SCREW TO OPEN ARMS

the distance of centres must be increased or the pallets pushed away from the wheel, and decreased if there is no inside shake or freedom.

In most of these clocks there is a turntable which carries the front pallet-arbor pivot, this giving the necessary adjustment because the pivot hole is planted off centre. The locking is increased by closing the arms and eased by opening; it should, however, take place right on the centre of the pad or on what would be the perpendicular to the flat face. This is very important, because if the tooth fails to lock it falls on the impulse plane and will stop the clock, the reason being that the tooth recoils from the impulse plane up on to the locking face, and as it gets only a part of the impulse the resistance exerted by the motive power is too great to be overcome.

In the best-quality clocks the arms are sometimes made adjustable by two screws fitted through them. One screw passes freely through one arm and screws into the other, and will close the arms by drawing them together, whilst the other screw is screwed into one arm and exerts pressure on the other to open the arms. However, in each case both screws have to be adjusted, because if it is desired to close the arms the latter screw has to be eased as well, and if it is necessary to open the arms the former has to be eased as the latter screw is turned.

The Impulse or Lift Varies with the Number of Teeth

In the Graham the angle of lift remains constant irrespective of the number of teeth in the wheel or the distance of centres, but in the Brocot pin-pallet the impulse varies with the number of teeth, and one cannot avoid this. The distance between two consecutive teeth varies, and as the distance between two teeth less drop is the impulse plane, the pallet pad decreases in diameter as the impulse plane gets shorter. Increasing the distance of centres also alters the length of impulse; if the distance of centres is 1 in. and the impulse $3°$, by making the distance of centres double, $i.e.$ 2 in., the impulse will be $1\frac{1}{2}°$; thus there is considerable scope.

One must remember that with all escapements the impulse or angle of lift is measured from the pallet-arbor centre or, as it is termed, the pallet hole.

$Usual$ $Repairs$—With the Brocot pin-pallet escapement the pivots must be smooth and round, and the holes or bearings must be quite round and must fit the pivots freely but closely. The pivots must be quite straight and not tapering, for with a tapering pivot the action is different and varies with the amount of endshake.

The wheel teeth, which are as a rule very delicate, must be quite sound and must be accurately spaced or divided. A bent tooth, even if only very slightly out of true, is often difficult to detect, because if the clock stops on a particular tooth it may be the one engaged by the other pallet which is the offender, so both must be closely examined.

Cutting the Wheel

The wheel teeth are cut in the same way as the Graham 'scape wheel, but the set-up is slightly different because the Graham teeth are slightly back cut or undercut, whereas with the Brocot pin-pallet dead-beat escapement the front of the tooth is radial.

Sometimes the tops of the teeth are rounded so that only a small part of the tooth is engaged; this is a mistake, and only adds unnecessary delicacy to an already delicate wheel. The teeth are sometimes cut in two parts, the top half being appreciably thinned but the bottom half being left much thicker. There is no advantage, however, in this, and the wheel is more difficult to cut (see Figure 45*a* and *b*).

As in all escapements, the wheel must be true both on the flat and in the round, and, last but not least, accurately divided.

Putting in Beat

Clocks with the Brocot escapement are what is called self-setting, *i.e.* by giving the pendulums a big swing they will put themselves in

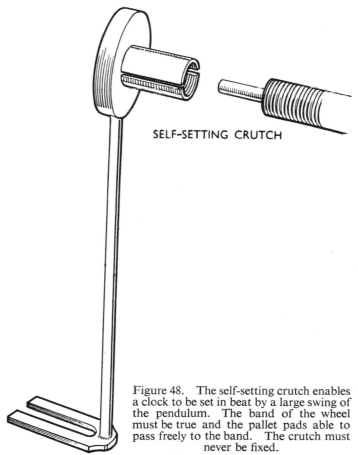

SELF-SETTING CRUTCH

Figure 48. The self-setting crutch enables a clock to be set in beat by a large swing of the pendulum. The band of the wheel must be true and the pallet pads able to pass freely to the band. The crutch must never be fixed.

beat. The crutch is screwed on to the pallet arbor instead of being a fixture as in most clocks.

The pendulum with a big swing forces the pallet pads to bank against the band of the 'scape wheel, continuing this action until the vibration eases off. As the pallet banks on the wheel the crutch carries on and banks on each side until it eventually settles down with the crutch equidistant, the escapement then being in beat.

The collet on the crutch is cut through so that the fit on the arbor can be adjusted; if the crutch is easy the pipe on the collet can be squeezed in very slightly until the fit is correct. The pipe should always be closed with a broach or by a piece of wire being put through it so that it is not squeezed too far. The crutch must not be an easy fit and yet not so tight that it will break the pivots when the pendulum is swung. In no circumstances whatever should the crutch of a Brocot pin pallet or like escapement be lead soldered; this is a habit of some clockmakers if they cannot find the fault, but it only makes matters worse, and should not be tolerated. If the clock will not keep going there is a fault, and soldering the crutch will not put it right.

THE PIN-PALLET ESCAPEMENT

This escapement, although called pin-pallet, is very different from the Brocot. In the dead-beat escapements so far dealt with the impulse plane has been on the pallets, but with this pin-pallet there is no impulse on the pallets and it is all on the wheel teeth. The escapement is mostly used for silent clocks, and gives very good results.

In this case the pallet pins are replaced by gut lines stretched between two pairs of arms similar to pallets, the wheel running between the two and engaging the gut line. At first glance it would be thought that the gut would wear very quickly, but this is not so, although new lines are put in when the clock has been running for some considerable time. When putting new lines on pallets care must be taken to replace with the correct size. This is most important, because the inside and outside freedoms or shake will be altered by any alteration in the size of the line or pins.

As with the other dead-beat escapements, the intersection affects the inside and outside shake, and the width of the pallet arms affects the locking. Thus if the escapement mislocks, the arms are closed, but the intersection or distance of centres must not be altered. Where lines are used there is a spring screwed to the outside of the arms and the lines are attached to the spring and are thus held quite taut. In a cheap clock the pallet pins are of steel.

Another point which the pin-pallet has in common with other dead-beat escapements is that as the distance of centres increases, for the same amount of impulse the impulse planes lengthen and the friction increases, but the amount of power required is less. This point, however, does not apply in the case of the Brocot pin-pallet. As has been seen, the lengthening of the arms decreases the angle of impulse, but the length of the impulse plane remains the same. As with the other escapements, a drawing will help to simplify the actions.

Drawing the Escapement

A wheel of 30 teeth is again taken as an example. The distance of centres will be 1·7 times the radius of the wheel, but the correct point can be arrived at by the usual tangents. The escapement can be drawn in a similar way to the Graham, and an opinion can be formed as to the advantages of either. There will be 11 teeth outside or spanning the pallets, with the pallets spanning 10 teeth inside.

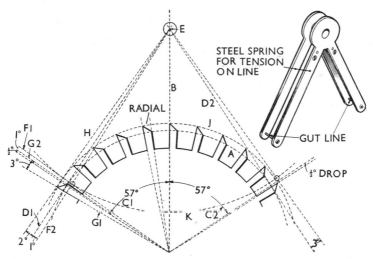

Figure 49. Pin-pallet escapement for pendulum movement. This is a silent escapement when gut line is used instead of steel pin. The gut is stretched between two pairs of arms and a spring keeps the gut taut.

A circle is drawn for the inside path of the wheel or what is the locking corner of the teeth, A, and then a centre line B is drawn, and extended a little farther than required. The two lines C_1 and C_2 from the wheel centre form an angle of 57° to the centre line, and are carried beyond the circumference. The lines D_1 and D_2 are tangents to the circle which meet C_1 and C_2 respectively, and where these lines meet on the centre line is the pallet-arbor centre E.

There is $\frac{1}{2}$° drop, and the pin or gut will be 2° in thickness. $1\frac{1}{2}$° is marked off along line D_1 towards the pallet hole E from the wheel centre and the line F_1 is drawn, then from the pallet hole E another line is drawn 1° from D_1 towards the wheel; this is the locking, F_2.

Where line F_1 meets F_2 is the centre of the pallet pin. A line drawn 1° either from the pallet centre or the wheel centre will give the outside of the pin.

3° is marked off on line C_1, line G_1 is drawn and above C_1 $\frac{1}{2}$° is marked off G_2; this will make the distance from G_1 to G_2 equal $3\frac{1}{2}$°, which is the width of the tooth. Now from the pallet centre E a line is drawn 2° above D_1, which will give the impulse or angle of lift H. Where G_1 meets H is the highest tip of the tooth.

A circle J is now drawn with the wheel centre as one point and G_1H as the point in the circumference; this will give the highest tip of all the teeth and also the full circumference of the wheel. G_1H is now joined up with G_2D; this is the impulse plane of the tooth, and the first tooth can now be completed.

As all of the teeth are 12° apart, both the front and the back of all of the teeth can be marked off in 12° segments. The fronts are only brought up to the inside circle, but the backs are brought up to the outside circle. On joining up the points where the backs meet the outside circle with the points where the fronts meet the inside circle all the teeth will be completed. Now with the pallet centre E as the centre a circle is scribed passing through the centre of the pallet pin and right across the wheel K. On this circle will be the exit pallet pin. From the pallet hole a line is drawn 3° above D_2, and where this line crosses circle K is the centre of the pallet pin. The pin is drawn the same as the entrance pin and the drawing is finished.

As will be noticed, the face of teeth both back and front are radial and must be so. This escapement can be made to be self-setting like the Brocot pin-pallet escapement.

Repairs to the Escapement

For this escapement to give satisfactory results the pivots must be a close fit in their holes or bearings; a wide hole will make the freedoms uncertain and may also cause mislocking. The pallets must not be removed and the train allowed to rush away, because the teeth may be damaged, and if the pallet pins are steel they may be broken off. The most serious damage would be to the wheel teeth, because the outside corner could be knocked off, and this would reduce the impulse and also cause the wheel to mislock, in which case the only remedy would be a new wheel.

To Make a New Wheel

The wheel is made from good hard brass and can be purchased in blank form or as a stamping. The blank must be turned to the exact outside diameter; the inside or locking circle is controlled by the angle at which the cutter is set.

The wheel can be cut using only one cutter, but it means filing the bottoms out to circle; the best way is to use one cutter for the impulse plane and another for the faces and the bottom or band of the wheel. In cutting the wheel shown in Figure 50, as the impulse

70

plane is 52° to the radial the cutter must be set 52° off the radial. The cutter can be set up by using a dividing plate of 360 divisions, or 13 divisions of a 90-division plate can be used instead. The front of the cutter must in any case be perfectly straight.

The impulse planes are cut first, and the space cutter must be reset

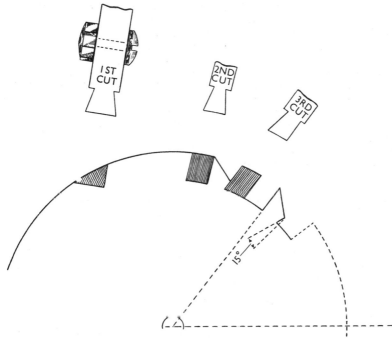

Figure 50. Method of cutting a pin-pallet 'scape wheel for a lever escapement, using 3 cutters.

to cut perfectly radial and also to follow the cuts made for the impulse planes. It is best for the backs of the teeth to be cut first, using a cutter about half or less than half the thickness required. By this means the correct amount of metal can be taken away without making the teeth too thin and thus reducing the impulse.

If the cutters are nicely polished the wheel need not be touched after cutting, but it is important to make sure that the wheel is perfectly true and accurately divided.

New Pallets

There is only one way to make the pallets, and that is, of course, by first making an accurate drawing and then securely sticking the drawing to the required metal and filing and drilling precisely to the

71

drawing; there are no short cuts. It is essential that the springs which provide tension are of hardened and tempered steel. They must be strong enough to keep the lines quite taut and must be screwed firmly in position.

In the case of steel pins the pins must fit the holes tightly and should be all but glass hard, and of course nicely polished. Both lines or pins must be replaced if they become worn.

THE CHEAP PIN-PALLET ESCAPEMENT

Another type of pin-pallet is in common use in alarm clocks and similar types of cheap clocks. This type is used with a lever and is a cheap form of lever escapement. It is really best termed a pin-pallet lever escapement, and has been used as a silent escapement. In this case the wheel, which is made of hardened fibre, has a very slow train, and as such requires very little motive power, whilst the drops are as close as possible and are almost silent. It is, of course, the drop which makes the noise or tick in a clock, thus the more drop, the greater the noise.

The wheel in the lever-type escapement usually has 15 teeth, and the distance of centres is, of course, very small; they are in fact made as close as possible so that the maximum arc of the balance can be obtained. This is a detached escapement, whereas the pendulum is almost always completely attached or in contact.

In the escapement previously described 2° of impulse was allowed, whereas in this type it can be as much as 8° or 10°. This impulse is transmitted to a lever attached to the pallets, and this is again transmitted to a balance, which is a wheel mounted on an arbor called a balance staff. In the cheaper grades the balance staff has two pointed ends which revolve in conical holes sunk into screw tails. In the better grades the staff has pivots which run in holes of either brass or jewel and having endpieces on which the ends of the pivots are supported. This method prevents the shoulder of the pivot coming into action, and only the ends of the pivots and sides are in action, thus reducing friction and increasing the freedom of the balance.

The lever engages an impulse pin by means of a notch at its end. The pin is usually fitted into the balance, but is sometimes fixed into a roller fitted tightly on to the balance staff. Where the pin is fitted into the balance the lever is provided with horns which bank against the balance staff and so prevent the lever getting on the wrong side and stopping the pin entering the lever notch. In the case of the roller a pin called the guard pin banks on the roller edge.

In either case the lever can pass across from one side to the other only when the impulse pin is in the notch, unless the escapement is out of order, when the lever can and does pass with the pin out of the notch, thus stopping the clock, which is said to have overbanked. In the cheaper grade there is no roller in the true sense of the word, but the impulse pin is fitted into the balance itself, and in this case the balance staff acts as a banking roller, and is so arranged that the

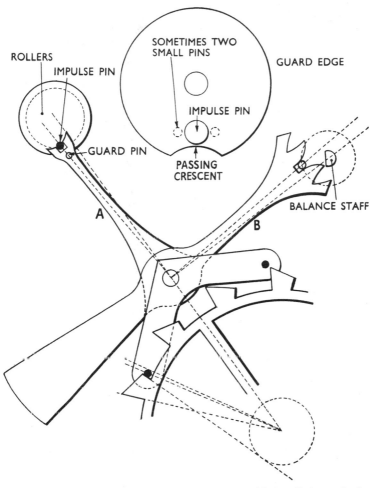

ROLLERS

SOMETIMES TWO SMALL PINS

GUARD EDGE

IMPULSE PIN

IMPULSE PIN

GUARD PIN

PASSING CRESCENT

BALANCE STAFF

A

B

Figure 51. The cheap pin-pallet escapement used in small alarm clocks sometimes has a separate impulse roller, and this is a definite improvement. The drawing shows the roller superimposed on the escapement. The pallets span 3 teeth and are spanned by 4. A has lever and roller, B has balance staff as guard.

lever cannot pass except when the impulse pin is in the lever notch. The balance staff has the part opposite the impulse pin made flat, and this flat section allows the lever to pass. Thus in this case the lever horns and the balance staff are the bankings, or part of them, as well as the safety action.

The Bankings as Cause of Stoppage

Where the clock has a separate roller, banking pins are usually provided, but with the cheaper escapements there are no banking

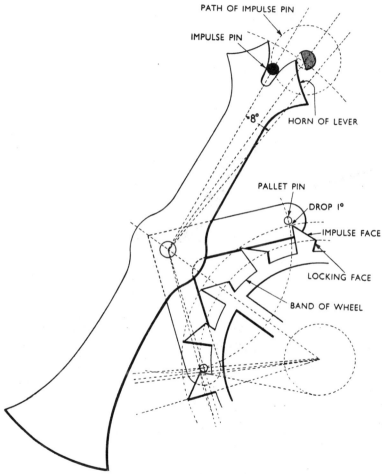

PATH OF IMPULSE PIN

IMPULSE PIN

8°

HORN OF LEVER

PALLET PIN

DROP 1°

IMPULSE FACE

LOCKING FACE

BAND OF WHEEL

Figure 52. Cheap pin-pallet as used on larger clocks. The pallets span 4 teeth and are spanned by 5.

pins, the pallet pins and the band of the 'scape wheel acting as the banking pins. Thus as the wheel tooth drops on to the pallet pin

74

the pin moves a little more until it is arrested by coming into contact with the band of the wheel. Now when the pallet pin is resting on the band of the wheel the horn of the lever should be just nicely clear of the balance staff. If the lever horn is touching the balance staff the clock will stop, but as long as the horn is definitely clear the less shake the better.

A similar thing can happen if the pallets mislock. If the pallet pin is not engaged by the locking face of the wheel tooth the horn of the lever is forced against the balance staff and will again stop the clock.

When the wheel tooth is dropped or drops off one pallet pin the opposite pallet pin should be in a position to be engaged by the locking face of the wheel tooth and about its own diameter inside the locking corner.

Sometimes the pin is engaged just on the corner of the tooth. This is unsafe, and the escapement must be deepened. If, however, the escapement is too deep the lever horn may again be forced against the balance staff and this will stop the clock. It must be remembered that with this escapement all of the actions are dependent on one another, rather more so than usual.

If the locking is correct and the lever horn is touching the balance staff the lever may be too long or not in angle. If it is tight on one side and correct on the other side of the staff the lever is out of angle. It should be tried on both sides of the staff. If incorrect the lever can be moved on the pallet arbor until correct. If, on the other hand the lever has the pallet pins fitted into it, as is the common practice, the lever must be bent to correct this angle fault.

If, however, the lever is tight against the staff on both sides the lever is too close to the balance staff. This condition must be carefully checked before alteration. The first step is to make sure that the wheel and pallet depth is not too deep. If this is in order the lever must be shortened, but a file should not be used, because if the horns are interfered with trouble may follow. By using bending pliers a small hump can be put in the thin part of the lever, and this will shorten the acting length. When shortening, however, it is necessary to make quite sure that the lever cannot pass across to the other side of the staff except when the impulse pin is in the notch; if it does the lever is too short and the hump must be flattened again until the lever is correct.

The lever must not be bent indiscriminately, because it may break with constant bending.

The Draw

This type of escapement has another function not present in the pendulum type, and this is called draw, *i.e.* the front or locking face of the wheel tooth instead of being radial is undercut about 15° from the radial. Thus as soon as the wheel locks on the pallet pin it draws the pin to the band of the wheel, where it is banked. The idea of this is to allow the balance perfect freedom after it has been given impulse by holding the horn of the lever clear of the edge of the balance staff.

Where the locking face becomes worn this function may not be effective, and the only remedy is a new wheel. Also, where the locking corner becomes worn a new wheel is necessary.

The Roller Type

Where the escapement has a roller the lever itself is not interfered with at the place where the guard or safety action is unsafe, but a perpendicular pin in the head of the lever is bent forward slightly until it is safe. This pin is the guard pin. Where there are banking pins the shake on each side of the roller can be altered by slightly adjusting these pins.

The roller edge must be examined, because this edge must be quite smooth. If it is rough or marked with pliers it must be smoothed up, otherwise the guard pin in the lever may become wedged owing to catching on the rough roller edge. Sometimes two thin pins are substituted in place of the impulse pin. These pins must always be inspected to see that they are quite straight and parallel to each other, as many troubles are caused by faulty pins.

This escapement does not give very good results, one of the main reasons being the difficulty of keeping it properly lubricated, and another reason being that the escapement is seldom well made; thus if serious repairs are necessary it is better to scrap the escapement and to buy a new one. If such a position does arise the method of cutting a new 'scape wheel is very similar to that used in the previous escapement, the differences being the length of the tooth, the angle of impulse and the locking face, the latter being undercut as stated earlier. The impulse face is cut 55° off the radial, and the locking face of the tooth is undercut by 15°. The length of the locking face or depth of cut should be three times the diameter of the pallet pin, although in the case of a thick pin twice the diameter may be enough. If the old wheel is available this can be used as a pattern. The pallet pins should, however, be as thin as possible, as thick as is necessary for strength and no thicker. Any thick pins mean serious loss of impulse.

THE PIN-WHEEL ESCAPEMENT

The pin-wheel escapement is a useful one, and is very good. It is a dead-beat, but instead of having teeth on the wheel is has pins fitted through the band which act instead. The impulse is generally reckoned to be all on the pallets, but with the English type the pins are so shaped that a certain amount of impulse is given by them. The pin-wheel has one fault in common with other escapements already discussed, i.e. the difficulty of keeping it lubricated.

The English type, which will be considered first, has the pins all on one side of the wheel, with the result that the pallet arms are of different lengths, the difference being half the space between two pins. In the escapements already dealt with the pallet arbor was planted over the centre of the wheel or radial, but with the pin-wheel the pallets are on one side or tangential to the wheel pins or the path of the pins. This has certain advantages inasmuch as the pallet holes need not be so critical with regard to fitting and the hole must wear quite a lot before the escapement is faulty.

The pallet arms differ from those already mentioned in that they are two separate pieces of steel instead of being in one piece. One

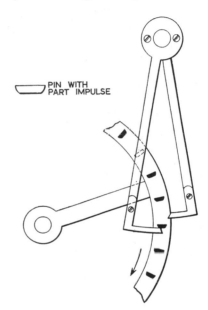

PIN WITH
PART IMPULSE

Figure 53. English type of pin-wheel escapement. The pins on the 'scape wheel are shaped to give impulse.

arm is usually on a higher plane than the other, thus reducing wear, as one arm is acted upon by one part of the pin and the other by another or higher part of the pin.

Like the Graham, the pallet faces are circular with the pallet arbor and are chords struck from it. The impulse planes are usually 2°, but they can be more or less to suit requirements, although by experience it has been found that 2° of impulse gives the best result because of the smaller arc of vibration. The pins are made of hard-drawn brass tightly fitted into the band of the wheel and then halved in a wheel-cutting engine.

It is possible to do the halving by hand, but it cannot be advised because it is a lengthy process and accuracy is essential in order that the drops are kept as small as possible. With quite a number of

77

these escapements not only are the pins halved but the underneath round of the pin is also flattened, which, besides reducing losses, gives impulse where there would be losses. The reduction of losses or drop means less motive power is required, with the result that there is less friction in the train and less jarring from the wheel teeth as they drop on to the pallet. This jarring or shock is present all the way through the train, and contributes greatly to worn wheel teeth and pinion leaves. The worst effects, however, are the shock to the pendulum and the resulting interference with the time of vibration.

It must not be forgotten that as the motive power varies through divers factors, so the effect of the drops varies and there is an uncertain rate. Thus the greater the drop, the greater the variations to be expected in the rate of the clock. The drops in a pin-wheel can be taken up by fitting larger pins, but this will be at the expense of impulse, and the pins must be as small as is consistent with their necessary strength.

The length of the pallet arms is usually about the diameter of the wheel, *i.e.* the mean length, because the arms are of different lengths. The space between the two pallets is, of course, the same as the depth of the pins plus the necessary drop, and this is the difference in length of the two arms. If there is 1° locking the clearance or opening between the two pallets must be a little less than half the full diameter of the pins.

The opening between the two pallets controls the locking, and as with the Brocot pin-pallet, if the escapement mislocks the arms are closed to narrow the opening, and vice versa. The inside and outside shakes are controlled by the length of the arms or rather by the relation of the length of one arm to the other. If the drops are equal but excessive the correct way to put this right is to fit new and thicker pallets. Another way is, of course, to use larger pins, but as stated earlier this is not a good method, although better than excessive drops, and as in most cases the pallets are screwed on to the pallet arms, the fitting of new pallets is the easiest and most economical way of correction, especially as it takes a long time to re-pin a pin-wheel.

The pallet faces of the pin-wheel escapement, which are of hard steel, will become worn and must be repaired, but when repolishing care must be taken to keep the impulse angles unimpaired. Obviously if the pallet faces have to be repaired the locking will be reduced and the drop increased, so there are limits to the amounts of repair that .can be carried out; however, if the pallet faces are highly polished and are hard it takes a long time for serious wear to take place.

As already mentioned, increased drop through repair means excessive wear owing to the jar or shock as the pin drops on to the locking face. This makes pits in the face and adds increased friction or resistance to unlocking.

THE FRENCH-TYPE PIN-WHEEL ESCAPEMENT

This escapement is a French one which has been universally adopted. It was invented by Amant, a French clockmaker, about 1741, but was very greatly improved by another French clockmaker, Lepaute, about 1750. Since then very little improvement has been made, and the escapement remains essentially as Lepaute designed it.

However, quite a number of French pin-wheels were made with

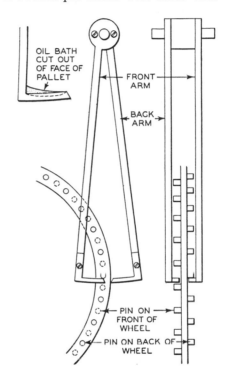

OIL BATH
CUT OUT
OF FACE OF
PALLET

FRONT
ARM

BACK
ARM

PIN ON
FRONT OF
WHEEL

PIN ON BACK OF
WHEEL

Figure 54. French pin-wheel escapement. Round pins are situated on both sides of the 'scape wheel, and the arms are therefore the same length. The little oil bath should be noted.

pins on both sides of the wheel face, the idea being to enable both pallet arms to be the same length. It meant, of course, that there had to be double the number of pins, because each pin was engaged only once, unlike the previous type, in which each pin was engaged by both pallets in turn.

The pins had to be thinner, and in fact two pins took the same room as one pin in the other type of escapement. The action of the two escapements was the same, but where the double quantity of pins was used the losses were greater because the pins were usually round and the extra impulse was lost by shaping the pins.

79

Another objection to the pins on each side of the wheel was that, being thinner, they were more easily bent and damaged, although, being round, they were easier to replace. Again there was the question of lubrication, which was a real problem, as with thinner pins the oil more readily ran away. This trouble was alleviated by a clever French horologist named Robin, who made the pallets in such a way that an oil bath or reservoir was provided on each pallet which kept the pins oiled in a very effective manner. Just behind the locking corner the pallet was hollowed out, and every time the pin locked it was oiled, any surplus being left behind. The author has known a particular clock by this maker which was still oily after 15 years, and there was very little wear even after this period.

TYPE OF PIN-WHEEL BY GALILEO

A type of pin-wheel escapement has been credited to Galileo, the famous astronomer. Whether it was designed for a clock or just to keep a pendulum vibrating seems uncertain, but in any case it was a frictional escapement.

The 'scape wheel had a type of ratchet teeth cut in the periphery and pins standing out from the band like the usual pin-wheel. The wheel was locked by a click-shaped pawl actuated by the teeth on the periphery, and the impulse was given by the pins through the band of the wheel. It would seem that this type of escapement would give the pendulum a very large arc.

SINGLE PIN ESCAPEMENT

This escapement was invented by McDowall, and although simple, had lubrication troubles which made it unpopular.

A roller or disc with just a single pin was substituted for the 'scape wheel and the pallets were made in the crutch itself. The advantage with this escapement was that the main impulse took place on the centre line and the locking took place on an almost flat plane, depending on the length of the crutch. There were no angles of impulse, the pin just resting against a straight perpendicular face and being given an almost straight push. This escapement was modified and fitted into a watch, and for a period gave very good results, the reason for failure, of course, being lack of lubrication.

CHOPPER DEAD-BEAT ESCAPEMENT

This escapement was invented by Gautier, a French horologist. It earned its name by the shape of the 'scape wheel teeth; where a balance and balance spring are used, as in the case of a carriage clock, the impulse is almost all on the wheel teeth.

The pallets, which are in the form of a roller or often a solid jewel, are fitted on to the balance staff. The roller, which is cut away, leaving about five-ninths of a circle to provide the locking, and also ground away on each side of the centre to provide partial impulse, is engaged at right angles by the wheel. This wheel is actually two wheels mounted on one arbor with spacing between to keep them a certain distance apart.

The action is easy to follow; as the wheel revolves, the tooth of one wheel is first engaged, and then as this drops so the tooth on the other wheel drops on to the roller. The balance has to be banked

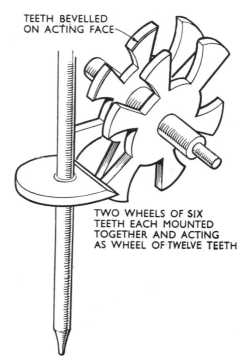

TEETH BEVELLED
ON ACTING FACE

Figure 55. Gautier or chopper escapement. This type is used in French carriage clocks and drives a balance. It dispenses with the contrate wheel, and gives a fair performance but is a frictional rest escapement. The roller is often made with jewel. All of the impulse is on the wheel teeth.

TWO WHEELS OF SIX
TEETH EACH MOUNTED
TOGETHER AND ACTING
AS WHEEL OF TWELVE TEETH

so that it cannot revolve too far, as otherwise the tooth may drop behind the roller and so prevent the balance returning.

To get the best results the position of the roller in relation to the wheel is very critical; if planted too high or low the locking is affected, and in either case becomes unsafe; also the drops and freedoms are reduced, and if the escapement is at all closely made it may not allow the wheel to pass. The angle of impulse is also affected because the impulse angles vary according to the manner in which the roller is presented to them.

These clocks often come in with a broken roller; it is hardly practicable to replace this with a jewel because a hard-steel roller will answer just as well. A jewel roller is hardly justifiable in any case, because a steel roller is so easily replaced when it becomes worn.

The only real advantage with this escapement is that a contrate wheel is dispensed with, and the balance runs perpendicular, with the minimum of friction at the pivots.

GAUTIER ESCAPEMENT WITH PENDULUM

This escapement lends itself very readily to the type of pendulum swinging from back to front instead of the usual side to side. It has on occasion been used to incorporate a swing with the figure of a girl sitting on it, the backwards-and-forwards motion of the swing

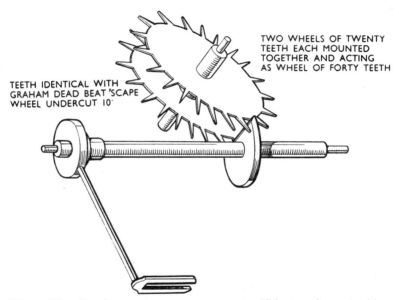

TWO WHEELS OF TWENTY
TEETH EACH MOUNTED
TOGETHER AND ACTING
AS WHEEL OF FORTY TEETH

TEETH IDENTICAL WITH
GRAHAM DEAD BEAT 'SCAPE
WHEEL UNDERCUT 10˚

Figure 56. Gautier or chopper escapement. This type is used with a pendulum often as a figure on a swing. All of the impulse is on the roller or pallets.

acting as the pendulum. This type of escapement usually has all of the impulse on the roller or pallets and none on the wheel teeth.

There are two wheels spaced apart on the same arbor or pinion, and one wheel must be in advance of the other by half of the space between two teeth. The thickness of the roller or the pallets must be a little less than half the distance between two teeth and the two 'scape wheels must be identical. The pallet arbor must have an endpiece or support at the end which takes the thrust, and the end-shake of the pallet arbor must be as close as freedom will permit.

The pallets or roller become worn both on the flat face and the impulse planes, and this wear must be polished out or a new roller fitted. The steel ones can be repolished on the flat face by rubbing them on a zinc block smeared with diamantine, and a very high polish can be obtained this way. The impulse planes can be polished with a flat zinc polisher by hand or on a zinc lap in the lathe.

The roller or pallets must be glass hard, because this escapement is not only a dead-beat but is also a frictional-rest type, especially when used to impart impulse to a balance where the vibration consists of perhaps three-quarters of a turn, *i.e.* three-eighths of a turn each side of the centre. As a timekeeper the pendulum type is the better.

THE DEAD-BEAT ESCAPEMENT USED IN SO-CALLED VIENNA REGULATORS

This type of dead-beat escapement embodies all the principles of the Graham, with the exception that the pallet pads are a separate unit and are clamped in position on the pallet arms. When these pads

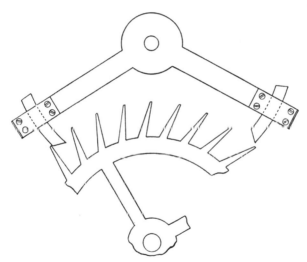

Figure 57. Dead-beat escapement with adjustable
pallet pads as used in Continental clocks.

become worn they can be reversed and readjusted, and the result is the equivalent of a new pair of pallets.

When the pads are worn out they are not difficult to make, although the operation takes some time. They can be bent round out of flat steel, but must be correctly curved, both to comply with

83

the circle struck from the pallet hole and also to fit nicely into the curved slot cut in the pallet arms. A brass disc can be turned in the lathe to the same size as the inner circle of the pallet slots, and the steel can then be bent round to correspond, the disc acting as a template.

When hardening there is less likelihood of the pads warping if they are covered in iron binding wire, made red hot and plunged into water, making sure that they are plunged edgewise and not flatwise. A high polish must always be given to the acting faces, and they must, of course, be quite hard. The adjustment of these pads affects only the depth of locking, and one is ill advised to attempt any adjustment for inside and outside shake; the shakes are adjusted by the turn-table which contains the front pallet-arbor pivot hole.

FRENCH DEAD-BEAT ESCAPEMENT WITH IMPULSE ON ONE PALLET ONLY OR A SINGLE-BEAT ESCAPE-MENT

There is a very interesting French clock escapement which is often met. It is usually in a complicated clock having more functions than just showing the time of day and striking, and is often provided with a 10-in. or half-seconds pendulum. It always gives very good results and is always centre seconds. In some cases the Ellicott type of pendulum is used with this escapement.

The 'scape wheel has 10 teeth very similar to the Graham, although they are sometimes of a more elaborate shape at the backs, which does add strength, although the tips of the teeth are very thin (see Figure 58).

With nearly all escapements the entrance pallet requires the most power or has more friction, but this escapement does not use the entrance pallet except for locking, all the impulse being on the exit pallet, which requires less power for the amount of impulse.

There are two sets of actions on the 'scape wheel; the teeth on the wheel are for locking only, but the impulse is given by perpendicular pins on the band of the wheel; when the wheel is in the clock these pins are, of course, horizontal. The impulse plane is mounted on a higher plane than the entrance pallet to allow the wheel teeth to pass underneath.

The impulse plane is again out of the ordinary, inasmuch as it is curved instead of flat and has a concave face. The idea behind this, which is to make the impulse equal over the entire length of the plane, is quite sound, but there is not a great deal of advantage in it. In the case of a flat plane the impulse varies in intensity with the maximum in the centre, the total impulse being the same in all cases, but in this case the impulse is 4°, *i.e.* the same as 2° on each of two pallets. There is, of course, no difference in the train calculation, although there is impulse on one side only, and apparently the wheel moves only once every two vibrations. The pendulum, as stated

84

earlier, is a half-seconds one, and the seconds hand beats seconds. However, there is discernible movement other than the beat.

From observation over long periods this escapement gives very

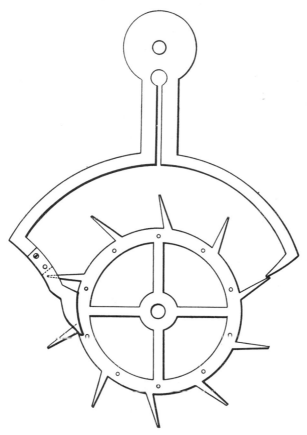

Figure 58. French single-beat escapement having impulse on one pallet, the other acting as locking only. This escapement gives a very good performance. The impulse pallet is raised above the plane of the locking and is engaged by the pins. Both pallets are jewelled.

good results. As in any good escapement, the pivots must fit the holes well and be perfectly smooth and straight, also the locking on the entrance pallet must if anything be heavy, otherwise the pin may not fall on the right side of the impulse plane.

This action is a very critical one, and the pallet arms are often adjustable in the same manner as some of the Brocot pin-pallet arms already described. These clocks must be nicely in beat, although of course this applies to all clocks.

In Beat—To test for in beat the pendulum is led from rest towards the locking pallet, when the pin will drop off the impulse plane and the tooth will lock. At the instant that this happens the pendulum is released, and if in beat the clock will start and keep going. The procedure is now reversed and the pendulum moved in the reverse direction until the pin drops on to the locking corner of the impulse plane, when the pendulum is at once released and the clock should start.

If it does not start in the first instance the crutch must be moved towards the locking pallet thus to favour the impulse pallet, whereas if it fails to start in the second instance the reverse procedure must be adopted. The crutch in these clocks is usually adjustable, but where this is not the case the adjustment is made by slightly bending the crutch.

This test can be applied to all clocks, *i.e.* the pendulum can be led from rest until the tooth drops, when the pendulum is released and the clock starts. The directions can then be reversed from rest until the opposite side is freed, when the pendulum is released and the clock started. In other words, if the movement is the same both sides the clock is in beat.

In most clocks an aural test is very good. To amplify the beat a watch brush can be used. If one end of this is placed on the centre arbor and the other end to the ear the beat will be found to be many times louder. Where the drops are unequal this test is, of course, uncertain, and the pendulum test is essential.

There should, of course, never be unequal drops, but unfortunately where the price is limited the commercial side makes it necessary to leave inequalities in some cases.

DEAD-BEAT ESCAPEMENT USED IN GRAVITY CLOCKS WITH SHORT PENDULUM OR BALANCE

This type of escapement is a dead-beat escapement and is reminiscent of the cylinder escapement, the latter having the impulse on the wheel teeth, whereas the type now to be examined has the impulse faces on the cylinder or the pallets.

The pallets proper are part of a cylinder with a base into which the pallet arbor is fitted. The cylinder is about five-ninths or is said to be cut away four-ninths, the pallet faces or impulse planes being on the remainder.

The thickness of the shell is a little less than half the distance between two teeth. This is decided by the thickness of the tops of the teeth, but it must also be remembered that the teeth become progressively thicker from the top to the root, thus if the impulse is full the corners of the cylinder may make or foul the back of the teeth. As these escapements are invariably applied to gravity clocks, the impulse is under control, *i.e.* one can add or subtract weight. Thus if the impulse is too large a little weight can be removed.

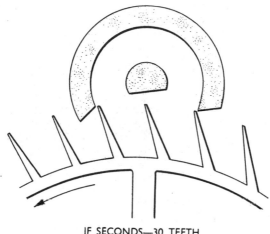

IF SECONDS—30 TEETH
IF ¾ SECONDS—45 TEETH

BRASS COLLAR

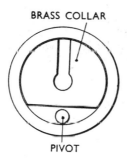

PIVOT

Figure 59. Dead-beat escapement giving very small arc of vibration. This is used in cheap gravity driven clocks with a bar type balance or pendulum. The lower inset shows the bearings for the pivots of the balance or pendulum.

Another very important point is that if the locking is too deep the factor of thick teeth comes into consideration. When examining these escapements it is imperative to make sure that when one tooth is resting on the locking corner, *i.e.* precisely on the corner, there is

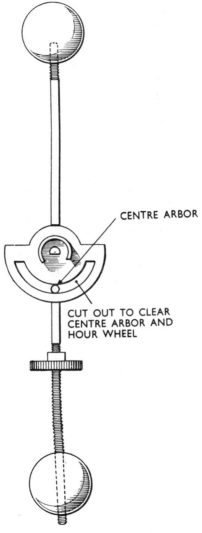

CENTRE ARBOR

CUT OUT TO CLEAR
CENTRE ARBOR AND
HOUR WHEEL

Figure 60. Dead-beat escapement.
This is a complete balance unit for a
gravity clock. The nut on the lower
half is for regulating.

only a little shake, the less the better, although there must, of course, be some present. This is tried again when the cylinder is embracing 3 teeth and then when the cylinder is between 4 teeth. These shakes should, of course, be equal.

Another point is that the pallet-arbor pivots do not run or revolve in round holes, but run on the edge of two large holes which have a plug filling about three-quarters of the hole, this plug being to prevent the pivots coming out should the clock be disturbed when being carried about.

The pendulum is like a balance adjusted to be out of poise and often takes about three-quarters of a second for each vibration; in this case the 'scape wheel has 45 teeth, but some were made to beat seconds and had a 'scape wheel of 30 teeth.

The angle of impulse is usually about 5°, but it will function with lower angles. It is not advisable to go higher than 5° because the arc of vibration will increase too much, and this must be kept small,

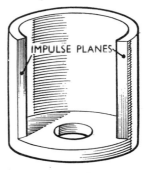

Figure 61. Pallets of a dead-beat escapement. These are similar to a cylinder but have impulse planes. They are made of glass-hard steel.

because as the pendulum vibrates it rolls along on its pivots and takes up different positions relative to the 'scape wheel. If there is too much movement the pivot may slide back and cause the cylinder lips to butt on top of the teeth and stop the clock. As is usually the case, the 'scape wheel is made of brass and the cylinder or pallets are of steel hardened and left almost dead hard. The outside and the inside of the cylinder where the wheel engages must be polished, as must the impulse planes, which must also be quite flat.

If one has to make new pallets a piece of steel rod a little larger than the distance between 4 teeth is used A hole is drilled truly central to fit the pallet arbor, then the end of the rod is turned perfectly level and flat and a piece which corresponds to the length or height is cut. The end of the rod which had been turned flat is placed in a step chuck in the lathe and the centre is turned, or rather the middle is sunk out until 3 teeth of the wheel will be quite free inside and the depth is as required, leaving the bottom quite sound.

It is now taken out of the lathe and filed on the side until 3 teeth of the wheel will fit closely in the gap. It is then tried with 4 teeth of the wheel against the outside; if the pallets pass into the 4 teeth by about the thickness of 1 tooth at its tip all is in order. If, on the other hand, 4 teeth will not embrace, then the outside is too large; it must therefore be put back in the lathe and, using a cutter in the slide rest, the outside of the shell must be trimmed until the 4 teeth will embrace it with the necessary tip-of-tooth intersection.

If the shell has been filed straight across, the impulse plane on the entrance side will be correct. It only remains to file the other impulse plane until the lockings are equal. This can be tested by putting the pallets on the pallet arbor and trying them in the frame. When all is in order the pallets are hardened and polished; if they are bound up in iron binding wire while being hardened there is little fear of them warping. Sometimes the hole for the pallet arbor shrinks or expands, but this is not usual. If it shrinks the pallet arbor can be reduced, but in the case of expansion a new pallet arbor is called for.

This is not a precision escapement, but it will give a reasonable performance. The adjustment of the pendulum of this sort of clock is opposite to the usual, *i.e.* the adjusting screw or nut is screwed in to make the clock slower, and vice versa.

THE HALF DEAD-BEAT ESCAPEMENT

This is so called because it embodies actions contained in both the dead-beat and the recoil escapement. It is an admirable escapement for bracket clocks because it gives a good performance with the shorter 6–10-in. pendulums.

The foundation of the escapement is the dead-beat, but the construction follows the recoil and the distance of centres is the same as a recoil, *i.e.* 1·4 times the radius of the wheel. The pallets span $7\frac{1}{2}$ teeth the same as the recoil. Whilst with a dead-beat the angle of lift is 2°, with a half dead-beat one can allow more than this if the pendulum is 6 in. long, but only 2° for a 10-in. or half-seconds pendulum.

With a dead-beat the locking face is on an arc struck from the pallet centre, but in the half dead-beat the raised curve is struck from a different centre. The main object of the half dead-beat is to counteract the various changes in motive power that one is bound to get in a spring-driven clock. However good the train in the limited scope of a bracket movement, there are bound to be variations of power owing to a not absolutely perfect fusee and low-numbered pinions.

This escapement gives a good performance under not too good conditions, adjustments to counteract changes in motive power being carried out by raising the locking face so that the wheel recoils as the vibrations increase. This puts a resistance to the increased vibrations and of course also on the lesser vibrations, so that when the power is less the resistance is less. Thus the greater the motive power, the greater the resistance, and so the mainspring or motive power is used by the escapement to counteract itself, a sort of self-compensating escapement.

Unfortunately these pallets become worn like all of the others and have to be repaired and repolished. When this is necessary the angles must be kept correct, as it is very easy to alter the escapement into a poor recoil with no advantages at all, and distinct disadvan-

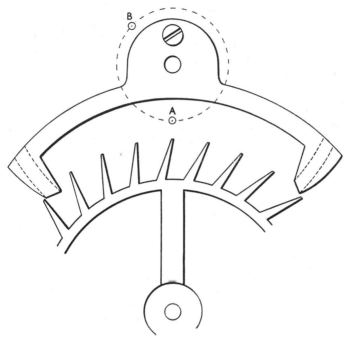

Figure 62. The half dead-beat escapement is a very fine escapement for shorter pendulums. The impulse is the same as the dead-beat, but the locking only is recoil, and the dead-beat is superimposed. A is centre for the arc forming the recoil face of the exit pallet, B is the centre for forming the entrance pallet.

tages. If the angles are changed the movement will become a very high-angled recoil and the clock will probably refuse to go, or if it does keep going it will not give anything approaching a reliable performance. Like all escapements, a good polish to the pallet faces is a great help to performance, and they will take a lot more work before becoming worn.

The recoil locking faces vary with different makers. The French make them to span a variable number of teeth from 5 to 8, and some have a very slight recoil, whilst others have a very heavy recoil. It is very difficult to alter this angle, and it can be done only at the expense of shorter impulse planes and excessive drop, which is bad at any time.

If the drops become excessive through wear the pallet and 'scape wheel depth can be deepened or the pallets closed and polished up correctly again as with the recoil, but much more care is required in order to make sure that the impulse angle and the recoil face are correct. To preserve the impulse angle it is best to polish by using a zinc lap in the lathe with the pallets held in a holder on the slide rest. Wettish diamantine is used at first, and when the wear is removed the diamantine dries, resulting in a real black polish. If the pallet faces are kept against the lap when the diamantine is dry they will be covered with scratches and score marks, so they must be disengaged just as the diamantine dries. The recoil faces can be polished by hand using a flat zinc polisher and diamantine.

Like all escapements, the drop must be at a minimum, and the crutch must be a close but free fit on the pendulum rod, and must be smooth and not worn. A final point is that careful watch must be kept to see that in the case of a large vibration the pallet dropping-off corner does not foul or rake the back of the wheel tooth. Where this does happen less motive power is required or a weaker mainspring.

4

THE GRAVITY ESCAPEMENT

THERE ARE VARIOUS TYPES of gravity escapement, but the outstanding type is, of course, the double three-legged, and for turret clocks this is the best under all conditions. It was invented by Lord Grimthorpe and was installed in the great Westminster clock known as 'Big Ben'. The principal advantage is that there is no direct connection between the train or motive power and the escapement.

The impulse is provided by the weight of two arms which fall alternately on each side of the pendulum rod, whilst the function of the train is to lift these two arms clear. The escapement consists of two 3-armed wheels back to back, and joined by 3 studs forming a pinion of 3 leaves. These 3 arms, legs or teeth are the locking teeth. This unit is mounted on the 'scape pinion, as also is a fly or fan. The object of this fly is to steady the speed of the 'scape wheel because the amount of movement is so great that without the fly the escapement would trip or knock the locking out of action, with consequent damage. The main function of this unit is to lift the impulse arms and to hold them until the required time.

The two impulse arms are pivoted at their top end and are planted as close to the centre of the frame as possible and close to the suspension spring, or to that part of the suspension where the bending takes place. The action is thus: as the pendulum moves across it passes the centre, and as it rises it engages the gravity arm (which is held up and locked) and unlocks this by moving the locking block free of the locking leg and the 'scape wheel runs. As it runs, one of the three pinion leaves proceeds to lift the opposite gravity arm until the locking leg meets and locks on its locking block.

Meanwhile the gravity arm resting on the pendulum is now quite free to fall, and it proceeds to do so, resting on the pendulum and adding its weight to it. The weight of the gravity arm is the total impulse. Now as soon as the pendulum reaches the centre or zero point it leaves the gravity arm and proceeds to run on by its own momentum until it meets the raised and locked gravity arm on the other side. As the pendulum carries on it again moves the gravity arm, unlocks the wheel and the sequence starts again. The only real connecting link between the train and the pendulum is the locking. The amount of interference here is negligible, and can be ruled out of any calculation.

The 'scape wheel is planted so that the gravity arms work midway between the two 3-armed wheels which form the unit. One wheel is locked above one of the gravity arms, and the other is locked below

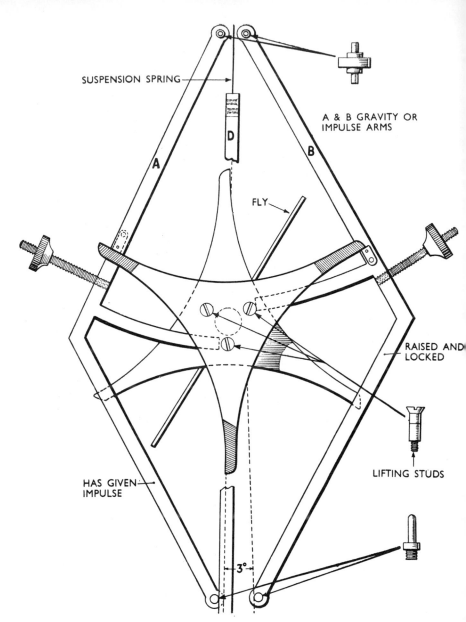

SUSPENSION SPRING

A & B GRAVITY OR
IMPULSE ARMS

D

A

B

FLY

RAISED AND
LOCKED

LIFTING STUDS

HAS GIVEN
IMPULSE

3°

Figure 63. The double three-legged gravity escapement. This is the best turret clock escapement and is used in 'Big Ben' on the Houses of Parliament. It is often used in regulators but is hardly suitable. When this is used in regulators it has adjustments to vary the effective weight of the impulse arms. It is a partially detached escapement, and the weight of the arms is the impulse. D indicates pendulum rod.

or underneath the other arm, and so the unit acts as a wheel of 6 teeth.

The length of the lifting part of the gravity arms is critical because this controls the locking. To increase the locking these arms are shortened, and of course the position of the lifting leaves of the pinion of 3 leaves must be correct so that only the minimum amount of supplementary arc is required to unlock. The weight of the gravity arms controls the arc of vibration, and where the gravity escapement has been fitted to regulators and smaller clocks an extra arm with an adjustable weight has been added. The arm is left very light, and if more weight is required the weight is unscrewed to stand farther out, thus adding extra weight by leverage.

Another type which is much favoured is one in which the gravity arms are replaced by arms mounted on steel springs; otherwise the action is the same. The gravity arms would seem to be preferable because the impulse would appear to be a more constant factor. The great Westminster clock has gravity arms, and its performance would certainly seem to give justification for this claim. There is no doubt that for turret clocks a double three-legged gravity escapement is best.

In repairing these escapements it must be seen that the tips of the locking teeth and the locking blocks which are screwed on to the gravity arms are quite hard. When these become worn they must be repaired and made quite smooth.

The sides of the two studs or pins which engage the pendulum rod on the bottom end of the gravity arms must be smooth and not pitted; they must not be oiled. They can sometimes be turned round 90° and a new part engaged. Sometimes these studs are rollers, but it is unnecessary for them to be so.

SIX-LEGGED GRAVITY ESCAPEMENT

This is a modification of Lord Grimthorpe's double three-legged gravity, and was invented by Thwaites and Reed, turret-clock makers. It has given very good results, and is a very good escapement, differing from the previous gravity inasmuch as impulse is given only on one side, the other arm acting as locking only. There are 6 lifting pins instead of 3, and 6 locking teeth. The wheel in the six-legged gravity turns half as fast as the double three-legged, and less weight is required to drive it.

The action is that as the pendulum moves across it engages the impulse arm, unlocks the wheel, frees the lifting arm from the lifting pins and the impulse arm is free to add its weight to the pendulum and give the necessary impulse. As the pendulum returns and reaches its peak it unlocks the neutral arm, the wheel runs and lifts the impulse arm to its peak. The pendulum returns and again unlocks the impulse arm and the process is repeated.

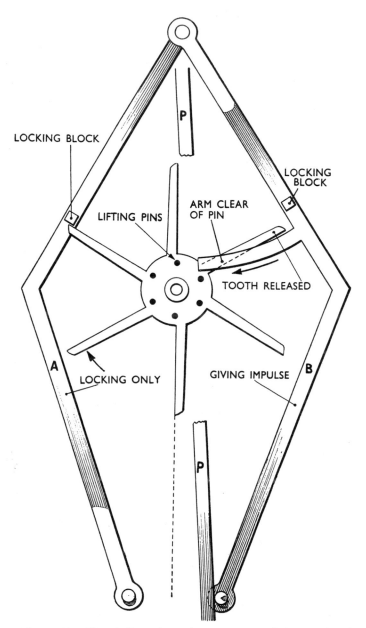

LOCKING BLOCK

LOCKING BLOCK

LIFTING PINS

ARM CLEAR OF PIN

P

P

TOOTH RELEASED

A

LOCKING ONLY

GIVING IMPULSE

B

Figure 64. The six-legged gravity escapement is a very good escapement. One arm is for locking and the other gives impulse.

The locking is controlled on the neutral arm by a banking pin, and thus the locking and the amount of engagement is controlled.

THE SINGLE THREE-LEGGED GRAVITY ESCAPEMENT

As stated earlier, the double three-legged gravity acts like an escapement with three teeth on the wheel, but its action is spread out more and is lighter. There is, however, an escapement with but three legs performing similar functions.

Instead of a pinion of 3 leaves, the centre is usually of triangular shape. These three sides act as the lifting agent for the impulse arms, and act on rollers pivoted on the lifting arms themselves. The locking is performed on the gravity arms much in the same manner as with the double three-legged escapement. The movement of the arms is, of course, greater than that in the double three-legged, and the wheel unit is provided with a fly to steady it and prevent tripping.

As with its brother, the double three-legged, the acting pins at the bottom of the arms which engage the pendulum can be studs or rollers.

There must be no oil at the point of engagement with the pendulum rod, but with both escapements the locking faces must be oiled.

THE FOUR-LEGGED GRAVITY ESCAPEMENT

This escapement will be found on regulators or long-case clocks fitted with a seconds pendulum. It is difficult to say whether it was used on turret clocks to any great extent, but it is ideal for them. Not many were made, because it needed high numbered wheels or even another or extra wheel and pinion. With a seconds pendulum the wheel would turn once every 8 beats or 8 seconds.

It scores over the Graham escapement inasmuch as the changing condition of the oil does not affect its rate. The principle of this escapement is not difficult to follow, especially if the double three-legged escapement has been understood, because the actions are very similar. Each gravity or impulse arm is lifted and falls alternately, and the wheel unit is provided with a fly to steady it and prevent tripping. In one way the gravity escapements can be likened to remontoires or constant-power escapements but there is a difference, as will be seen from Figure 65, which shows this escapement with spring arms and working on the pendulum bob instead of the rod itself.

REMONTOIRE ESCAPEMENTS

This is really a misleading term, because any escapement can be used with a remontoire. There are various types, but the principles are fundamentally the same, so the two main types will be examined.

Most remontoires have a separate source of power driving the

97

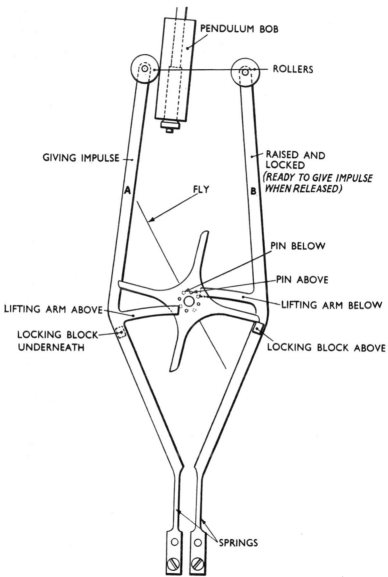

Figure 65. The four-legged gravity escapement has an action very similar to the double three-legged but requires an extra wheel in the train. The drawing shows the escapement working with spring arms and giving impulse to the pendulum bob instead of to the rod.

fourth wheel or the wheel next to the 'scape wheel, and this often consists of a weight running on a pulley on the fourth pinion arbor. As the escapement releases, so the 'scape and fourth wheel turn; as the fourth wheel turns a quarter turn, the main driving train is

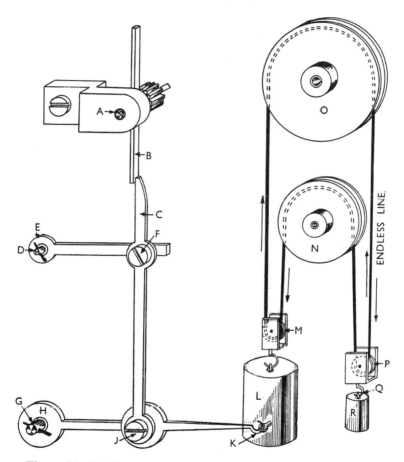

Figure 66. Robin remontoire. In this escapement the going train is geared back from the 'scape pinion. A = Fly pinion pivot; B = Locking arm mounted on fly pinion arbor of setting-up train; C = Locking piece; D = Stud and pin; E = Collet; F = Shouldered screw; G = Stud and pin; H = Collet; J = Shouldered screw; K = Hook and eye; L = Main weight; M = Small pulley; N = Pulley on 'scape pinion arbor; O = Pulley on arbor of train; P = Small pulley; Q = Hook and eye; R = Counterpoise weight.

released and immediately rewinds the supplementary weight, and this process is repeated every quarter turn.

With a seconds train the supplementary weight is rewound every fifteen seconds, and these clocks usually have a dial noting seconds, although individual seconds are not shown.

Sometimes a very weak mainspring is contained in a barrel, with the fourth pinion acting as the arbor. At a set period the barrel containing the mainspring is rewound, and as only a small section and the most equal-pulling part of the spring is used, an almost constant power is continuously on the escapement.

The last wheel of the main train usually has a fly to steady it so that the locking can be safe. This type is often used, even when the main train is weight driven.

Where it is desired to show true seconds or half-seconds, especially where a centre seconds hand is used, a pinion is unnecessary and the supplementary power is on the 'scape wheel arbor.

Mounted on the 'scape arbor is a pulley with small pointed studs so that the grip is certain and the line will not slip. Running over this pulley is an endless line or cord which also runs round a pulley on the main train. This line also has on it the main driving weight of the supplementary train with its counterpoise weight, i.e. a smaller weight to keep the line from being slack on that section of the line not pulling.

The main train ends in a fly with either an arm or a double arm on the opposite end of the arbor. Pivoted on a stud is another arm on which the main weight of the remontoire rests. A part of this arm is directly in line with the arm or double arm on the main train, and locks it. The principle is that as the 'scape wheel is released it turns, and as it does so the main weight gradually falls. As soon as it falls a certain distance (the arm falling with it), and the locking end of the arm moves out of the path of the arm on the main train, thus releasing it, the train runs and by means of the endless line winds up the main weight of the remontoire until the arm becomes in line with the double arm on the fly on the main train and locks it. This action is continuously repeated, and thus the power on the escapement is absolutely constant.

Unfortunately these remontoires do not get over all of the troubles, such as oil, temperature, barometric errors, etc., but they are no doubt a very great help. One of the disadvantages is that they have to be very carefully moved about, otherwise the line comes off the pulley. Another point is that the line, which is in action about every half-minute 24 hours a day, becomes worn and has to be replaced, and being an endless line has to be spliced very nicely, otherwise it will get badly cut up at the join.

There are other types, but they are mostly applied to chronometers and other instruments of a similar nature, and will be dealt with later in this book.

5

THE CHRONOMETER DEAD-BEAT
ESCAPEMENT

THE CHRONOMETER DEAD-BEAT ESCAPEMENT is a combination of the Earnshaw chronometer and the Graham dead-beat, and is understood to be a product, if not the invention, of that well-known firm E. Dent & Co. Ltd.

It is no doubt an extremely good principle, and has given a very good performance as a standard clock at the Royal Observatory.

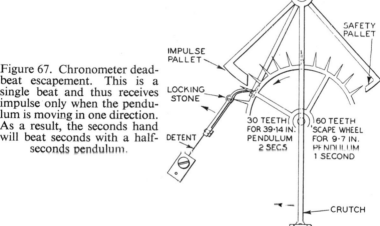

Figure 67. Chronometer dead-beat escapement. This is a single beat and thus receives impulse only when the pendulum is moving in one direction. As a result, the seconds hand will beat seconds with a half-seconds pendulum.

The pendulum receives impulse only when moving in one direction, and the return vibration is called the passing or dummy vibration. Thus with a half-seconds pendulum the clock beats true seconds and with a seconds pendulum the clock beats every two seconds.

Naturally a cheaper edition has been made, but the same results cannot be claimed for it as for the original; it will, however, be examined later. As will be remembered, the Graham dead-beat had a 'scape wheel of 30 teeth and the clock beat seconds. With the chronometer dead-beat there must be 60 teeth on the 'scape wheel for it to beat seconds. The teeth are identical with the Graham, so there is no need to go into detail again.

The 'scape-pinion arbor, as with the Graham, carries on its pivot the seconds hand. The pallets are constructed in a similar way to the Graham, with the great exception that all the impulse is on one pallet and none on the other; in fact, the one pallet is cut very thin and acts only as a ' safety ' in case of disturbance and to prevent running through and damaging the wheel teeth. The main locking is carried out on a jewel locking stone usually of sapphire which is fitted into what is called a spring detent.

The detent is planted tangential to the 'scape wheel teeth, and consists of the locking stone, the passing spring (invariably called the gold spring because it is made in gold), the horn of the detent, the body of the detent, the spring and the foot.

The foot, spring, body and the horn are all of one piece of steel, and the locking stone is fitted, wedged and fixed with shellac into the detent pipe, which is part of the body of the detent. The gold spring is screwed to a slightly raised platform at the back of the detent body and lies parallel and close to the body of the detent and meets at the end of the horn, just slightly overlapping. The detent is an extremely delicate piece, and must be handled at all times with great care.

When the clock is taken down for repair the first action after the escapement has been examined is to remove the detent and put it in a box for safety. A wedge is then put in the train so that it is safely held and cannot run, after which the crutch and pallets, *etc.*, are removed.

If the crutch is removed with power on the train the 'scape wheel may be damaged as it rushes down, by hitting one of the pallet pads. If this same thing happens with the detent in place, the damage will be much greater, as the detent, locking stone and wheel may be completely smashed up, which would be a very expensive accident.

The action is fairly simple, because on the active vibration the action of the wheel on the pallets is the same as the Graham. After release the wheel tooth drops on the locking face and then gives impulse and drops off, but instead of dropping on to the other pallet it drops on to the locking stone of the detent. Then as the pendulum changes its direction an arm on the crutch engages the passing spring on the detent by means of a jewel pallet fitted into the arm. While the pendulum still carries on, the passing spring is just lifted and drops back into place again as soon as it is disengaged. Again the pendulum reverses its direction and the passing spring is again engaged, but on its opposite side.

As stated earlier, the passing spring lies parallel with the detent. As the pendulum progresses it lifts the passing spring and also the detent; as the detent moves, the locking stone is lifted out of the path of the wheel teeth and the wheel moves forward and drops on to the locking face of the impulse pallet. The pendulum still moves on, and the detent is released to drop back into the path of the wheel; by this time the wheel tooth is giving impulse to the pendulum, and at the end of its run the tooth drops off the pallet, locks on the detent locking stone and the sequence starts again.

When it is said that a particular tooth is released by the detent or locked it is often confusing, because one is inclined to think of one tooth only, but actually there are two teeth involved in each case. The tooth locked on the detent and the tooth engaged on the impulse pallet are a distance apart, usually the third tooth in advance is the tooth locked on the detent as against the tooth giving impulse. It may be wondered where the advantage lies, but if the action is examined it will be realised that the pendulum is only in action on every alternate vibration and is almost detached or free on the other or dummy vibration. In fact, the interference on the dummy side is very slight and only for so short a period that its effect is almost negligible. The only improvement which could be introduced would be that of dispensing with the crutch, and this cannot be done.

The fault generally to be found with this escapement is mislocking. Like the Graham, when the wheel is released by the detent the appropriate tooth must fall on the locking face and not on the impulse face. The lighter it locks or the nearer to the corner, the better, of course, because it is a necessary loss.

Another point is that the locking on the locking stone must be safe but also as light as possible, as any unlocking action is loss and extra friction. The gold spring or passing spring must lie on the horn of the detent with no gap, but not hard on, because this will increase friction on the passing or dummy vibration.

Again the passing spring must be the correct length so that it is only long enough to release the wheel tooth plus a little extra to be sure of release If say 2° is required to unlock and 1° extra, making 3° in all, this is quite sufficient.

With a half-seconds pendulum the angle of lift on the impulse plane wants to be about 3°, but with a seconds pendulum the impulse angle should be 2°.

The replacing of a detent or any of its sections is not a job for a clockmaker, but is an extremely delicate operation and even for a watchmaker a delicate and skilful job. If the locking stone becomes broken and a jewel is not available in no circumstances whatsoever must a substitute in steel be fitted, because it will ruin the wheel. It will not harm the wheel if a locking stone is made in gold, but obviously it is not nearly as good as a jewel.

Unfortunately the wheel teeth have to be oiled because of the impulse pallet, but only the necessary amount of oil and no more should be used, because if it spreads to the body of the detent the gold or passing spring tends to stick to the detent, and this does not help to give a good rate.

THE CHEAPER TYPE OF CHRONOMETER DEAD-BEAT

The previous escapement had a crutch giving impulse to the pendulum, but with the cheaper type the impulse was given direct to the pendulum rod. This no doubt had its advantages, but even these are uncertain, as this type of dead-beat was only made up as a cheaper

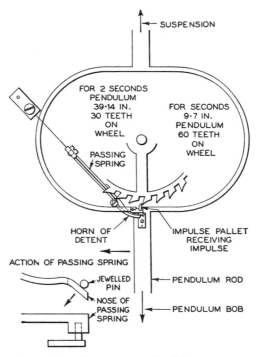

Figure 68. Chronometer dead-beat escapement. The 'scape wheel engages the pendulum rod direct and does not employ a crutch.

edition of the previous escapement by Messrs. Dent, which was a really first-class regulator with first-class workmanship.

The principle of the cheaper type was that instead of a single rod for the pendulum the rod opened up into two sections, the 'scape wheel fitting between these two sections and in the same plane. The same idea of impulse on one side only was adopted, and a detent was used in just the same way to lock the wheel when not in action giving impulse.

There was, however, no safety pallet, and if the pendulum did not hang perfectly upright there was always a chance of the wheel

104

getting free, with disastrous results. Some were provided with stepped blocks, one on each side, which kept the pendulum from moving from back to front and also ensured the pendulum being in the correct position; if it were not so, the pendulum would foul one or the other. The impulse was given to a jewelled block at the lower part of the pendulum rod, and the discharging or unlocking pallet was also planted near.

The passing spring presented a problem because the engagement was not perfectly straightforward. The spring was stepped and presented at an angle in such a way that the discharging pin acted as though on an impulse plane, *i.e.* the pin engaged moved along and dropped off the other end of the step and lifted the spring in the process. On the return it engaged where it previously dropped off, pushed the spring the other way as it moved along and dropped off where it was previously engaged. Thus the length and angle of the stepped part of the passing was very critical, and great care was needed when making any adjustment.

Often these escapements were made visible, *i.e.* the pendulum and 'scape wheel were visible just below the dial in the front of the case, and it must be said that it would have been very difficult to adjust the escapement if the clock had not been constructed in this way. There were, however, adjustable feet on the clock case to allow alteration of the level in order to make the pendulum perfectly free and in its correct position. One of the objections to this type of escapement was the length of time the passing spring was in action and the excessive friction involved.

6

PLATFORMS OR PLATFORM ESCAPEMENTS

THE PORTABLE CLOCK BROUGHT the platform escapement into general use. In many cases pendulum clocks have been converted from a pendulum to a platform escapement. The conversion is usually not difficult, but some movements are much more difficult to alter than

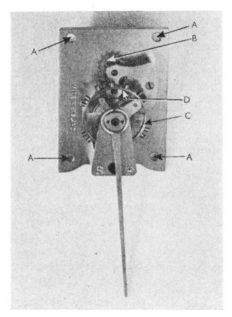

Figure 69. Lever platform escapement.
A = holes for securing platform to move-
ment ; B = 'scape wheel ; C = balance ;
D = lever and pallets.

others, the main trouble often being the count of the train wheels and pinions.

A platform escapement is a plate on which is built an escapement like a large watch escapement. They are often Chronometer, Duplex, Lever or Cylinder, and come under the category of watch escapements. As such they will therefore not be dealt with in detail in this section of the book, but only in their application to clocks. These platforms have a long 'scape pinion, and the bottom pivot is run or supported in a drop cock. The long pinion is to enable the 'scape pinion to pass through an aperture or slot in the clock plate and take drive from the fourth wheel, which would be the 'scape wheel in a pendulum clock.

In quite a number of these clocks the platform is screwed flat to the back plate, usually by four platform screws. Although this is a cheaper way of using a platform escapement, it is not a good way, because the balance is always hanging, *i.e.* the balance is vibrating or running on the sides of both balance-staff pivots. The result of this is that the balance does not have a large vibration owing to the increased friction, and also the pivots become worn much more quickly. In addition, owing to the increased friction, the rate or performance is not as good as it ought to be.

The best way to fit a platform is across the two plates or horizontally, the balance then being subject only to the friction of the

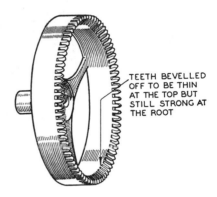

Figure 70. Contrate wheel as used with a platform escapement when the platform is planted horizontally.

TEETH BEVELLED OFF TO BE THIN AT THE TOP BUT STILL STRONG AT THE ROOT

end of the bottom pivot, with the result that there is a better vibration and a better rate. To plant the platform horizontally what is called a contrate wheel must be used.

A contrate wheel has its teeth at right angles to the body of the wheel, whereas the ordinary wheel has its teeth in the same plane. This contrate wheel and 'scape-pinion intersection or depth are very important.

The teeth must always be thinned from back to front so that only one size of wheel is in action. The best way is to bevel them so that the root of the tooth is still strong and only the tops thinned. The tooth is thinned from inside to outside and not on the profile of the tooth, which must not be altered. The diameter of the contrate wheel is, of course, the same as that of the flat wheel which it displaces.

107

A contrate-wheel pinion must always have an endpiece or end screw working on the end of the back pivot so that the endshake of the pinion is kept to a minimum. The endpiece controls the engagement of the contrate wheel and 'scape pinion; if excessive endshake were present the depth could vary between shallow and deep or correct and shallow.

A good platform escapement will have all the bottom pivots running on endstones as well as in jewel holes; the holes are jewelled so that wear is considerably reduced, and the endstones are to keep the shoulders of the pivots from coming into action. These pivots are quite straight, but the shoulders are conical and are made thus for strength. With a cheaper type of escapement, such as the cylinder, the jewel holes are of a cheap variety and the lower pivots are not endcapped, with the exception of the cylinder pivots, which must, of course, be endcapped, otherwise the clock will not go owing to the very great friction on the pivot shoulder.

PART II
WATCH ESCAPEMENTS

INTRODUCTION

WHEN DEALING WITH WATCH escapements the principles to be followed are the same as those used for clock escapements, but the manner of their application is different. Whereas clock escapements are predominantly dead-beat or recoil, watch escapements are detached or frictional-rest types.

When the detached escapement was brought into use it seemed to be the answer to the watchmakers' prayer, but as the escapements improved, so the demand for even greater accuracy in timekeeping became more insistent.

The detached escapement was first introduced by Thomas Mudge. His invention was not detached according to present-day standards, but it was a step in the right direction. His next escapement, which was a lever type, had distinct advantages, although it was rather complicated. It seems surprising that when in 1765 Mudge invented his remontoire or partly attached escapement he did not realise the possibilities of his invention, which contained all of the ideas used in modern escapements; others did realise this fact to their advantage.

A detached-lever watch was made by Josiah Emery, but it is generally understood that this was made with the co-operation of Mudge, and it was certainly made to his pattern.

As stated at the beginning of the book, the verge was the earliest known form of escapement. It had been used for clocks for a number of years before it was applied to watches or portable clocks as they were then called. The first of these is understood to have been made by Peter Henlein in about 1510. The verge escapement was in vogue for many years, and was still sometimes used in 1850 or even later.

John Harrison, Mudge, Emery and others all experimented with the verge until Mudge invented his detached lever.

The cylinder escapement, which was also called the 'horizontal' because of the verge being a vertical escapement, was invented in 1695 by Thomas Tompion, and with its various improvements gave a very good performance. A L. Breguet, Ashley and others all added various improvements to endeavour to perfect this type of escapement.

The lever escapement invented by Mudge followed the cylinder escapement, and also about this time a Frenchman named Julian Le Roy invented an early form of detent escapement, which was perfected in about 1780 by Earnshaw and Arnold as the chronometer escapement. This was essentially the same as the form in use today. Arnold's earlier escapement was not so good as his later one, which

111

as far as can be ascertained was made at the same time as the one made by Earnshaw. This escapement is unsurpassed, and many watches are known as half-chronometers, whilst many fine watches with lever escapements are known as chronometers. In England the name chronometer always means an instrument fitted with the spring detent or chronometer escapement.

The next type of escapement was the Duplex. This was invented about 1720 by Dutertre and others, and was a frictional-rest escapement. It gave exceedingly good results, but was very delicate and expensive to repair.

Experiments were still being carried out on the lever escapement, and in 1791 Litherland invented the rack lever, but this was not detached and had only a short life. J. F. Cole brought out several forms of lever escapement during the early part of the nineteenth century, including a form of resilient lever, and Charles Curzon was another one who added to the perfection of the lever escapement.

Upon the re-introduction of the double roller previously invented by Mudge the lever escapement became more detached than it had previously been, and this roller has been adopted on all of the mass-produced watches of today.

There are two types of lever escapement: (1) the ratchet tooth, and (2) the club tooth. It is difficult to say which of these is the better, but the club tooth is more popular with manufacturers because it is easier to mass produce by machinery.

THE VERGE ESCAPEMENT AS FITTED TO WATCHES

IN THE FIRST SECTION of this book the verge escapement for clocks was described and examined, and the same type of escapement as used in watches will now be considered.

The early watch escapements were made in a similar manner to the lantern clock, and with a balance, the timekeeping being controlled by variation of the motive power, in the same manner as with the earlier clocks.

The escapement consists of the verge, the balance which is mounted on the verge, the balance wheel ('scape wheel) and pinion. In the early watches the balances were made of brass or steel and were usually very heavy.

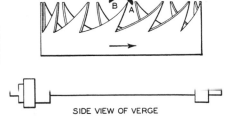

Figure 71. Verge escapement. Pallet A is receiving impulse and pallet B is falling into position to receive the next tooth.

SIDE VIEW OF VERGE

The Balance Wheel

The balance wheel, like the crown wheel in a clock, must have an odd number of teeth, otherwise the escapement cannot function. The number of teeth in the wheel is controlled by the amount of room available, although the French made their wheels with high numbers of teeth, but with these the teeth were extremely delicate.

In the old thick watches 17 teeth were not uncommon, but any odd number between 9 and 17 is quite usual. The crown wheel in a clock has the acting face of the teeth upright, but in its counterpart in the watch the teeth are undercut usually about 30° so that only the tips of the teeth are in action.

The Pad or Pallets

The verge is twisted so that the two pads are at an angle of 90° to each other, just as with the clock verge. They could be 95° or

113

100°, but there is no real advantage in this. The length of the pads, or the amount that they stand away from the centre of the verge, is as critical as it is in the case of the clock escapement. If they are too long the teeth will fail to pass because the action will be the same as

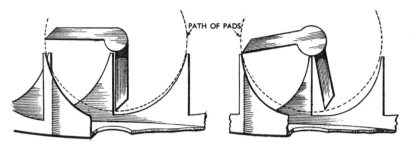

PATH OF PADS

Figure 72. This illustration shows how the incoming pallet comes on top of the incoming wheel tooth if the pads are too long.

a proportionately large pinion in a gearing depth. To get the best results the teeth of the balance wheel should pass through the centre of the verge or as close as possible to it, providing the verge arbor has sufficient strength.

The Drops

The drops must be kept to the minimum required for freedom, because as mentioned in previous chapters this drop is all loss. In action, as one pallet reaches its maximum lift the wheel tooth drops off and a tooth on the opposite side of the wheel drops on to the other pallet on that side; when this second pallet reaches its maximum lift this tooth drops off and the whole process is repeated. In each case the drop on or off must be equal and at a minimum.

There was no adjustment on the older watches, and all that could be done to equalise the drop was to move the holes supporting the verge, and thus move the verge over a little until the drop was correct. This is the reason why in so many old verge watches the balance was not upright, but was in fact leaning over one way or the other.

The Dovetail

In the later verges the front pivot of the balance wheel pinion ran in a hole drilled in a slide which was dovetailed into the front of the pottance. The reason for this was that it made it possible to move the wheel across the verge to equalise the drops: when the drops are unequal the verge does not pass across the dead centre of the balance wheel. The disadvantage of unequal drops is the fact that if the drops are unequal they must be excessive, because if the escapement is as close to the wheel as it should be the wheel will not pass on one

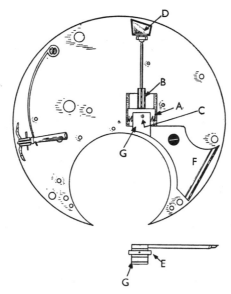

Figure 73.   English verge escapement
with   dovetail.   A = balance   wheel
('scape wheel);   B = balance wheel
pinion;   C = lower verge plug with
partly drilled hole in head of pottance;
D = tongued follower;   E = dovetail
containing   front pivot of balance
wheel pinion;   F = pottance;   G =
head of pottance.

side.   Another point is that excessive drop means that there will be
excessive wear on both the pads and the wheel teeth.

The Pottance

The pottance is the drop cock between the frames which support
the lower verge pivot and also the front pivot of the balance wheel
pinion in a dovetailed slide.   In the older watches the lower verge
hole was simply a partly drilled plug, but in the later models,
particularly the French verges, the lower bearing consisted of a hole
with a steel or jewelled endpiece screwed on.   This supported the
end of the pivot and kept the pad and pivot shoulder clear of the
pottance.

In the older pattern watches the pottance was often dovetailed and
riveted in place, but in later models it was screwed and steady-pinned
in place.

115

The Balance Cock

The top verge pivot was supported in a half-drilled plug fitted into a balance cock. In some of the older watches these balance cocks were very beautiful pieces of work and were pierced, engraved and mercurial gilded. Many of these have remained in first-class condition for two or three hundred years, but others have fallen into the hands of vandals in the shape of inexpert watchmakers and have been maltreated. In some cases these lovely examples of craftmanship have been broken and lead soldered together again, whilst others have been hammered up to create burrs. There are also examples in which a three-cornered punch has been driven into the underneath to ' correct ' endshake, *etc.*, and this has mutilated them for ever.

There is no excuse for this sort of treatment because it is always possible to manipulate the plug in the balance cock without any damage being done, and this is in fact the correct procedure.

The Balance Spring

The first verge watches did not have balance springs or hairsprings as they are commonly called. The balance spring was invented by Dr. Hooke about 1660 and was used by Tompion in all his watches, with the result that other watchmakers soon followed suit. The earliest controller was, of course, the hog's bristle.

In a verge watch the balance spring does not take complete control; it is still under the influence of the motive power. Therefore a verge watch fitted with a balance spring must have as weak a mainspring as possible in order that the balance spring can exercise its full influence on the time of vibration of the balance.

Another factor which tends to neutralise the balance spring is the escapement action: if the watch is losing the escapement depth can be shallowed slightly, *i.e.* the balance wheel pinion can be given more endshake; if the watch is gaining and the escapement is shallow it can be deepened to slow up the vibrations; should this not correct the fault, a weaker mainspring will make a lot of difference, even if it does not give perfect accuracy.

Sometimes, through constant pinning up, the balance spring becomes shortened owing to the end breaking off. If a new spring is unobtainable the faulty spring should be unpinned from the collet, placed on a piece of roughened glass which has been smeared with oilstone dust and oil, and then rubbed thinner by resting a finger on the spring and rubbing it against the oilstone paste and glass. Care should be taken to see that the spring is not reduced too much. After this treatment the spring can be re-blued.

If a suitable glass ' tool ' for this operation is not available one can easily be made by rubbing together two pieces of glass with a mixture of oilstone dust and oil between them. This prepared glass can also be used as a burnisher for brass wheels, jewel settings, *etc.*

FRENCH VERGE WATCHES

The French gave a great deal of attention to verge watches, and some very good specimens are still in existence. The majority of French verge watches had a useful arrangement for adjustments to the escapement after the watch was completely assembled. The balance wheel front pivot was fitted into a long slide which was provided with a lead screw flush with the outside of the plates, enabling

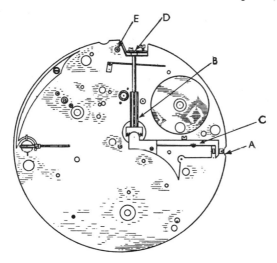

Figure 74. French verge top plate showing adjustments. A = adjusting screw; B = balance wheel and pinion; C = slide containing front pivot of balance wheel pinion; D = follower taking back pivot of balance wheel pinion; E = screw to fix follower securely when correct.

the drops to be easily adjusted. There was also a screw through the side to enable the escapement depth to be adjusted by pushing the balance wheel bearing nearer to, or away from, the verge. The latter adjusting screw was easily accessible for a long, thin-bladed screwdriver.

The English verges were not so well provided for, and with these it was necessary to make the adjustments prior to assembling the watches.

The Follower

The follower was the support for the back pivot of the balance wheel pinion, and in the French verges this was adjustable.

The English type verge had a follower consisting of a brass

117

block riveted to the top plate, with a straight brass rod ending in a flat tongue passing closely through the block with the flat tongue on the outside.   A hole was drilled in the rod to a depth of about three-quarters of the pivot on the inside, and this was the pivot hole or bearing for the back balance wheel pinion pivot.   An eccentric hole was sometimes drilled, but this was only advantageous under certain circumstances and could in most cases be a nuisance. The idea was that by pushing the rod through the hole the endshake of the pinion was decreased and deepened the escapement, or vice versa.   When an eccentric hole was drilled the contrate wheel and balance wheel pinion depth could be adjusted within limits.

The French verges had a cock screwed to the plate with a steady pin at the end which kept it in position at that end.   The screw hole was oval, thus allowing the cock to move, whilst beyond the screw was situated the pinion pivot hole, and beyond this was a screw tapped into the cock, banked against the edge of the plate.   By unscrewing this screw the cock could be pushed forward, by screwing it in the cock could be pushed back, thus adjusting the endshake. When the correct position was achieved the main cock screw was screwed home, so ensuring that the cock remained in position.

A New Top Verge Pivot

Sometimes a top verge pivot becomes broken off, and although this often necessitates a complete new verge, this is not always essential.   If the brass collet on the verge on which the balance is mounted is thick enough a hole sufficiently deep to take a plug and hold it securely can be sunk with a sinking tool into the brass. When the hole has been made deep enough the exposed arbor of the verge can be broken away and a steel plug fitted into the hole to the required depth, and a pivot turned on the end of the plug.

If the brass collet is short the treatment outlined above would not be possible because there would not be sufficient metal to hold the body of the verge, and it would become loose.   In such a case a new verge would be needed, for the old verge could not be secured in this condition.

Making a Verge for a Watch

There are several ways of making a verge, and the easiest of these will now be described.   To make the brass collet a suitable piece of brass rod is chosen, this rod being a little larger than the hole in the balance-spring collet, so that it can be turned true afterwards.   A hole is now drilled in the rod, preferably while it is in the lathe, about three times as large as the verge pivot.   Next, a piece of flat steel, lever steel or even mainspring thick enough to form an arbor for the verge is selected, and this is filed down until it is a little less than half the diameter of the brass collet.   The metal is now filed away in the middle to a square arbor, leaving the pads standing out.

Using the balance wheel ('scape wheel) as a guide, the pads are

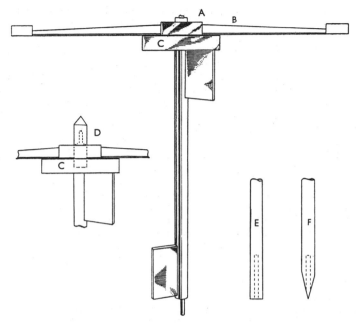

Figure 75. Pivoting a verge. The pivot is drilled out at A and the steel broken off in the root; B = balance; C = brass collet as balance seat; D = plug; E = round steel rod drill or sinker which is drilled as indicated by dotted line and filed to a knife edge as shown at F.

arranged so that the wheel teeth will work in the centre of the lower pad, leaving an arbor at the bottom for the pivot.

The balance wheel is now placed in the frame in position and the lower pad rested on the side of the pottance in line with the wheel. The top of the upper pad is now marked off; this will be only just above the top of the balance wheel or definitely free of the wheel. The top arbor is now filed, leaving it square in section. This leaves a square arbor at the top, the top pad, a square arbor in between the two pads a little shorter than the inside diameter of the wheel or about two-thirds of this inside diameter, the lower pad and then a square arbor. It is important that the direction in which the wheel runs should be carefully noted.

Direction of Pads—Looking from the pinion side, the wheel runs clockwise in most cases, providing the wheel is towards the centre of the watch and the pinion towards the outside. Sometimes, however, the pinion is towards the centre of the watch, and in this case the verge must be made with the pads reversed. In addition, in the case

119

of three-wheel trains the wheel turns clockwise in some cases and anti-clockwise in others.

Twisting the Verge—If the balance wheel turns clockwise when viewed from the pinion end the lower pad should be twisted clockwise when viewed from the top or balance end of the verge. In order to twist the pad the centre of the verge should be either red hot or nearly so. This can be done over the small flame of a spirit lamp, twisting until the two pads are at right angles to each other. After checking to see that it runs near truth and is not bent, it can be hardened and tempered, leaving it as hard as possible, *i.e.* until it can just be turned with a graver or just marked with a file. It should be tempered to a rich blue but not below this. When this has been completed the brass collet has to be fitted.

Fitting the Collet—After the rod has been drilled in the lathe a portion about the same length as the height of the balance cock from the plate is parted off. Some watchmakers open the hole in the collet until the square top arbor just passes through and then lead solder the collet to the verge, but the best way is to slightly taper the top arbor, and then to carefully broach the hole in the collet until the arbor will pass about three-quarters of its length through the hole, after which the verge is driven into the collet with a punch, lightly tapping it with a hammer. The punch used for this purpose is a piece of steel rod with a slot cut at an angle to ensure striking the verge as nearly central as possible. Care must be taken to hit the verge straight, otherwise the arbor may break, and this will entail starting afresh.

Fitting the Verge—The method of turning the verge has already been described in the author's previous book, and therefore need not be repeated again, but a few hints on the fitting will prove useful. It must first be ascertained that when the lower pad is flush with the inside of the bottom of the pottance the bottom of the brass collet is just clear of the balance wheel; if this is all in order the next step is to clean up the actual verge. The arbor between the pads will look like a corkscrew, so it must be filed or stoned up round and smooth. The other arbors can be turned true later.

Next, the pads have to be thinned by one-half, and this should be done by stoning across the verge and not lengthwise. Although this takes a longer time, it looks very much nicer. When the thinning is completed the pads are polished with diamantine using an iron polisher shaped to suit.

Care must be taken to see that the gap between the two pads is wide enough to clear the centre of the pottance, and then the verge is turned to fit the frame.

Making a New Balance Wheel

Sometimes the balance wheel teeth become damaged, thus necessitating a new wheel. This is a tricky job, because it is very difficult

120

to cut the teeth in an ordinary lathe, as they are back cut or undercut about 30°, and as the teeth (like a contrate) are at right angles to the body of the wheel, the lathe head itself must be tilted up the 30°. In addition, the wheel has to be cut at an angle, otherwise the teeth would be thicker on the outside, and the tops of the teeth would be triangular instead of parallel.

When a single wheel has to be cut a certain amount of reliance must be placed on trial-and-error methods, the best way being to make two or three blanks and to use these when setting the machine for the wheel required. There is no need to cut more than one tooth; after this has been cut it can be examined and the machine altered accordingly until it is correct. It is worth the time it takes to get the wheel right. Usually the cutter is set at about the distance between two teeth higher than for a radial cut, but with some of the French verges, where the wheel teeth are closer together, the cutter is not set so high.

The slide must be banked so that the cutter does not cross the centre, the reason for this being that the wheel has an odd number of teeth which are all in relatively opposite directions, as will be seen if the wheel is examined from one side looking across the face of the wheel.

Making the Blank—The first thing to do when making a blank is to select a piece of good-quality hard brass rod. This is put in the lathe and, using the slide rest, the face is turned perfectly flat. After this a true hole is drilled to the full depth of the blank, the hole being made smaller than the pattern, then, still using the slide rest, the outside is turned to the exact size of the wheel. In each case a polished cutter is used so that no finishing is required afterwards.

The inside of the wheel is sunk out, making sure that it is exactly the same as the old one, then, leaving the blank full for length, it is parted off from the rod. After the blank has been parted off it is put in a step chuck the reverse way round, *i.e.* the part for the teeth going to the face of the chuck. After making sure that the blank is quite true in the chuck it is faced off quite square.

Some of these wheels are what is called ' crossed out ', *i.e.* the bottom of the wheel is filed out, leaving 3 arms, this being done for lightness. If the wheel is being crossed out it should be done at this stage.

Cutting the Teeth—In order to cut the teeth the blank can be firmly fixed to a wax chuck with shellac. It must, however, be really firm. Alternatively, it can be held in a small step chuck which is perfectly true. It will probably be necessary to make the cutter, as this cannot be obtained commercially owing to the demand being too small.

The cutter must not be too thick, it is better to have one too thin and to make two cuts with it. This is generally the better way, as the first cut often tends to force the teeth over because it is cutting

121

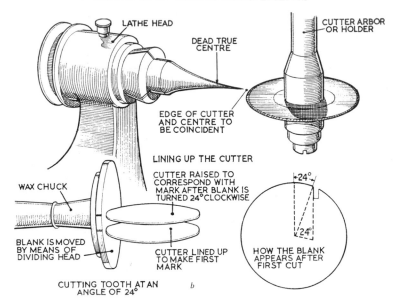

LATHE HEAD

CUTTER ARBOR OR HOLDER

DEAD TRUE CENTRE

EDGE OF CUTTER AND CENTRE TO BE COINCIDENT

LINING UP THE CUTTER

WAX CHUCK

CUTTER RAISED TO CORRESPOND WITH MARK AFTER BLANK IS TURNED 24° CLOCKWISE

BLANK IS MOVED BY MEANS OF DIVIDING HEAD

CUTTER LINED UP TO MAKE FIRST MARK

HOW THE BLANK APPEARS AFTER FIRST CUT

CUTTING TOOTH AT AN ANGLE OF 24°   *b*

Figure 76.   Procedure for cutting a wheel.   *a* setting up for wheel or pinion ;   *b* setting for cutting tooth off the radial.

both sides, or both edges are cutting together.   By using two cuts the second cut is only cutting on one side, and this will not force the teeth over so readily, but the lighter the last cut is, the better.

Mounting the Wheel—This is the most exacting job of all, because however accurately the wheel has been cut it will be hopeless if not mounted perfectly flat and true.   When opening the hole the wheel is put in a step chuck with the teeth towards the face.   The wheel must not be gripped enough to damage it, but should be held with just sufficient firmness.   Using a very thin cutter in the slide rest, the hole is turned out to fit the seat on the pinion closely.   A very deep undercut is turned in the face of the rivet so that the leaves can be easily pushed over the wheel.   When riveting only very light blows should be given with the hammer, and the wheel should be continually examined to see that it is going on flat.   When the wheel is quite firm the riveting is stopped.   If the wheel has gone slightly out of flat the riveting can be continued on the higher side to push the wheel down a little, but great care must be taken.

Trueing the Wheel—In spite of every care the wheel does not always mount perfectly true, and this can only be corrected in action.   The wheel is tried in the frame with the verge in place, and after finding

122

which tooth is the offender the incorrect tooth is marked with red polishing paste: it is altered very carefully by hand until it is correct.

The tooth should be altered only from the back, and a very small smooth and slightly rounded file should be used for this job. The alteration must, of course, be very small or the wheel may be completely ruined.

The Bankings

All verges have to be banked to prevent the verge going too far round and also to prevent the wheel running by as soon as the pads pass the centre. The balance usually has the banking pin, and this is situated underneath the balance and acts either against screwheads in the plate or against the circular block or plate covering the index. In quite a number of English verge watches the pin is above the balance, and banks on steps in the circle of the balance cock.

This banking limits the movement of the balance to a little more than half a turn, or a quarter turn each side, thus the wheel cannot get away or be damaged.

The pin must be in its correct position, which is exactly halfway between the two farthest points of its movement, otherwise the wheel can run through on one side although it is unable to do so on the other. This must be carefully checked.

From the point of rest the balance is led round to the banking and the wheel is tried to see if it will pass, then the direction is reversed and the other side is tried. If one side passes, the balance is moved in the same direction in relation to the verge so that it is banked earlier, or another pin is put in if this is easier. If the wheel passes both ways two banking pins are put in, one on each side of the existing pin.

To Put In Beat

A verge is not an easy escapement to set even when it is out of beat, therefore a verge can only be put in beat by having very little power on the escapement.

The point of rest of the balance without any power is noted and the balance is led round until the tooth drops, and the distance that the balance moves is noted. The direction is now reversed until the tooth drops and the distance of the balance movement once again noted. If the same movement from the point of rest is required both ways the escapement is in beat.

It is very difficult to decide whether the verge is in beat aurally, *i.e.* by sound, because any inaccuracies in the train depths will in any case make the beat sound uneven.

Contrate Wheel

It must not be forgotten that the contrate wheel in a verge watch is very important. A bad contrate depth will make a verge watch sound out of beat and make the drops appear unequal. The pinion

123

must not be small in proportion to the contrate wheel or the pinion leaves will butt on the wheel teeth on the recoil, but neither must the pinion be large unless the leaves are shaped to suit, *i.e.* the pinion leaves must be broad at the base or dedendum, with a thinner top or addendum.

Where some of the older watches have pinions of 5 leaves on the balance wheel pinion it is often very difficult to get a satisfactory action, and a watchmaker is very fortunate if he can keep such movements going without serious attention or alteration. It is no good being deceived into thinking that the escapement action is wrong, for obviously one cannot expect a close rate or even a regular rate from a verge watch, but one or two of those handled by the author have given remarkable performances.

Some of the verge watches were very small and could be mounted in a ring, and they were certainly comparable in size with a modern wrist-watch.

Repairs to a Verge Escapement

The pivots of the verge become worn, and, like all other escapements, must be repaired, also the verge pivot holes wear oval.

Inserting a new hole is a tricky operation, but if the position of the top pivot hole is carefully noted, or even marked, no trouble should be experienced. The old bush is pushed out and a new plug pushed tightly, but not riveted, in place. A hole is drilled about the length of the pivot in depth, and of the correct size to suit the pivot because it cannot be broached out afterwards.

The balance and balance cock are then put in place to make sure that the hole is in the correct position for drop, *etc.*, and, of course, endshake. If the endshake is too great the plug must be pushed through a little until it is correct. The hole is then chamfered on the part inside the balance cock to give clearance to the pivot shoulder.

When all is in order the plug is shortened from the outside, this being done in a lathe by waxing the balance cock to the wax chuck, and turning the outside of the plug to its correct length with a graver or slide-rest cutter. If a lathe is not available it can be filed off, but in this case a piece of paper must be placed over it and the filing done across the paper. As the plug stands proud, the paper will be filed off first and the plug can be filed away with perfect safety, because as soon as any other part of the paper is filed it will be noticed at once, and therefore there is no likelihood of the balance cock being spoilt by file markings.

Front Balance Wheel Pinion Pivot

The front pivot and hole of the balance wheel pinion are often worn and have to be corrected. It is necessary to dismount the balance wheel to repair the pivot. The pivot is repaired in the usual way, but it must be quite straight, *i.e.* perfectly cylindrical, and not bent or tapered.

If the hole or bearing is in a dovetail it is often easier to make a new dovetail and to drill this with a hole to fit the pivot, this being in the same relative position as the one in the old dovetail. Some dovetail pieces are stout enough to enable a new bush to be fitted with ease.

The difficulty now is to remount the balance wheel, as upon remounting on to its pinion it may possibly prove to be out of true and not flat. In this case the leaves of the balance wheel pinion are turned away and a brass collet is put in their place on which the wheel is mounted. This will be found to be quite easy and will save a lot of time.

The position in which the contrate wheel gears into the pinion must, of course, be ascertained, for if the action is close to the balance wheel any error may involve a new pinion, therefore before the turning is commenced it is wisest to ascertain how far the leaves of the pinion can be reduced.

Contrate Wheel and Pinion

Sometimes, after a new hole has been fitted to the top contrate wheel pinion of a verge watch it is found that the bush has drifted towards the balance wheel pinion arbor, and this fault has been the reason for many obscure stoppages. This is caused by the contrate wheel arbor touching the balance wheel pinion arbor.

If the arbors are thick this fault can be remedied by thinning them where they cross each other, but very often the contrate arbor has to be moved slightly to give clearance.

Oil

Although it has been advocated that a verge should not be oiled, it is usual to lightly oil the pads, and from experience it would seem that this is necessary as long as the oiling is not excessive, *i.e.* enough oil should be used to keep the wheel teeth slightly damp but not enough to pick up dust and dirt.

8

THE MUDGE REMONTOIRE ESCAPEMENT

THE ESCAPEMENT INVENTED BY Thomas Mudge was made into a marine clock or ' chronometer ' in an endeavour to win the Admiralty prize for a marine timepiece for navigational purposes. This escapement gave really fine results, and Mudge spent quite a lot of time trying to improve on its performance.

There is no doubt that his escapement gave ideas to other watchmakers, culminating in the invention of the ' Gravity ', ' Lever ' and ' Spring detent ' or chronometer escapement.

The remontoire escapement is so called because the impulse to the balance is given indirectly from the mainspring, but the main object is really to provide the balance with a constant impulse, and thus with a constant vibration.

Action of the Escapement

It is fairly easy to understand the action of the escapement. The balance staff is in the form of a crank with a brass pin tightly fitted into each end. The impulse is given to these pins alternately by pivoted arms, on the arbors of which are fitted hairsprings and also the lifting pallets. These lifting pallets are in some cases hardened and polished steel, and in other cases made of ruby, which was the material used for the first ones.

The 'scape wheel, or to call it by its correct name, the balance wheel, is very similar to the balance wheel of a verge escapement, the teeth, however, which are very strong, are shaped like the dead-beat in clocks or the ratchet tooth in a watch escapement. This wheel is the connecting link between the train and the escapement itself, and with the lifting pallets its action can be likened to a verge escapement with the verge in two halves, each half pivoted at each end, and yet apparently working as though a single unit. As the balance wheel, which is driven by the train, revolves it lifts the pallet in the same way as the pallet of a verge is lifted, with the difference that the pallet ends in a hook; as the pallet is lifted to its full extent the wheel tooth is locked by this hook with the pallet raised, and as the pallet has the impulse arm and the hairspring on the same arbor, the result is that the impulse arm is raised and the hairspring wound up. Now as the balance turns, the brass pin on the crank of the balance staff engages the impulse arm and lifts it up, and so moves the hook on the lifting pallet and unlocks the wheel, which proceeds to run. At the same time the impulse arm is resting on the brass pin with the hairspring pressing on it.

This pressure from the hairspring provides the impulse to the balance by pushing the impulse arm against the crank of the balance staff. Now as soon as the balance wheel teeth are released the wheel turns and the tooth on the opposite side of the wheel proceeds to set up the other pallet, and again locks on the hook as before. As the balance is given impulse it proceeds to run, with the impulse arm pushing until it reaches the centre of its vibration, when it leaves the impulse arm which has given impulse and proceeds until it engages the other arm already set up and locked. As before, it pushes the impulse arm, unlocks the wheel, the other pallet is engaged and set up, the balance receives its impulse from the released arm and the sequence starts all over again.

Arc of Vibration—The arc of vibration, as in the verge, is a little more than a quarter of a turn each way, or a total of a little more than half a turn. The balance, however, is detached or in free vibration for about a quarter of a turn, or the distance between the disengagement from the one impulse arm until the engagement and release of the other arm.

Its vibration is, of course, restricted by the resistance of the set-up hairspring. As the balance engages the impulse arm to unlock it also carries the arm a little more than necessary to unlock, and it does this against an already set-up spring. The balance is, of course, banked, but it is carried out through the cranked balance staff, which is banked on the pottance. The pottance is cut away to allow about seven-eighths of a turn, but the crank will not reach this maximum, and the idea seems to be more of a guard against accidental swinging of the balance whilst it is being handled or wound up.

As the vibrations of the balance are equal, they do not play so important a part, and their greatest asset is the fact of their being constant.

The Motive Power—Although this escapement is a constant force or remontoire, it is very particular in regard to the force or motive power which it receives from the train. One of its faults is that the impulse spring may not be fully set up, and on observation one comes to the conclusion that the wheel fails to lock, or it is said to trip, or at least appears to do so. The reason for this action can be either that the motive power is not strong enough or that there is a hold-up somewhere in the train.

Another fault if it can be so called is a lack of oil on the lifting pallets. If these pallets are left dry the impulse springs will be readily set up at first, but will soon fail, therefore the lifting pallets, whether jewelled or of hard steel, must be lightly oiled in much the same way as the teeth on a lever 'scape wheel should be oiled.

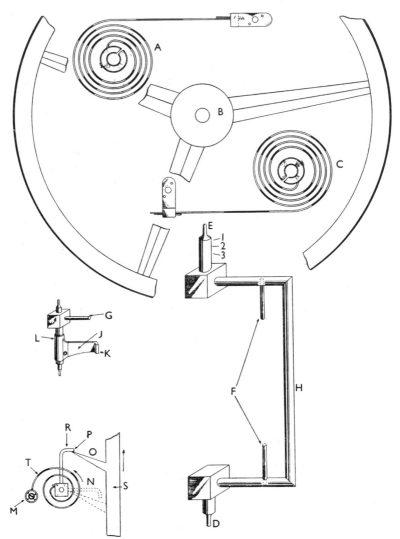

Figure 77. Mudge Remontoire partially detached escapement as used in his first marine clock. A = upper hairspring; B = balance; C = lower hairspring; D = long staff pivot running in roller bearings and resting on diamond endstone; E = top long staff pivot which is the same as the bottom pivot D; F = the brass posts in the balance staff which receive impulse and also unlock wheel tooth; G = impulse arm; H = balance staff; J = lifting pallet which is sometimes of jewel; K = locking hook; L = pivoted arbor; M = stud; N = tooth about to lift and set up hair-

128

When these escapements have been running for a long time the sharp or clean locking corners of the wheel teeth become worn, and when this happens the escapement will definitely trip or mislock. A usual sign that this has happened is that the instrument gains very much on its rate. The tops of the teeth are usually thicker than those in a normal 'scape wheel, and therefore the front of the tooth or the locking face can, within limits, be cleaned up.

Refacing the Wheel Teeth—The wheel teeth are best refaced in a wheel-cutting engine, or in a lathe fitted up as such. Failing this, the wheel must either be touched up by hand or else by a swing tool adapted for the job. This will, of course, ensure that the face is flat. The maximum amount of care must be exercised, otherwise the condition of the wheel will be worse than before.

Putting in Beat

As these escapements set very heavily and take a large swing to start them, they must be carefully set in beat.

To test for beat the procedure to be adopted is very much the same as usual. The balance is led from the point of rest towards the impulse arm, which is raised or set up, then the balance is carefully moved until the tooth is released, and on that instant the balance itself is released. It should then move far enough across to just release the tooth on the other side and carry on going. This should be tried both sides, and if it starts on both sides it is in beat. If it fails to start on one side the balance-spring collet should be moved so that the balance is a little nearer to the side which it has failed to release.

The Set-up

It is inadvisable to interfere with any of the impulse hairsprings if the balance appears to have a poor vibration, and great care must also be taken to see that they are not distorted or out of flat, for this would lead to a possibility of the impulse arm becoming fouled when they were set up.

Before taking them to pieces it is essential that the amount that the mainspring is set up should be noted, because the whole action of the escapement depends on it. It should be ascertained that the impulse arms and also the brass impulse pins on the staff are quite tight.

The balance wheel pivots have to be repolished, but as the balance wheel is usually screwed to its collet this presents no difficulty. The depth of engagement of the balance wheel is adjustable because it is

spring; O = wheel tooth; P = locking tooth; R = lifting pallet; S = balance wheel or 'scape wheel; T = impulse hairspring. The upper hairspring A, balance B and lower hairspring C fit on the top long staff pivot E in positions 1, 2 and 3 respectively. The inset drawing bottom left indicates how the impulse is set up.

on a slide and has a screw to fix it firmly in position. The endshake of the balance wheel pinion must be close but free, and the wheel teeth must be sufficiently oiled to keep them damp with oil but no more.

The balance-staff pivots run on roller bearings, and as they have diamond endstones there is very little wear. The roller bearings are mounted on arbors pivoted in the frame of the balance cock and the lower pottance. These pivots become worn and have to be repaired, and new holes fitted, otherwise there is a great loss of vibration.

When these instruments are being cleaned they should not be given a severe cleaning-machine treatment, but great care should be exercised, each instrument being treated as an individual job.

9

THE CYLINDER ESCAPEMENT

THE CYLINDER ESCAPEMENT WAS invented by Thomas Tompion about 1695. It was, however, greatly improved by George Graham, and improvements or modifications were carried out by other horologists later. It was at first called the horizontal escapement because the verge was a vertical escapement, and this was the first distinction between the two.

The escapement consists of a cylinder which is a steel tube partly cut away to form pallet faces or lips, and a 'scape wheel which has its teeth raised up as though on stalks, with their edges shaped to form the impulse planes.

The wheels were at first made of brass, but are now mostly made of steel, and these can be much lighter in weight and also the acting faces are thinner. Obviously the thinner the wheel teeth, the more room or clearance is available.

Types of Cylinder

The cylinders are now mostly made of steel, but quite a number were made in ruby, and these were in three types. The first of these was one where the whole cylinder was made of ruby, the second type consisted of a shell fitted into a steel skeleton, whilst the third type was found only in watches made by A. L. Breguet and was totally different. This latter cylinder consisted of a section of shell which was fitted into a channel at one end but which was unsupported at the other end and stood proud of the cylinder frame. This will be dealt with again later in the chapter.

Mounted on the cylinder body is a brass collet on which is fitted the balance. The brass collet also has a reduced part on which the balance-spring collet is fitted.

The Cylinder Plugs

The cylinder is supported and revolves on pivots which are turned on plugs fitted into each end of the cylinder. When this cylinder is made in steel it is hardened and tempered to a point where it can only just be cut or turned.

The plugs are not quite so hard, and when they have to be replaced the steel should be hardened and then tempered to a dark-blue colour bordering on a light blue. The body of the plugs should be almost straight, but should have a very gradual taper so that they have the maximum grip without being viciously tight.

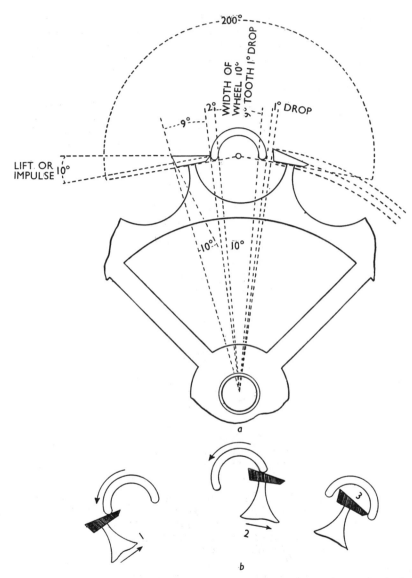

Figure 78.   Cylinder escapement with 10° impulse or lift using a wheel of 15 teeth.   The impulse given to the entrance lip is shown at (1).   Impulse given to exit lip (2) and (3) shows the tooth locked inside the cylinder.

When the 'scape wheel is made of steel it is left very hard, but the centre is softened near the hole through which the 'scape pinion is fitted. This pinion generally has 6 leaves, but there can be any number to suit the particular train that it controls.

Description of the Escapement

The cylinder escapement is what is termed a frictional-rest, *i.e.* after the 'scape wheel tooth has given impulse the wheel is stationary but is resting on the body of the cylinder, and as such the balance is never detached, that is to say that at no time is the balance running freely and it is always in contact with the escapement.

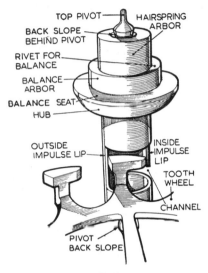

Figure 79. Cylinder escapement showing details of the cylinder.

The balance is banked so that it cannot revolve a full turn. The banking pin is usually fitted into the balance rim and stands out horizontally, or in some cases vertically. At the full turn this pin comes into contact with either a pin set vertically under the balance cock, on the arbor of the fourth wheel pinion, or on the edge of the balance cock.

In quite a number of the older English cylinder watches the banking pin is fitted through the body of the cylinder, and banks against a pin in the pottance or drop cock supporting the lower cylinder pivot. As with the verge escapement, the position of the banking pin in relation to the cylinder is very critical.

133

The Cylinder

The cylinder itself is cut away to make what is called ' the great opening ', which forms the lips and the lesser opening or the channel. The great opening is four-ninths of the cylinder shell, leaving five-ninths or 200° of the full shell for the lips. The 20° in excess of half a shell is for locking and also to help the wheel when giving impulse. It is, however, wrong to have too much locking, and this should be only sufficient to be perfectly safe on all teeth, but no more The wheel teeth have all of the impulse, and are usually at an angle of 10°, or 10° of lift. It is quite common to find wheel teeth with a higher angle, but in such cases the watches usually set very heavily.

Action of the Escapement

The sequence of events in a cylinder escapement is that as the balance moves the wheel tooth is resting on the outside of the cylinder, and as the balance continues to turn, the point of the 'scape wheel tooth reaches the lip, so that the impulse plane of the tooth proceeds

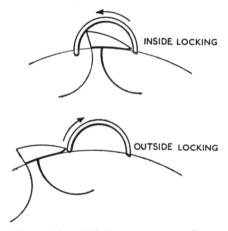

INSIDE LOCKING

OUTSIDE LOCKING

Figure 80.   Cylinder escapement showing how locking takes place.

to push the cylinder round, and turns the balance. As soon as the end of the impulse plane is reached the tooth drops off, and then drops on to the inside of the cylinder. The balance continues to revolve until it reaches the end of its momentum, when the balance spring drives the balance back, unlocking the tooth inside the cylinder, and the tooth proceeds to push the cylinder and help it on its way. As soon as this tooth reaches the end of its impulse plane it, too, drops off, and the tooth following it drops on to the outside of the cylinder and the sequence starts all over again.

134

Mislocking—When the tooth drops, or is dropped by the cylinder, it must be ensured that the point of the tooth drops on to the shell itself either inside or outside the cylinder. If the point misses the shell and the impulse plane of the tooth falls on the edge or lip of the cylinder it will stop the watch. This action means that the escapement mislocks, and this is caused by either a worn wheel, a worn cylinder or because the escapement is pitched too shallow or the cylinder and wheel are too far apart.

The Chariot

In most foreign watches the cylinder and balance cock are fitted on to a chariot. This is a plate sunk into the pillar plate which is steady-pinned in place and secured by a screw. Although this plate is fixed, it can be carefully adjusted if necessary by slightly bending the steady pins the appropriate amount in the direction required. Sometimes this chariot is fitted on the top of the plate and has a screw with an eccentrically planted pin to enable adjustment to the escapement depth to be made. As the balance cock is mounted on the chariot, the uprightness of the balance unit will not be affected by any adjustment made.

Drop

It has been stated earlier that the 'scape wheel teeth have drop like all escapements, and that this is freedom and loss of impulse, and must therefore be kept to a minimum. The drop is controlled by the size of the cylinder, *i.e.* the inside and outside diameters of the cylinder shell. If the cylinder is too small there will be no inside drop, and if the cylinder is too large there will be no drop when there are two teeth on the outside of the cylinder, or when, in other words, the cylinder is between two teeth.

A number of watchmakers shorten the wheel teeth to correct this, but although this gives freedom, it does not equalise the drop but increases the one already free, so that the drop which is already excessive is increased still more. This results in excessive wear on the cylinder and very little impulse. The only way to equalise the drops is to replace the cylinder with one which is the correct size.

Repairing the Wheel Teeth

The points of the teeth of a cylinder 'scape wheel often become worn, and when this occurs they act like a brake, especially when on the inside of the cylinder, and this fault will often stop a cylinder watch. When repairing these teeth the impulse planes should not be touched, but the points should be brought up again from the inside of the teeth. The points can be ground up sharp again by rubbing them on the inside with a thin steel polisher on which oilstone dust has been smeared.

Some watchmakers shorten the teeth by rubbing off the sharp

135

locking corners, and this will cause the same trouble.   This can also be cured by use of the same treatment as for worn teeth.

If there is no alternative to shortening the teeth each tooth should

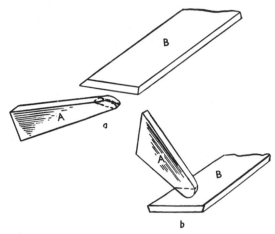

Figure 81.   Wrong way *a* and right way *b* of repairing   worn   cylinder   'scape   wheel   teeth. A = tooth; B = polisher.

be shortened from the heel, making certain that the point of the next tooth is not touched.   It must always be born in mind that if the tooth is shortened the wheel will often mislock as well as the drops increase.

The Motive Power

The motive power plays an important part in a good-quality cylinder escapement.   If the mainspring is too strong the balance may strike the bankings or rap on the banking pin, *i.e.* the balance will vibrate a full turn and the banking pin on the balance will strike the banking block, and in this case a weaker mainspring is the only remedy.   When a poor-quality cylinder escapement has too strong a mainspring the friction will increase so much that the watch will stop, therefore a weaker mainspring is again the only remedy, although a bad escapement can never be made into a good one.

If either a cylinder watch or a carriage clock with a cylinder platform escapement is to keep reasonably accurate time its vibration must be fairly constant at two-thirds of a turn, *i.e.* one-third of a turn each side.

Worn Cylinder

If a cylinder is badly worn it more often than not means that a new one is required.   With some cylinders having a wide channel, however, it is possible to move the wheel from a worn part of the cylinder to an unworn part. With English-made cylinders it is easy to lower the wheel on its collet, or to raise the wheel by fitting a new collet on the 'scape pinion and remounting the wheel higher, but with foreign cylinders it is often easier to move the cylinder up or down.

In order to lower the cylinder the lower pivot is reduced and the top plug is pushed out as much as the lower one is shortened; to raise the cylinder a new bottom plug and pivot are fitted and the top is shortened. If the balance becomes foul by either of these alterations the collet on which it is mounted can be knocked down on the cylinder to lower it, and the cylinder can be knocked through the collet a little to raise it. The balance must not be bent about, because this may lead to all sorts of trouble.

Shortening the Pivot—When shortening either the top or bottom of the pivot it is often necessary to turn back the cone shoulder to allow the pivot to pass well through the jewel hole to reach the endstone.

The pivot itself must be sufficiently long for the pivot shoulder to be quite clear of the jewel sink when the end of the pivot rests on the endstone. A falling-off in vibration is often due to the shoulder resting on the jewel hole. The idea of the endstone is to keep the shoulder clear of the jewel so that only the end of the pivot and the sides are in action, thus causing only the minimum of friction.

New Cylinder Plugs

When a cylinder watch is dropped the cylinder itself is very often broken, necessitating a new one, but sometimes it is not the actual cylinder which breaks but only the pivots. These are much easier to replace than a complete cylinder, and the only difficulty is in removing the plugs.

Removing the Plugs—The first requirement for removing a plug is a stake with the same size hole in it as the plug, or alternatively one which is just too small for the cylinder itself to pass through. The

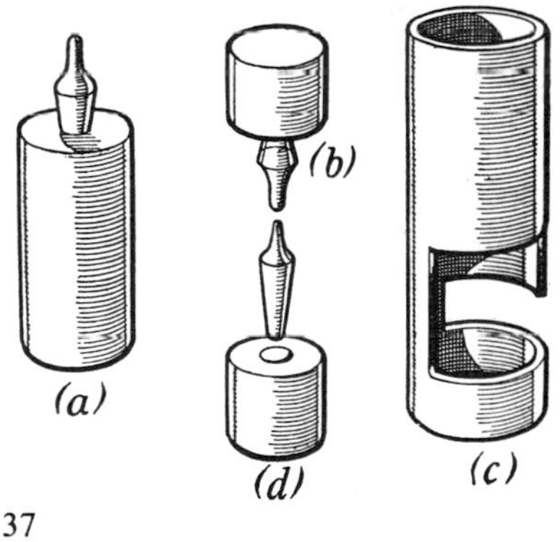

Figure 82. Cylinder plugs: (*a*) Swiss top cylinder plug, (*b*) Swiss bottom plug, (*c*) cylinder ' shell ', (*d*) English type plugs.

edge of the hole should be slightly chamfered so that the cylinder can be easily located.

Knee Punch to Remove Plug—The plug itself is driven out by means of a punch called a ' knee punch '. This is a punch which is filed up so that the section remaining will pass cleanly into the cylinder. There should be a pivot or punch proper at that end of the punch which passes into the cylinder.

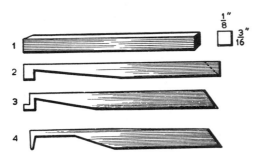

Figure 83. Cylinder plug punches: (1) steel rod, (2) recess filed out, (3) filed away to leave pivot, (4) filed away to form punch to drive cylinder into brass collet.

In order to remove the plug the cylinder is rested over the hole in the stake, and the pivot of the punch is laid on the plug. When the punch is given a blow with a hammer the plug should drive out.

It is quite easy to carry out this operation if a staking tool is available, because the work can then be steadied with the disengaged hand, but in the ordinary way one hand is required to hold the punch whilst the other one holds the hammer.

Removing a Tight Plug—The blows should be light ones, otherwise the punch or even the cylinder may break. If the plug does not readily move it is a good plan to rest the cylinder on its side on a flat stake and to tap the outside of the cylinder very lightly with a hammer. This must, of course, be done after the cylinder has been removed from the balance. This will stretch the shell of the cylinder very slightly, and it is often possible to push the plug out with the points of a pair of tweezers.

Fitting a New Plug—When fitting a new plug is must be remembered that a cylinder is very delicate and is easily broken, therefore a new plug should not be fitted to be viciously tight, but should just be a good fit. The plug must be almost straight, and should be lightly pushed in until about 0·005 in. from its final position flush on the inside with the edge of the channel. The plug can then be pushed firmly home with the aid of the flat end, *i.e.* the end without a pivot, of a knee punch whilst the outside of the cylinder is resting on a stake. When this has been done the pivot can be turned on the plug.

English Cylinder Plugs

The English cylinders had the plugs in two parts, the cylinder itself being first plugged or bushed with brass, after which steel plugs were fitted into the brass. This method of fixing makes the removal of the plugs a much more simple proposition.

Another difference between the English and Continental cylinders was the top plug. The majority of English cylinder watches were full plates, *i.e.* the balance and balance cock were on the top of the plate, and the rest of the mechanism was between the plates, the balance spring being fitted underneath the balance and not above as in the modern watch.

This type of watch was referred to as an undersprung watch, and the brass plug was solid with both the balance seat and the balance-spring seat or arbor. These were first drilled and then turned on an arbor to fit tightly into the top of the cylinder. The steel plug was then fitted into the brass plug and the whole turned true with the body of the cylinder. The balance-spring collet was fitted first, and this controlled the size of the balance seat. The balance was then fitted as high or as near the end as possible.

If when the cylinder was finished the balance was a little high it would not be difficult to lower the seat until the required height was reached.

The Cylinder Height—When fitting a new bottom plug it is most important to see that the height of the cylinder is correct. The height, or relative position, of the cylinder depends on the lower plug; if the watch is a flat or thin one the aim is to position the cylinder in such a way that the plane of the wheel passes midway through the channel. If there is any error at all the channel must be a little low, so that when the watch is lying on its back the endshakes will bring the action central; if the watch is a thick one the position can be arranged to have the action high or low, so that when wear takes place the cylinder can be raised or lowered accordingly to bring an unworn part of the cylinder into action.

THE RUBY CYLINDER

The Breguet ruby cylinder is a really good escapement, and although it is a very delicate piece of work, this is allowed for in its construction.

Unlike the usual cylinder, in which the pivots are more or less part of the cylinder, the Breguet has its pivots on what is more or less a separate unit. The pivots are part of an arbor which is driven friction tight into the balance collet, so in the event of shock the cylinder itself is unaffected, and the only way it is possible for it to get damaged is by careless handling.

The cylinder is mounted in a grooved frame on a steel stalk which is part of a unit mounted on the balance, the stalk forming part of the banking. The lower pivot, on which the cylinder revolves, runs in a partly drilled jewel fitted at the bottom of a pipe, the cylinder running

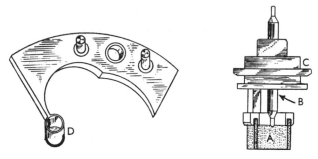

Figure 84. Breguet ruby cylinder. A = ruby cylinder standing proud; B shows how the arbor fits into the centre of the cylinder frame like an ordinary balance staff; C = brass collet as usual; D = lower jewelling and banking for cylinder frame.

round the pipe, *i.e.* the pipe is inside the cylinder, and so cut away that the stalk can move round and bank against each side. If this jewelled cylinder does become broken it is difficult to replace.

Making a Breguet Ruby Cylinder

It is not suggested that the average watchmaker would make one of these cylinders, but some may want to do so, and the procedure to be followed will now be given.

The first thing to be done is to make a template or gauge. This can be made in steel, and after testing it out to see that it is in order the jewel can be made to pattern or measure.

Selecting a Stone—A rough stone should be selected, large enough and to spare, either sapphire or light-coloured ruby. This is ground flat on two opposite sides to make any black marks or streaks in the stone clearly visible, and if any marks do show another rough stone should be selected and the operation started again. When a satisfactory stone has been found one of the flat sides is fixed with shellac against a brass wax chuck with a hole drilled in the centre slightly larger than the internal diameter of the finished cylinder.

The stone is waxed up near true and a hole is drilled through the centre, using a piece of copper wire with a small piece of ' bort ' *i.e.* a diamond chip set in place in it with shellac, as the drill. The drill must be smaller than the inside diameter of the cylinder, and should be operated at a high speed, using water or thin oil as a lubricant. Only sufficient pressure should be exerted to cut the stone, and of course it will take longer to drill a hard stone than it would take to drill a soft one.

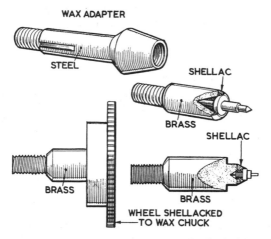

Figure 85.   Wax chucks for use in the lathe.

Enlarging the Hole—When the hole has been drilled through it must be enlarged to the exact inside diameter of the cylinder.   This is done with a piece of iron wire, slightly tapered and about 0·02 mm. smaller than the required size of the hole, which has been charged with a mixture of diamond cutting powder and oil.   If the hole is very much smaller than its finished size a piece of copper wire with cutting powder hammered into it will open the hole very quickly, but plenty of water or oil must be used, otherwise it will bite.   When opening a hole the wire should be inserted in the hole and pushed carefully through until the friction is felt; at this stage the wire is pulled back and the operation repeated.   The wire must be kept wet, and no force should be exerted.   Care must also be taken to see that the wire does not bite into the hole and either break off, splinter the jewel or both.

When the hole is all but to size the wire should be changed for a special sizing polisher.   This is a piece of soft iron wire (and it is essential that only iron wire is used) with its acting end shaped like a small ball, and with its outside diameter the exact size of the finished inside of the cylinder.   It is smeared with the finest diamond polishing powder and oil; it must not be charged with this, or it will not polish.   The same procedure of approaching and taking away is adopted as in the previous operation, until the polisher will pass through.   The hole should now be exactly the size required, perfectly straight and highly polished.

Turning the Outside of a Ruby Cylinder—The stone is now removed from the chuck.   Next, a piece of brass rod about three times the size required is turned down in the lathe, and a straight pivot is

141

turned to fit the hole in the jewel easily, or at least not tightly. The next operation is to put shellac on the jewel with its hole on the brass pivot; when the shellac sets the jewel can be turned.

The turning rod or graver consists of a suitable piece of bort fixed into a piece of brass or copper rod with a sharp edge standing proud, and the jewel is turned in the same way as a piece of steel or brass would be turned. Of course, very little pressure is used, the main thing being firmness, and very great care must be taken until the rough edges are brought down true. Only powder comes off during turning, but although is seems slow, it is in comparison quite a quick job. It is important that the stone is kept parallel or quite straight.

Polishing the Outside of the Cylinder—When about 0·05 mm. above size it is smoothed, first using a copper file, *i.e.* a flat strip of copper into which diamond cutting powder has been hammered or burnished. This is used as an ordinary polisher until all of the deep marks are out and the cylinder is only about 0·02 mm. over size. At this stage an ivory polisher with diamond polishing powder smeared on it is brought into use, and the stone is rubbed with this at high speed until the cylinder is to size and a high polish has been attained. A lap can, of course, be used for this, but it takes time to set up.

It is now time to polish one end, and this is done by means of a piece of lead solder on which polishing powder has been smeared. As before, a high and a very light touch are needed, otherwise the shell may easily be broken. It is only necessary to finish one end, because the other end will grip the shellac better if left with a grain from the grinding.

The jewelled cylinder is now to size, and the next step is to cut the lips, and for these, as with the steel cylinder, only five-ninths of the full cylinder is required. Before proceeding with this the brass rod with the cylinder on it is cut off, leaving about $\frac{3}{16}$ in. standing beyond the cylinder itself.

Cutting and Polishing the Lips—The brass rod is held in a tool such as the one used for pallet polishing, but any other tool which can be placed at will in exactly the same position without any risk of failure will do. The full diameter is measured with a micrometer, and then with the aid of a diamond grinding mill held in the lathe the jewel and brass are ground away until only about 0·02 mm. over size.

The shellac is now softened until the cylinder can be moved, and it is then very carefully turned so that one part stands proud by about 0·02 mm. The outside of the lip is now rounded until it just meets, but only just meets, the inside.

When this lip is polished the shellac is again softened and the cylinder turned until the other lip stands proud. The procedure is repeated as before, but from the inside to the outside, again only just reaching the outside. If either of these edges are reduced the cylinder will be less than five-ninths, and may probably mislock and be useless.

142

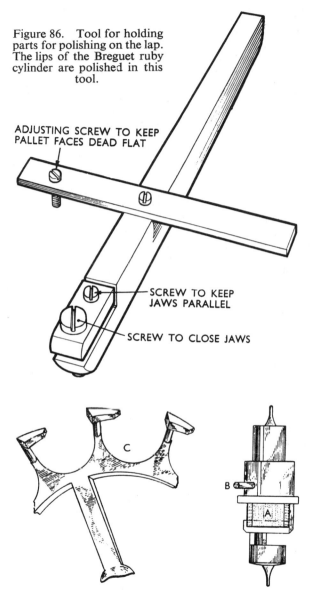

Figure 86. Tool for holding parts for polishing on the lap. The lips of the Breguet ruby cylinder are polished in this tool.

ADJUSTING SCREW TO KEEP PALLET FACES DEAD FLAT

SCREW TO KEEP JAWS PARALLEL

SCREW TO CLOSE JAWS

C

B

A

Figure 87. English ruby cylinder. A = jewel cylinder fitted to steel skeleton; B = banking pin fitted through body of cylinder; C = 'scape wheel.

To make a complete cylinder in jewel is a formidable job, and once having made a shell in the manner already described it means making special laps for cutting the lips and the channel. Where the cylinder is made of steel the plugs are driven in place, but with a jewel cylinder the plugs are fitted and fixed in place with shellac.

Where the jewel is fitted inside the skeleton the procedure is much the same as that already described, but the length is extremely critical.

Making a Steel Cylinder

In order to make a steel cylinder or an ordinary cylinder a piece of steel rod is chosen which can be hardened and tempered, and which is just tight when measured or compared to the space between two teeth, *i.e.* between the heel of one tooth and the toe of the next one.

The length of one tooth is measured, and a drill is made so that when a hole is drilled it will be exactly the same size as the length of the tooth. The steel rod is centred in a lathe and a dead true hole of a length corresponding to the required length of the cylinder is drilled. This is parted off to length from the rod, and the result is a tube of steel. A piece of brass rod is filed or turned to fit the inside of this, and is allowed to pass right through the tube, making sure that it fits both ends. The brass is pushed right into the tube so that it is quite tight.

Making the Impulse Lips—In order to file the impulse lips the tube is laid on the filing block and a slot is filed with the aid of a narrow-edged file; a square file will answer the purpose.

The width of the slot should be the same as the total thickness or height of the wheel when measured from the underneath to the flat of the top teeth, whilst the depth of the slot should be four-ninths of the diameter of the tube, or to put it another way to leave five-ninths intact.

Direction of the Slot—The slot is left perfectly smooth, flat and square. Now the channel is cut to clear the band of the wheel, and it is essential to see that this is cut the right way round, because the direction of this cut is dependent on the direction in which the 'scape wheel turns. The object of the channel is to allow the cylinder to run round when a tooth is inside the cylinder, and it is not needed when the teeth are on the outside. Thus when the 'scape wheel turns clockwise the channel is on the left of the cylinder, or, looking from the top of the cylinder straight down, the channel will be anti-clockwise. When the wheel turns anti-clockwise the reverse is, of course, the case.

To give the maximum amount of freedom with safety, the channel should be cut leaving about one-eighth of the tube sound, and no less should be left at this stage. The width of the channel depends upon the thickness of the band of the wheel, but the channel should not be cut unnecessarily wide, because this will weaken the cylinder. At this stage the wheel and cylinder can be tried in the depth tool by using the male centres to support the cylinder. The cylinder should be tight when a tooth is inside, and tight when between two teeth. If all is in order the cylinder can be hardened and tempered.

Hardening the Cylinder—To harden the cylinder it is placed on a piece of steel wire which closely fits the inside, then both the cylinder and wire are brought to red heat and plunged into oil. The reason for putting the cylinder on the steel wire is to minimise the risk of warping. While the cylinder is still on the steel wire it is brightened with an emery stick, care being taken because it is very brittle. It must be ensured that the cylinder is free of oil, because any grease will deceive when tempering.

To temper the cylinder it is placed with the wire on an iron or brass plate, and almost covered with brass filings, leaving just enough showing so that the colour can be observed. This is now heated over a spirit lamp and on closely watching the cylinder it will be seen to change colour as the heat increases. First it will turn light straw colour, then in turn dark straw, brown, purple and finally rich dark blue.

It should not be heated in the flame until it reaches rich dark blue, but should be taken out of the flame when purple, otherwise one is sure to make it too soft. It will turn a little after it is taken out, but if below dark blue it will be too soft and is best rehardened.

Polishing the Cylinder—The lips of the cylinder which were left square must now be rounded and polished. The easiest way to do this is by using a thin, flat polisher, first, with oilstone dust and oil, and then diamantine. This is best done in a depth tool, using a very small bell-metal lap as the polisher in one side and the cylinder in the other.

By working the lips against the revolving lap smeared with diamantine and oil a high polish will result. When the lips are polished the inside of the cylinder has to be dealt with. In its unpolished state the wheel tooth would be tight in the cylinder, and the polishing will give the necessary freedom.

The cylinder is placed in the lathe and a piece of very slightly tapered iron wire about the size of the finished inside is used as a polisher. The wire is first charged with oilstone dust and oil, or triple washed emery and oil. The polisher is pushed in and out, care being taken that it does not bite and possibly break the cylinder. The cylinder is first treated from one end and then the other. When it is smooth diamantine is used to give a high polish.

To polish the outside of the cylinder it is placed on an arbor and polished over its whole length, using a flat steel polisher and diamantine. A backwards-and-forwards motion of the arbor will give a quicker and also a higher polish. When the cylinder has been polished it is placed with the wheel in the depth tool and the shakes are checked to see that they are equal; if the outside is too close a

145

little more polishing will ease it, and if the inside is too close it must be polished until free.

Fitting the Plugs—By polishing the inside of the cylinder from both ends a slight taper is created, and this enables nicely fitting plugs to be inserted. The plugs are made of hardened and tempered steel of suitable size, and a piece of metal a little larger than the finished plug should be used, because it can then be turned to size and will be sure to be perfectly true and of the correct taper to fit over its whole length.

The lower plug is the one which must be treated with the greatest care, because this end of the cylinder is shorter and is thus more easily split. The plug is turned until it will pass about three-quarters of the way, then smoothed with oilstone dust until it almost reaches the channel. The end is now stoned dead flat and polished if this is required.

The length of the main part of the plug is marked off on the steel, then the total length, *i.e.* the main plug, pivot and shoulder, is marked off, tnen the portion between the main plug and the end of the plug is thinned, after which the total length is cut off, leaving an almost cone centre. Next the plug is placed in the cylinder and pushed home. In order to do this a knee stake is put in a staking tool, making sure that it is in the correct position, then, using a punch with a small hole, the plug is pressed home. It must not be driven, otherwise the cylinder may break, and if it cannot be pushed home it is too tight and must therefore be placed in the lathe again and a little more ground off.

The same procedure applies to the top plug, but before fitting this the length of the cylinder must be ascertained, otherwise the plug may have to be shortened, and in the process it may become loose or the cylinder may break.

When the cylinder has had the plugs inserted the brass collet on which the balance and balance spring are to be mounted is fitted.

Fitting the Brass Collet—The collet is made from a suitable piece of brass rod, the size of this depending on the size of the watch or the balance, but it entails unnecessary work if too large a rod is used. A piece of rod the same size as the balance centre is usually about right; some centres, however, are a little large.

The brass rod is placed in the lathe collet and a hole is drilled in it slightly smaller than the size of the cylinder. The rod is now cut off almost to length, leaving it just a little longer than required. The drilled brass is now put in a lathe and the hole is broached until the end of the cylinder will pass about halfway through it.

The collet is now put in the staking tool, and with the aid of a flat knee punch the cylinder is driven into the collet up to the lips or the limit that can be reached with a flat knee punch. In no case should a pivoted knee punch be used, because this is certain to knock the plug out.

146

Fitting or Turning in the Cylinders

Whether one is turning in a cylinder in the turns or using a lathe the principle is the same. When using a lathe a wax chuck must be used to avoid breakage and also to ensure perfect truth; it is certainly a mistake to use a split or wire chuck, because they are very seldom true enough.

The procedure is the same in either lathe or turns, *i.e.* the lower height, as it is called, must be ascertained. This is the distance from the lower endstone to the channel through which the band of the wheel passes. A height tool for measuring this was described in the author's book *Watch and Clock Making and Repairing*, page 131, Figure 115.

Using the Height Tool—To use the height tool its base is set on any suitable part of the frame and the pump centre is released until its pivot passes through the jewel hole and rests on the lower endstone, care having, of course, been taken to see that the jaws of the tool are closed. The pump centre is now secured and then raised by the setting screw until the end of the pump centre reaches the centre of the band of the 'scape wheel. The distance apart of the jaws will now show the exact position of the centre of the cylinder channel in relation to the end of the finished lower or bottom pivot.

The Bottom Pivot—The first operation, therefore, is to shorten the cylinder from the bottom until it agrees with the tool. When this has been completed the great shell, *i.e.* all of the cylinder which is cut away for the lips and channel, is filled with shellac; it will be quite strong like this and less likely to be broken.

The bottom pivot is now turned and fitted, remembering to turn it until it fits the hole closely, when it is polished or burnished till quite free. A point should always be made of turning a pivot very smooth so that the minimum of burnishing or polishing is required, for it is in these operations that a pivot becomes oval or out of truth, and their use should always be kept to an absolute minimum.

Height of the Balance—The balance is fitted with the aid of the height tool, which has already been set for the lower endstone. The tool is placed as before and the pump centre raised by the set-screw until it is nicely above the 'scape cock. The jaws will then show the distance between the lower endstone and the balance seat. By resting the end of the pivot on one jaw it is possible to check the correct position of the balance by the other jaw, and this is marked on the collet with the sharp point of a graver.

Ascertaining Total Length—The total length has now to be ascertained. For this purpose the two-screw tool is used, and the distance between the outside of the two balance jewel holes is measured with, of course, the balance cock in place (see *Watch and Clock Making and Repairing*, page 115, Figure 97). The top end of the complete cylinder is now shortened until it coincides or fits closely between the two arbors of the two screws. This must be exact, and no additional allowance should be made.

The cylinder can now be put into a cone wax chuck with the cylinder inside the cone and the brass collet and the top of the cylinder standing proud. The brass collet is turned to fit the balance, making sure that the seat coincides with the mark previously made. The hairspring collet is now fitted and the undercut for the balance riveting or rubbing over is turned.

The Length of the Brass Collet—The brass collet is shortened until it is just below the hairspring collet (the collet will go down a little lower when the balance is riveted). The cylinder itself can be shortened if necessary, then the top pivot is turned and finished off. It is as well to put a back slope or a back cut behind the pivot shoulder to prevent the oil running down on to the hairspring by way of the collet.

The procedure when using the turns is similar, but the ferrule and cylinder are fixed with shellac across the great shell and left there until the finish.

Removing the Shellac—To remove the shellac the cylinder and ferrule are in both methods placed in a deep pan with methylated spirit, which is boiled until the shellac is dissolved, leaving the cylinder and ferrule clean. It is advisable to hold the boiling-out pan in a vice in case it catches fire, as anyone holding the pan when it caught alight would be liable to jerk the flaming liquid over himself or the bench. Above all, the operation must be carried out well away from a benzine bath if this is being used in the workroom.

The cylinder is now finished, so the balance is placed on the cylinder and the unit put in place in the movement, with the balance in its correct position in relation to the cylinder and banking pin, wherever it may be.

To See if the Balance is Correct for Banking

In order to place the balance correctly it is led round until the banking pin is resting against its banking, then it is tested to see if the 'scape wheel tooth can be pushed round the back. If a tooth can be pushed past, the balance must be moved on the cylinder so that it meets the pin earlier.

This is tried on both sides, and if the tooth cannot pass either side the balance can be riveted in place, making sure that the position does not vary in the riveting. It is as well to lightly rivet it at first and then try it, and if all is in order it can be properly riveted.

If a mistake is made another pin can be put in the balance in the correct place. If the wheel can be made to pass on both sides a larger banking pin can be fitted, or another pin can be put close beside the other.

Wheel Teeth on Different Planes

As has already been mentioned, the cylinder becomes worn through continual action of the 'scape wheel teeth, and necessitates a new cylinder or moving the wheel or cylinder to work on a different and unworn part.

Ashley 'Scape Wheels (E. Ashley)

To minimise this wear Ashley, in or about the year 1800, devised a method having the planes of the 'scape wheel teeth at different heights. In some of these there were 3 teeth raised and in others 5, or in other words in the first case only 5 of the 15 teeth in the wheel worked on the same part of the cylinder, and in the second case only 3 of the 15, and thus the life of the cylinder was proportionately increased.

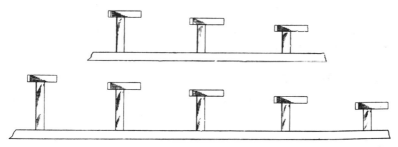

Figure 88.   Ashley cylinder 'scape wheels with teeth on different planes.

Most of the watches of this period had brass 'scape wheels, but these were later superseded by steel wheels. The majority of cylinder 'scape wheels were of 15 teeth, but some were made with 8, 10, 11, 12, 13 and 14 teeth.

Chronographs recording $\frac{1}{100}$ second were fitted with cylinder escapements using a 'scape wheel of 10 teeth, and, of course, the 'scape pinion carried the $\frac{1}{100}$-second hand, providing an easy method of recording this period.   From an efficiency point of view 15 teeth give the best result.

Another point about these 'scape wheels is that they often turn in the opposite direction to the usual one.   Most wheels turn clockwise, and where the wheel turns anti-clockwise the wheel cannot be turned upside down as can be done with the lever escapement. Thus a replacement for a 'left-hand' wheel can very rarely be obtained, which means either having one made or making it oneself.

Making a New 'Scape Wheel

The French had a method for making cylinders and 'scape wheels very cheaply on a mass-production basis, but where only one wheel has to be made it is a lengthy business, and as it is not an easy job it is costly.

To make a wheel a suitable piece of plate steel which will harden is chosen. This is placed on a wax chuck in the lathe and the outside is turned perfectly true and to size. Next a hole is drilled in the centre and trued with a thin cutter held in the slide rest. Again with the aid of a slide rest the centre of the wheel is turned or sunk, leaving the ring on the outside the correct width of the tooth. All of this work must be done accurately, as there is no way of making corrections afterwards.

When the blank has been sunk out to the correct depth it is taken off the chuck and reversed. This entails using a smaller wax chuck or one which is very nearly the size of the sink in the blank. The blank is waxed on to the chuck and the edge is turned, leaving a flange which will be the correct thickness for the finished teeth.

Cutting the Impulse Planes—The impulse planes of the teeth must now be cut. Much experimental work was done to decide the most favourable angle for the wheel teeth, and the majority of makers were in favour of 10°, thus the majority of 'scape wheels for the cylinder escapement have an impulse plane of 10°, or 10° lift. It must, however, be noted that there is a vast difference between the length of a tooth being 10° and a 10° angle of lift, and it is possible to have a tooth 5° in length but still to have a lift of 10° on that length. Likewise a tooth can be 10° long with only 5° of lift.

With the cylinder escapement of 15 teeth there is 24° between two teeth, *i.e.* 24° between the toe of one tooth and the toe of its neighbour. This is divided between the cylinder and the teeth. In most cylinder escapements the wheel tooth occupies 9°, the cylinder shell 4°, *i.e.* 2° each side, the inside of the cylinder 10°, which is 9° for the tooth and 1° drop, and the drop from the outside of the cylinder 1°. Thus if the cylinder and wheel are correctly matched, the inside and outside drop or freedom will be equal at 1° each.

The 9° of impulse plane on the wheel tooth turns or lifts the cylinder 10°, which means that the angle of the impulse plane must be at least 8° to the radial line of the 'scape wheel. If the watch is a small one a high angle is better than a low one, owing to the balance being smaller or of less mass, but in a large watch, such as a pocket model, this 8° is enough. As the impulse planes are the first thing to see to when cutting a 'scape wheel, the cutter, which can have either a flat or concave face but which must never be convex, is lined first to the radial. A mark is made on the blank with the cutter, then the wheel is moved round 8°. The cutter is relined to the original mark, which will set the cutter at 8°.

Quite a number of cylinder 'scape wheels have the impulse plane quite flat, but it is generally reckoned to be slightly curved to minimise the wear on the lips of the cylinder. One thing is certain, and that is that the teeth must not in any circumstances be concave.

150

The impulse planes can now be cut, and the first thing to do is to line up the cutter and once again use the mark which has already been made. The wheel is now turned 9°, and then the blank is marked with a line which should be light but quite visible. Next, the blank is brought back again to its mark or to where it is coincident with the cutter. The planes are now cut until the second or 9° line is just reached but not eliminated.

The blank is now turned 24°, and as the cutter is set for both depth and length and next impulse plane can be cut. This operation is continued until 15 impulse planes have been cut.

Cutting and Separating the Teeth—The blank is still solid, so the band is cut through, leaving the teeth separated. The heel of the tooth is cut back at an angle of 10° so that when it is inside the cylinder there is proper clearance, therefore the cutter is set 10° in the opposite direction. As the cutter is already set at 8°, the blank has to be moved backward 18°, bringing the cutter to line up on the new setting.

The cutter which has so far been used would have had a flat face and would have been about 9° wide, or even a little wider. The second cutter should be the diameter of the cylinder at its edge, and should also be tapering so that there is a little scope.

This second cutter must cut the blank in the correct place, so the blank must be moved round to bring the mark for the beginning of the impulse plane or the heel of the tooth coincident with the edge of the cutter. If this is not carefully done the impulse plane may be spoilt and the wheel made too small.

When all is in order the band is cut through until the marks set for the heel and the toe are just eliminated. All of the spaces are now cut, leaving only the stalks of the teeth to be attended to.

Cutting the Stalks—This is another operation involving very careful setting. The cutter used is a small cylindrical miller which cuts only at the end; it must, however, be back cut for clearance. The cutter is set at right angles to the wheel or perpendicular if the wheel is being cut on a horizontal table, the blank is moved so that it is in the correct position, and the cutter is adjusted for depth. This depth adjustment is critical, and there must be a stop screw to prevent the cutter going too deep, or the tooth will be cut right away.

The depth is arranged so that it just reaches the flange which has been turned to decide the thickness of the tooth plane. Once it has been set the first space or U-space is milled out, and if this is in order the whole can be milled out. This completes the actual cutting of the wheel.

Hardening and Tempering the Wheel—If the wheel is a steel one it is best hardened with the aid of two brass plates, one of which is sunk out to take the shape of the wheel and the other to fit inside the wheel and lay against the teeth. The plates and the wheel are tightly wired together, then they are brought to a red heat and plunged into oil. The teeth should be tempered to a brown not lower than red, while the rest of the wheel should be a light blue.

The impulse planes of the teeth are polished in a tool which will provide protection against breakage and yet maintain accuracy. The flat faces of the teeth can be polished with a flat zinc polisher, with the wheel body resting in a sunk-out brass block.

Before any finishing is attempted it is as well to check up to see if any adjustments are required. Another important point is that when making the blank all turning and filing must be left as smooth as possible, thus saving a lot of trouble and time. To try to finish up anything which has been left too rough in the roughing-out stage is a heart-breaking job.

The Total Impulse

When cutting the wheel a 10° lift was mentioned, but actually there is more lift than is apparent. The cylinder is 20° more than half a circle, *i.e.* 10° each side, and therefore if the point of the 'scape wheel tooth passes through the centre of the cylinder the total lift is 20°. It is therefore said that the apparent lift is 10° but the total lift is 20°. As has already been stated, the smaller watches require a greater lift and are often given a total lift of 40°.

There are many cheap cylinder watches in use today whose principles are anything but correct. If a new 'scape wheel is required for one of these and the correct replacement cannot be obtained but an apparently suitable substitute is available, one is well advised to notice the planes of the teeth, for if these are lower than those of the original wheel it will be difficult to obtain a good vibration, and the watch will stop at the slightest provocation.

Faults with a Cylinder Escapement

Most cylinder watches have an adjustment of some sort so that the depth of the wheel into the cylinder can be adjusted. In the better-quality foreign watches the balance cock is mounted on an adjustable ' chariot ' as it is called. The idea is to allow the depth to be adjusted if it is too deep or too shallow.

Care must be taken to see that the wheel tooth drops on to the solid part of the cylinder and never on to the lips; if it does so it is termed ' mislocking ', and may stop the watch. In any case it will trip through very quickly and the watch will gain rapidly. The cheap watches usually have a slot cut on each side of the lower hole which enables an adjustment to be made, but it is a very poor way of correcting the fault, because it puts the balance out of upright. There was no adjustment in old English cylinder watches, which were made in such a way that adjustment was unnecessary.

A fault often found in cylinder watches is caused by the band of the 'scape wheel fouling either the top or the bottom of the channel. If it fouls the top it is usually fairly obvious because it causes the 'scape wheel to recoil. Where it fouls the bottom the watch will generally stop when turned dial up. Sometimes when the channel is not long enough the back of the channel will recoil the wheel when the balance has a large vibration.

The Brass Collet—When a cylinder has to be replaced a finished shell is sometimes obtainable from the material dealers, and it would seem that all that has .to be done is to knock the old cylinder out of the brass collet and knock the new one in.

This is not quite so simple an operation as it sounds, and often when the cylinder is knocked in the collet is very much out of truth, and of course the balance is a lot out of flat; when the balance is made flat by bending the arms the balance runs much out of truth in the round and the watch or clock loses appreciably. When this happens there is only one thing to do, and that is to fit a new brass collet, which must be turned while fitted on to the cylinder, and between dead centres. Besides being the correct way to do the job, it is also the quickest and most efficient, however cheap the escapement may be. By bending the balance there is not only the risk of breakage but the balance is also spoilt, .and this should not be tolerated.

Broken Top Pivot—The top pivot of the cylinder sometimes becomes broken or worn, and requires replacement. This can be carried out by knocking out the top plug far enough to enable a new pivot to be turned on it. If the plug is not tight enough when partly out it can be taken right out and the body of the plug rolled with a file on a boxwood block. The burr created will sufficiently tighten the plug to make it quite sound when knocked back.

This cannot be carried out with the bottom pivot because there will be insufficient metal to hold the plug. Care must always be taken with the bottom plug because the cylinder will very easily split. The only thing to do if the bottom pivot should be broken is to use a complete new plug.

10

THE VIRGULE ESCAPEMENT

HAVING DEALT WITH THE cylinder escapement, it is most logical to follow on with details of the virgule, which has much in common with the cylinder, from which it differs only in two respects. First, whereas with the cylinder practically all of the impulse is on the wheel teeth, a virgule has no impulse on these teeth, and secondly, all of the impulse is on the exit vibration and none on the entrance. Thus the first vibration is termed a dummy vibration, and the escapement is called a single-beat escapement.

It is a frictional-rest escapement like the cylinder, and as such the balance is never detached. Although the frictional-rest escapement has been obsolete for many years, there are several kept in running repair, and a few details about this interesting type of escapement will no doubt be appreciated.

The Virgule 'Scape Wheel

The 'scape wheel teeth resemble the stalks supporting the teeth of the cylinder 'scape wheel, and stand proud from and, like the cylinder, perpendicular to the band of the wheel. The teeth resemble a square which has had two opposite sides squeezed together to make a sort of diamond shape, but as will be seen, it is easier to cut them triangular. The front is cut back, or undercut about 30°, so that only the extreme point is in action.

It is a nasty wheel to make, and, like the cylinder 'scape wheel, can only be made singly. The virgule on which the balance and hairspring are mounted is the heart of the escapement. It is like a very thin cylinder and has the pivots turned on plugs in the same way as the cylinder, and the plugs fit into the virgule proper.

On one side of the virgule is the impulse pallet, which is curved and resembles the beak of a toucan; this receives the whole of the impulse from the wheel. The length of this pallet is very critical and, as will be shown, is in some ways akin to the impulse pallet of the duplex escapement; the impulse pallet of a virgule is, however, solid with the body and is not a separate unit.

The action of the escapement is that as the balance turns a tooth is resting on the circular body of the virgule, and as the balance continues to turn the wheel tooth drops off the body and into the inside, thus giving no impulse; the wheel tooth is resting on the inside and the virgule revolves round it. As the balance changes its direction at the end of its vibration the tooth reaches the end of the shell as it may be called, and drops on to the hook or impulse plane, proceeding

154

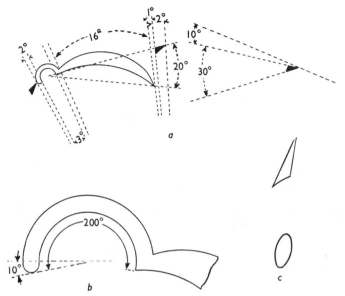

Figure 89. Theoretical drawing of a Virgule escapement:
a shows method of setting out, *b* shows how the body is set
out, *c* shows in the upper diagram the eventual shape of the
tooth which is in some cases also finished something like the
lower illustration.

to push the pallet round, thus giving impulse. As the balance progresses the tooth drops on to the body of the virgule, where it rests
as the balance continues on its path. As soon as its momentum is
exhausted the balance again reverses, and as the corner of the lip of
the virgule is reached the wheel tooth drops inside and the sequence
is again repeated.

Action of the Wheel Tooth

As with the cylinder, the wheel tooth, whether inside or outside,
must drop on to the body of the virgule. If it fails to do so it is said
to mislock, and this fault will stop the watch. The virgule becomes
worn like the cylinder, and has to be replaced, but if not too badly
worn it can be repolished and then slightly deepened by moving the
virgule nearer to the wheel. The 'scape wheel should not be moved,
however, because if it is moved there will sure to be trouble with the
fourth wheel and 'scape-pinion depth or gearing.

The 'scape pinion often has 6 leaves, and as such is a critical
gearing; this applies to most escapements, and the position of the
'scape pinion should never be altered in a hurry but only after considerable thought and examination. Most virgules have a 15-tooth

155

'scape wheel, and thus there are 24° between consecutive teeth. This 24° is occupied by the virgule body, the outside drop and the impulse.

To obtain the maximum amount of impulse the drop must be as small as possible, and also the body of the virgule must be small in

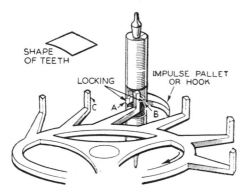

SHAPE OF TEETH

LOCKING

IMPULSE PALLET OR HOOK

C A B

Figure 90. Virgule or Hook escapement. Although now obsolete, a number of these escapements are still in existence. It is actually a cylinder escapement with all of the impulse on the cylinder and none on the wheel.

diameter.   Where the tooth engages the virgule a ring is left standing on the body so that only a small part of the wheel tooth rests on the virgule itself.

There appear to have been many different types made, but with most of them the following proportions seem to have been the commonest.

Proportions of the Virgule

The body of the virgule occupies 7°, but as a section is raised the body is actually $6\frac{1}{2}°$, and the other $\frac{1}{2}°$ is the raised portion.   This allows the inside to be 3°.   The wheel tooth occupies 2°, and there is the usual necessary 1° drop on the outside.   The inside drop is accounted for by the inside of the body of the virgule, which means that the maximum length of the hook or impulse pallet is 16°.

The angle of impulse also varies greatly, some have practically no angle of lift, whilst others have about 10° or even as much as 20°. It seems that about 10° would be correct, because this means a total impulse of 10°, which is all on one side, there being little if any on the dummy vibration side.

Making a Virgule

If a virgule is being made the angle of impulse can be altered by leaving the extreme end of the hook circular with the centre, instead of cutting it back, as is done when it is finished.   The impulse plane is concave and is an arc with the same radius as the 'scape wheel, the idea apparently being to lessen the friction.

The virgule is made from one piece of steel, and the procedure is very similar to that used in making a cylinder, with the exception that one has to start with a piece of flat plate steel instead of a round rod.

The hole is drilled first, this being slightly larger than the wheel tooth to allow for freedom and drop. The metal is then filed away, leaving the part for the hook. It is now put on an arbor and turned true with the hole which has been drilled. The blank can be turned above and below the hook, but the part where this comes must be carefully filed to shape and truth. When this stage is reached the hook can be shortened to length.

While the blank is on the arbor the part for the hook can be marked with a graver point so that it will be in circle with the centre. Next the hook is shortened until the whole blank will pass between two teeth, but it is as well to make sure that it passes with little or no freedom, as this can be given at the last finishing.

Making the Body of the Virgule—The body is now filed to a condition similar to what it would be if it were a cylinder, *i.e.* it is left a little more than half, filing the channel, of course, to enable the virgule to be free of the external band of the wheel as the virgule turns. It is now hardened and tempered in the same way as a cylinder and left fairly hard, *i.e.* it is tempered until it reaches a dark brown or purple shade under heat.

All the necessary parts are now polished, especially the acting face of the hook or impulse pallet, which is left slightly rounded so that the minimum surface is engaged. The lips are finished in the same way as the lips of a cylinder so that there is a suspicion of impulse. The brass collet is fitted on for the balance and hair-spring, and then the plugs are fitted as for a cylinder.

The virgule is now ready for the final turning in and fitting. About 20° impulse is left on the hook, as if it is a small watch it will need this amount; when the virgule and balance are placed in the frame this angle can be checked by using the balance as a guide.

If the balance is a 3-armed one there will be 120° between each arm, and as halfway will be 60°, it will be easy to judge 20°, which is one-third of the distance.

Care must be taken to see that the corner of the hook will just clear the tooth which is has last dropped. To reduce the impulse the acting face can be cut away, starting at the dropping-off corner and finally merging with the locking corner, which must not be reduced.

Cutting a New 'Scape Wheel

The procedure adopted for cutting a wheel is very similar to that used for a cylinder 'scape wheel.

The blank is turned to the full diameter and is then sunk out so that the rim remaining is stout enough for the teeth. Unlike the cylinder, there is no flange to worry about because the teeth are perpendicular to the body, whereas with a cylinder the teeth stand out.

When the blank is made and mounted up, the first cut is the opposite to the one made in a cylinder. In the latter impulse planes were being made, but with this wheel a clearance is being created, so the cutter must be on the opposite side, although still at 10°. When the clearances have been cut the cutter is set back another 30°, the blank and cutter are lined up again and the 30° cuts are made.

Setting the Cutter—The cutter is now brought back to the radial, and after the blank has been lined up with the cutter it is advanced 5°, the cutter being moved to coincide with it. The blank is now advanced another 2°, which will be the thickness of the teeth, and the final cut is made. The teeth should not require any finishing or touching up if the cutters are properly smooth and polished.

When mounting the wheel it is best to mount it on a brass or gold collet fitted on the 'scape-pinion arbor. By using this method the wheel can be mounted quite flat and perfectly true far more easily than if it were mounted on the pinion leaves direct, because it is burnished on instead of being riveted as would be necessary when mounting on the pinion leaves.

There is very little that can go wrong with a virgule providing that the wheel tooth locks properly on to the body and the hook clears the heel of the outgoing tooth. The lips of the body may become worn, but they can be repolished. If the wheel teeth become worn the wheel can be raised or lowered on its collet to bring a different part of the teeth into action.

Like the cylinder, the balance has to have a banking pin, otherwise the balance would turn a full circle and the hook would hit the incoming tooth or even go between two teeth and be locked solid. The 'scape and virgule pivots must fit their holes closely, or the wheel will mislock.

Of course the endshakes must be close, as in all escapements.

THE DOUBLE VIRGULE

This modification of the virgule was designed so that impulse was received on both vibrations. There were only a few of this type made, and it is an almost extinct escapement.

The virgule was provided with two hooks, and the teeth were in pairs, the impulse being given on one side to the concave hook and on the other to the convex hook. No advantages can be seen in this, and in any case if the virgule escapement is fully understood there will be no difficulty in understanding the double virgule.

When taking a virgule to pieces the balance must not be removed while there is power on the wheel, or the escapement will be ruined by the rushing down, and the wheel teeth are certain to be knocked off. If it is difficult to let the power down a wedge should be firmly placed in the wheels.

It is difficult to oil a virgule, as the oil creeps away from the teeth and leaves them dry. It should not be over-oiled, as the oil tends to run away very quickly, but the oil should be put on the raised portion of the body, the teeth picking it up from there.

158

11

THE DUPLEX ESCAPEMENT

THE DUPLEX IS A frictional escapement like the cylinder and the virgule, or rather it is a frictional-rest, but there is also recoil, as will be shown. Thus when the wheel tooth is locked it is still in contact with the balance staff, the balance therefore never being detached or free.

The escapement consists of a wheel with two sets of teeth, one set being horizontal and the other vertical. The first duplex escapement had two wheels mounted on the same pinion, hence the name.

There is a roller on the balance staff, usually made of ruby with a V-shaped groove cut vertically. This roller is termed the locking roller, and its only function is to lock the teeth, the V-slot allowing the wheel teeth to pass at certain times. Also fitted on the balance staff is a roller or pallet which receives the impulse from the wheel.

The action of the escapement is that the wheel tooth is locked on the locking roller (always referred to as the ruby roller), and as the balance is turned the V-slot comes into the same position as the wheel tooth and the tooth promptly drops into the slot; as the balance continues to turn the V-slot moves round and releases the tooth. The tooth is now free to run, and does so, but at the same time the impulse pallet has moved into the path of the second set of teeth.

The Impulse

As the wheel is released from the ruby roller so the impulse teeth give a blow to the impulse pallet and thus give impulse; as the impulse tooth drops off the pallet at the end of its impulse the next locking tooth is dropped on to the ruby roller and is again locked. As the balance returns the locked tooth drops into the V-slot, but as the balance is still carrying on, the wheel is pushed back or recoiled, and the balance carries on with the locking tooth resting on the roller edge. On reaching the end of its vibration the balance returns, the locking tooth drops into the V-slot, and as the balance carries on the tooth is released, the impulse is again given and the sequence is repeated,

As will be seen, the duplex is a single-beat like the virgule, but it has the impulse given in a very different way and is almost a blow with very little friction. The duplex scores in this, because, as has already been shown, the virgule impulse pallet has to be oiled, whereas the impulse plane of the duplex must not be oiled in any circumstances, as the oil would spoil the wheel and would be detrimental to performance.

159

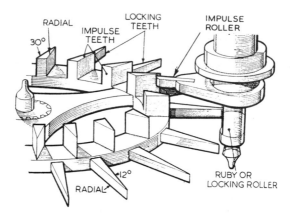

Figure 91. Duplex escapement.

Lubricating a Duplex

The ruby roller of a duplex must, however, be very lightly oiled because the locking tooth is always resting on this roller. When oiling, only a very small amount should be put in the V-slot, the teeth being allowed to collect it from there by contact. There is usually a back cut behind the seat for the ruby roller on the balance staff, so that the oil does not creep up on to the impulse roller and thus on to the impulse teeth of the wheel.

Most duplex wheels have 15 teeth, but there were several made with 10, 12 or 14 teeth. The early ones were often made with as few as 7 teeth, but with, of course, two separate wheels. The object of the single wheel was lightness, and these wheels are very light and delicate.

Removing the Balance

When a duplex watch comes in for repair the balance must not be disturbed while there is any power on the 'scape wheel, otherwise the 'scape wheel will be completely spoiled, because as the released wheel rushes round the wheel teeth will hit against the staff or pallet and will be bent or badly damaged, and a new wheel will be required. Therefore the power must always be removed or the train wedged up.

The wheel is really 30 teeth or 30 divisions, because the impulse teeth, with few exceptions, are situated midway between the locking teeth. Sometimes the locking teeth are referred to as the long teeth because they stand out by their own length beyond the circle of the impulse or vertical teeth.

The relationship between the two sets of teeth varies greatly, and there is no standard, each maker having different ideas.

160

Proportions of the Duplex

The best proportions for a duplex pocket watch are those where the diameter of the impulse roller is about three-quarters the diameter of the impulse teeth circle. With a smaller watch the roller should be smaller, owing to the necessary freedoms being proportionately greater. There must be freedom in the pivot holes whether the watch is small or large, but in a duplex as the size of the watch decreases these freedoms become serious losses.

The amount of the intersection of the impulse pallet into the wheel is at all times very small, and any excess freedom in the pivot holes of the balance or 'scape pinion pivots will cause the wheel to ' miss ', *i.e.* as the locking tooth is released by the ruby roller it will miss the impulse pallet altogether instead of engaging it, and no impulse will be given.

The size of the ruby roller plays a very important part in a duplex; not only does it lock the wheel tooth, but also, according to its diameter, so the position of the wheel is fixed. If the ruby roller is too large there is always a tendency for the tooth to wedge against the side of the roller owing to the intersection being too small. Therefore the golden rule is to have a ruby roller as small as is practicable. The usual proportion of the balance to the 'scape wheel is that the balance is twice the diameter of the locking wheel.

Objections to the Duplex

The objections to a duplex escapement are, first, that if it has a reverse swing while it is being worn it is liable to set, especially if the watch is a small one, and secondly, that it is so delicate that if it is dropped and the balance staff becomes broken the 'scape wheel may run through and become ruined, more especially so if the ruby roller is broken as well, and such an accident would be an expensive one.

Repairing a Duplex

Great care is required in handling a watch fitted with a duplex escapement, and as stated earlier on no account must the balance be disturbed until all power is removed from the escapement. If no other means are available a thin wedge should be placed firmly into the fourth wheel, making sure that the wedge cannot fall out and that the fourth wheel cannot move, but also taking care that the pivots of the fourth pinion are not broken off.

The first thing to do in this as in all watches is to examine the escapement to see what repairs are required and to check the action. With a duplex the pivots must fit their holes very closely, or in other words they must be only just free. There must be no visible side shake or freedom, and the endshakes must be close.

Recoil on the Dummy Vibration—In order to check the action a little power is put on the 'scape wheel, after which the balance is then moved in one direction and the action which takes place is noted; if it is the dummy vibration it will be seen that the long or locking tooth will drop just a little, and proceeding in the same direction, the wheel will recoil as the tooth is pushed out of the slot of the roller on to the edge.

The direction of the balance is now reversed and the long tooth will drop into the slot again. As the balance is proceeded with the tooth will again drop, but this time the upright or impulse tooth will engage the impulse pallet or roller and thus arrest the progress of the wheel.

At this stage the locking teeth are disengaged from the ruby roller. As one proceeds the wheel teeth will continue to engage the impulse pallet until it drops off the end of the pallet and the wheel is arrested by the next long tooth engaging on the locking or ruby roller. When a duplex becomes worn the impulse teeth may miss the impulse pallet and give no impulse, causing the watch to stop or trip through. If the impulse pallet is not too badly worn it can be moved round on the staff or given extra drop, and this may cure the trouble, but there are, of course, limits to the amount that the drop can be increased. Any excess of drop means loss of impulse, and as a result the watch will have a bad vibration.

Raising the Roller when the Wheel is Worn—The roller may sometimes be slightly raised on the balance staff so that it engages on an unworn part of the wheel tooth, or if the locking teeth become worn the intersection or depth can be altered. If the watch is of English manufacture this is easy to carry out: the 'scape wheel can be moved nearer to the balance staff. The jewel hole is set into a brass setting which fits into the plate. The small part of the setting, which is the vital part, is called the pipe and fits into the plate, but the larger flange does not and is usually just easy.

Therefore if it is desired to put the wheel closer to the balance staff the hole in the 'scape cock can be carefully scraped on the part nearer to the balance staff, after which the pipe on the jewel hole is burnished to swell it slightly until it fits the enlarged hole in the plate. This adjustment must always be carried out very carefully so that it is not overdone, and also the setting on the jewel hole must be kept truly round. In no circumstances should the setting be made eccentric, for should this be done a nasty trap will be set for anyone doing the job subsequently.

The Locking Teeth—The locking teeth must always be quite free in the slot of the ruby roller, and if they are found to be otherwise, must be thinned at the end until they are free. It is essential that these teeth are not thinned on their acting faces, but if they are thinned from the backs the accuracy of the wheel division will not be interfered with, and it is most important that the wheel should be accurate.

Another point of wear is the acting face of the impulse pallet; if

162

this is not badly worn it is best left alone, but if deeply pitted it must be repolished. This means that its length will be reduced and the escapement will therefore have to be deepened or given more drop, otherwise it will miss. The acting face should not be flat but well rounded, thus ensuring a constant action should anything be out of upright or out of square. It will not decrease friction, because the friction will be the same in any case.

Effect of Deepening the Escapement—There are certain things which one has to be careful about when deepening the escapement. The drop-off as it is called, *i.e.* when the impulse tooth has given impulse and dropped off the pallet, is, and must be, very close or very little. If the escapement is deepened this drop is reduced, and so after receiving impulse the pallet, on its return, will fail to clear this tooth.

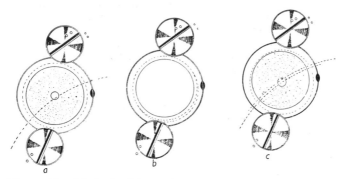

Figure 92. Method of deepening an escapement depth in an English frame or opposing the distance of centres when the pivots are endcapped. *a* shows original fitting of pivot hole in plate or cock, *b* shows fitting scraped towards balance, and *c* shows final position of fitting after trueing up.

This may mean that the locking teeth are relatively longer, or are too deep into the ruby roller, and if this is the trouble it can be adjusted by topping the long teeth and thinning again.

An old depth tool can be used to ensure accuracy. A piece of Water of Ayr stone is fixed firmly between one pair or runners, and the wheel and pinion with a ferrule fitted to it are put in the other pair of runners. With a light bow on the ferrule the wheel is revolved against the stone, which has some oil smeared over it, and the depth tool is adjusted until the wheel teeth just snick the stone on passing. By pressing the two halves of the tool together with the fingers the diameter of the locking teeth can be reduced without risk of damage and the wheel will be absolutely true.

The teeth can be thinned in the tool used for polishing the sides of the long teeth. It must always be remembered that when a duplex is being deepened the teeth are brought backwards by the action of the long tooth on the ruby roller, and thus the drop off the impulse pallet is always reduced, also the impulse teeth are brought in closer, which reduces the drop-off as well.

Making a Duplex Escapement

If one is called upon to make a duplex escapement there are certain rules to be followed, as there are in fact when making any escapement.

The balance should be of the same diameter as the barrel cover, *i.e.* the balance, including the screws on the rim, should fit the recess turned in the barrel to receive the cover, and the 'scape wheel in a duplex should be half this diameter, measuring it, of course, on the circle of the locking teeth.

The Size of a Duplex 'Scape Wheel—The impulse circle is usually two-thirds, and may be even three-quarters, the diameter of the locking circle, the point to remember being that the larger the impulse wheel, so the shorter the impulse pallet. Therefore as the wheel gets larger the impulse pallet acts deeper and safer into the teeth, thus helping the impulse and requiring less power. The fact of the wheel being larger means that less power is available, so the size of wheel must be that most suitable for the watch concerned. With a small watch the pallet is best longer, because there will then be less likelihood of it setting in wear, therefore the wheel will be smaller.

To proceed, the balance staff and 'scape pinion are turned in (or made), and the wheel is mounted tightly on its pinion, but not rubbed on. The ruby roller is fitted in place, then the staff and roller (without the balance) and the wheel are placed in the depth tool, which is adjusted so that the locking teeth are only just free in the notch of the roller. This is then marked off on the watch plate using the balance-staff hole as the centre, and an arc of a fair length is scored on the plate. The fourth wheel and 'scape pinion is then put in a depth tool, preferably a different tool from the one previously used, and adjusted to the correct depth. This is then scored on the plate, using the lower fourth hole as the centre. The precise position of the 'scape pivot holes is where the two arcs cross.

Making the Impulse Roller—The next step is the making of the impulse roller or pallet, this being best made by using the depth tool. This tool has already been set to pitch the 'scape pivot hole, so the operation need be described only from that stage. The balance should not be mounted on the staff until the last, because the staff can be used as the arbor for the final trial. The roller is made from a piece of flat steel which can be hardened and tempered. A hole large enough to pass over the ruby roller is drilled at one end and the excess metal is filed away to leave a rounded pipe which is put on an arbor and the pipe turned true. The hole in the roller will give an indication of the size of the ruby roller should this become broken.

The hole is opened until the roller passes about three-quarters up the arbor of the balance staff, or so that a part of the ruby roller is visible to enable a trial to take place. The end is filed away to a point and shortened until it is just not free of the impulse teeth of the wheel. The roller is then taken off the staff and the pallet is filed to its correct shape without shortening in any way. It should be left very smooth with the impulse face well rounded, but straight from the centre to the end, and of course quite radial to the centre of the roller. It is now hardened and tempered but left as hard as possible, or so that it can be worked only with difficulty. Next the impulse face must be polished to a high degree, then the back of the pallet is polished to a sharp edge with the impulse plane. It is now tried in place on the staff, and in the depth tool with the wheel, then the pallet is shortened from the back until it is only just free, but definitely free, from the impulse teeth.

Completing the Escapement—The escapement can now be completed. The balance is fitted on the staff and the escapement is put in place to see that all is in order, after which it only remains to mount the balance in its final position. As some balance staffs for duplex watches have a very thin hub, it is inadvisable to rivet the balance, so the riveting has to be burnished over the balance. The 'scape wheels in duplex watches, or for that matter those found in most English watches, should be finally fitted by burnishing the rivet over, and this makes a very sound job, without the distortion that riveting often introduces.

CRAB TOOTH DUPLEX

This escapement is a modification of the duplex inasmuch as exactly the same principles are present, the only difference being in the locking section of the 'scape wheel; there are two locking teeth close together instead of a single tooth between each impulse tooth, the idea being to give the impression that the watch is beating seconds.

The sequence of events is thus: as the balance turns the tooth drops into the slot in the roller, and as it continues the tooth is dropped, giving no impulse, but the second locking tooth is resting on the ruby roller; as the balance reverses the second tooth drops into the slot, and is pushed out again as the balance proceeds; as the balance returns the second tooth drops in the slot and moves with the balance until this tooth drops, and as this second tooth is released so impulse is given in the same way as is usual with a duplex. Thus the balance receives impulse only once in every four beats.

Crab Tooth Escapement Beating Seconds

If the watch train is of 14,400 vibrations per hour, the seconds hand apparently moves every second, but if very closely watched the slow progress and recoiling of the wheel by the hand until it gets its impulse and jumps a full second will be noticed.

165

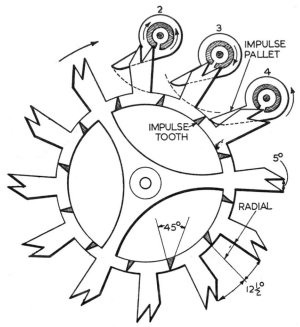

Figure 93. Crab-tooth duplex escapement. Beats
seconds with a 14,000 train.

The escapement has no advantages, rather the reverse is in fact
the case, but all that applies to the ordinary duplex applies to this
modification of it.

DUPLEX ESCAPEMENT BY FERGUSON COLE

This is a very complicated form of the duplex, and again it is hard to
see that it has any advantages. It is difficult to explain, but if one
knows the facts it will be easy both to recognise the escapement and
to deal with it.

The balance staff has the usual impulse pallet mounted on it, but
instead of a ruby locking roller a wheel, usually having 20 teeth,
although the number is not critical, is mounted. This wheel of 20
gears into another wheel of 20 which is mounted on a arbor pivoted
into the frame. A ruby locking roller is mounted on the same arbor,
and as the balance turns the ruby roller turns with it by means of the
two wheels of 20 gearing together. Now, also pivoted in the frame
is a pinion of 8 leaves, and on this pinion is mounted a double-ended
fly, flirt or arm which engages into the ruby roller like the locking
teeth of an ordinary duplex. Gearing into this pinion of 8 leaves
is a wheel of 60 teeth, and every fourth tooth in succession on this

166

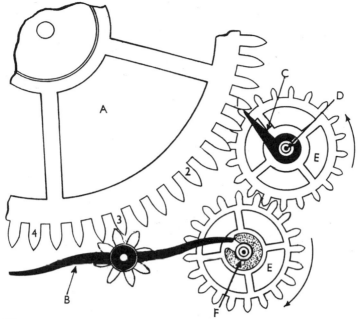

Figure 94. Ferguson Cole duplex escapement. A = fourth wheel with each 4th tooth double height (1, 2, 3 and 4 indicate the high teeth or impulse teeth); B = locking arm; C = impulse pallet; D = balance staff; E = wheel fitted on balance staff and wheel fitted to arbor carrying ruby roller. F = Locking or ruby roller.

wheel of 60 is raised above the plane of the wheel proper. There are thus 15 raised teeth on this wheel, and these are the teeth which give impulse to the balance.

Action of the Ferguson Cole Duplex

The action is that as the balance turns the locking roller is turned, the arm on the pinion is released and flies round, and the other arm is immediately locked. Thus the pinion turns half a turn and releases 4 leaves, and thus the 4 teeth of the wheel of 60. This means that the raised tooth gives impulse to the pallet on the balance.

Obviously the wheels and pinions have to be set up in mesh in the correct way, and this is often awkward. The correct way to do it is to use means to wedge the wheels in fixed positions; if this is not done a lot of time can be wasted in getting them right, as they always manage to move at the wrong time. One advantage of this escapement is that the wheels and pinions can be meshed in such a way that the drops can be very closely adjusted. It is a very interesting escapement, but its advantages are vague (*see chronometer escapements*).

167

12

THE LEVER ESCAPEMENT

THE DETACHED LEVER ESCAPEMENT was invented by Thomas Mudge, although not quite in its present form. The lever escapement will be dealt with first, and the early types discussed later.

Types of Detached Lever Escapement

There are two main types, one of which is called the ratchet tooth and the other the club tooth. The principles of both escapements are almost identical, but their construction is different. It is extremely difficult to decide which is the superior escapement, because the performances of both have been of the highest class under the same conditions; the club tooth, however, has been brought almost to perfection, whereas the ratchet tooth is now hardly ever made. The ratchet-tooth wheel is much more delicate and far more difficult to manufacture on a mass-production basis.

THE RATCHET-TOOTH ESCAPEMENT

If the ratchet-tooth escapement is dealt with first the advantages of the club tooth will be better understood and the reader can draw his

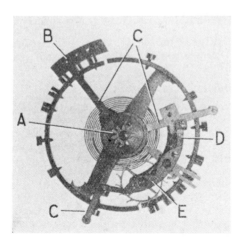

Figure 95. Carriage of a lever Tourbillon movement. The tourbillon carriage completes one revolution per minute. Carriage is driven by third wheel as usual, but fourth wheel is a fixture. The carriage driven round transmits power to 'scape pinion. A = fourth pinion on which carriage is mounted; B = piece of gold to poise the carriage; C = three lower arms or lower plate of carriage; D = lower 'scape bridge; E = steel plate with lower 'scape and pallet end-stones.

own conclusions as to the relative merits of the two types. The wheel usually used is of 15 teeth, but like other escapements it has been made with 12, 14 or 16 teeth, and in the case of some watches by A. L. Breguet it even has 20 teeth. Experiments were carried

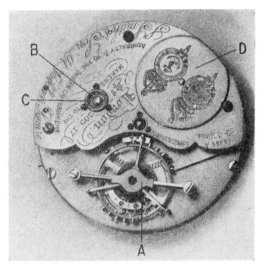

Figure 96. Typical English fusee keyless Tourbillon movement as seen from the back. Carriage is shown separately in Fig. 95. A = steel bar supporting top pivot of the carriage; B = fusee square; C = gunmetal fusee piece; D = raised barrel.

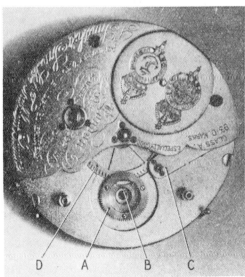

Figure 97. Tourbillon movement with carriage removed, showing fixed fourth wheel and part of third wheel which drives the carriage. A = fixed fourth wheel screwed to the plate; B — third wheel teeth just visible; C = third pinion cock supporting top third pivot; D = centre wheel.

out by many makers, and as a result of their experience the 15-tooth 'scape wheel was more or less universally adopted.

169

Distance of Centres

Another subject which involved a great deal of experiment was the distance of centres. The point considered was whether the escapement was better with the centres fixed by two tangents, *i.e.* at right angles, or above or below the right angle; if above a right angle the nibs would be farther from the centre and have longer impulse planes, but would require less power to drive them; if below the opposite would be the case and of course the freedom between the pallet staff and wheel teeth would be less, and as a result the pallets, being very thin in the centre, would be easily damaged or bent. Another consideration was that when above the right angle the friction was greatly increased and the effects of changing oil were more apparent. Thus the right-angled pallets were universally adopted.

Right-angled Pallets—The term right-angled pallets means that the pallet centre is fixed by the meeting point of two tangents struck from the path of the wheel teeth. Now the escapement consists, first, of

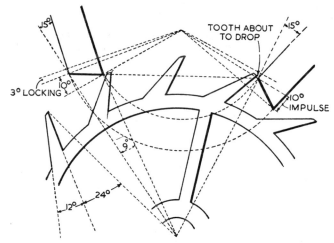

Figure 98. Ratchet-tooth lever escapement, showing necessary inside shake or freedom.

a 'scape wheel mounted on the 'scape pinion and receiving the motive power by way of the fourth wheel, gearing into it. The wheel has 15 teeth, which are to all intents pointed, but of course they would not last unless they had some thickness of metal at the tip, and this is usually reckoned to be $\frac{1}{2}°$. The teeth should, however, be as thin as is practicable, as extra thickness means a loss of impulse.

The wheel engages the nibs of a pair of pallets, these nibs being the two ends of the pallets which protrude from the body towards the 'scape wheel; the part of the body nearest to the 'scape wheel is termed the belly of the pallets.

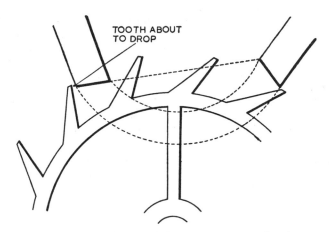

Figure 99. Ratchet-tooth lever escapement, showing necessary outside shake or freedom.

The pallets are often made solid with the lever, but sometimes the lever is a separate unit.

The Lever and Roller

The lever conveys the movements of the pallets to the balance and gives the balance its impulse, this being carried out by what is called the lever and roller action because the lever engages the roller which is fitted to the balance staff. This roller is a disc of metal into which is fitted an impulse pin which may be steel or jewel. The end of the lever is shaped into what is termed a ' fork ', *i.e.* a square notch to which are added what are called ' horns '; these will be discussed later.

The fork engages the impulse pin in the roller, and thus as the lever is moved to and fro by the action of the pallets so the roller is moved likewise and turns the balance, or causes the balance to vibrate as it is termed, *i.e.* to revolve first one way and then the other.

The Pallets

The pallets are the heart of the escapement, and if these are poor the whole escapement is bad. The nibs of the pallets are of a set width, and this cannot be increased; it can, of course, be decreased, but any decrease must be loss, so the nibs must be as wide as possible, as long as they have freedom, which is again loss. The sum of the two nibs is equal to the distance between two consecutive teeth, less the necessary freedom.

171

In order that the pallets may be moved or lifted they must be so shaped that the face engaged by the wheel has an angle of lift or, as it is called, an impulse plane. This angle varies with different types of lever escapements, but the standard angle universally adopted is 10°, which means that as each pallet is engaged by the wheel teeth it is lifted or turned 10°, and as the lever is joined to the pallets it also is moved 10°, and in theory the balance receives 10° of impulse.

The Locking

In action the wheel tooth is resting on a part of the pallets called the locking face. The locking is essential, so that the pallets are held while the balance is revolving; were it not for the locking, the lever would move backwards and forwards uncontrolled, and would obstruct the balance.

In the early escapements the locking face was like the Graham dead-beat, *i.e.* circular with the pallet hole, or on a circle struck from the pallet hole. The pallets could, however, be jerked out of the wheel, thus causing unlocking, so stopping the watch. The locking face is therefore cut back to provide what is called draw, and this pulls the pallets into the wheel, or causes them to be drawn into the wheel. The entrance pallet, which is the first pallet engaged, requires 12° of draw, but the exit pallet, which is the last engaged, requires more, usually 15°. Therefore the usual practice is to make the draw 15° on both pallets for ease of manufacture. The exit pallet is so placed that the wheel has a great tendency to throw or push the pallet away, hence the reason for the extra draw being required.

Types of Pallet

The pallets can be of three different types: the circular, the equidistant lockings or the semi-equidistant lockings, and it is difficult to say which of these is the best.

Circular Pallets—The circular pallets are generally reckoned to be the best because of the easy manner in which they are constructed, and are so called because the outside corners of the pallets are on a circle with the pallet centre, the two inside corners also being on a circle from the pallet centre.

Equidistant Lockings—With equidistant lockings the locking corners of both pallets are on the same circle, which is struck from the pallet centre. The dropping-off corners are on another circle also struck from the pallet centre. Thus the pallets appear to be moved over bodily by their own width when compared with the circular. The wheel has more work to do when raising the entrance pallet, and the equidistant locking tends to help unlock, but of course this pallet is nearer to the centre of the pallets, and it is natural to

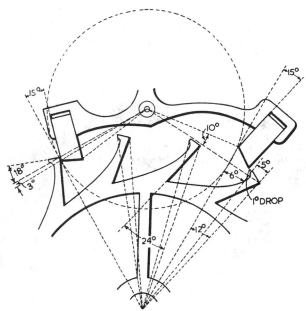

Figure 100.   Club-tooth escapement with 10° pallets and equidistant lockings.

suppose that it will require more power to lift it than if it were farther away.

The Semi-equidistant Lockings—The name actually speaks for itself, meaning a midway pallet, *i.e.* where the pallets are midway between circular and equidistant, or a modification of one or the other.

Very few watches are found with this type of pallets, and if a replacement was being carried out the original pallets would not be copied but would be replaced by circular ones.

The Pallet Staff

The pallets are mounted on a pallet staff or axle, as it would be called in engineering circles.   There are two types of pallet staff, the screw-in type and the slightly tapered, driven-in type.

The screw-in type was mostly used by the Continental watchmakers, and very seldom in this country, the only advantage being when the lever and pallets were separate units.   It gave a certain amount of scope where the wheel and pallet depths were incorrect, and the pallets could be manœuvred till correct, and then permanently pinned.   The pallet staff should fit the pallets, not the lever, but with the screw-in type the pallet staff screws into the lever.   This advantage is not present where the lever and pallets are a single unit.

Some of the early mass-produced watches were fitted with screw-in type pallet staffs, and this certainly saved the risk of distortion which could occur in a small pair of pallets when the pallet staff was driven

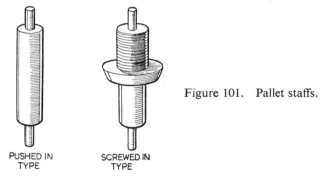

Figure 101.   Pallet staffs.

PUSHED IN
TYPE

SCREWED IN
TYPE

home too hard, or if the pallet staff was full size.   Of course, the same thing could have happened if the thread of a screw pallet staff was too large or the thread was crossed when carelessly screwed in place.

A pallet staff must always be very carefully fitted, and above all it must be true, otherwise the whole action of the escapement can be destroyed.   Many small watches are completely ruined by an out-of-truth pallet staff, especially when, as is often the case, the rest of the watch is made to suit it.   A pallet staff should always be made between dead centres and not in a split collet in a lathe.

Making a Pallet Staff—When making a very small pallet staff it is hardly practicable to use a wax chuck, and it is certainly not a commercial proposition, but doing the job between dead centres is correct and is a commercial proposition.   Pallet-staff pivots must be truly round and perfectly straight; they must also be a close but free fit in their holes, and even if the pivot is on an endstone it must be straight, although the shoulder should be conical.   If a pallet-staff pivot is worn it must be repaired and a new hole or bearing fitted.

Pallet-staff Pivots—Another important point is that the pallet-staff pivots must at all times be oiled.   It is not a good point to leave them without lubrication, but as in most cases there is no oil trap, the top pallet-staff pivot of a small watch must be sparingly oiled, the reason being that the oil may creep all over the body of the pallets, and by suction between the pallet cock and itself may stop the watch.

Pallet-staff pivots wear on one side only, and often have to be carefully examined for this to be noticed.   The vibration will often show any defect in the pallet-staff pivots, and will be laboured or sluggish.

174

Another point regarding a pallet staff is that it must be upright in its bearings, and most important of all, it must be perpendicular to the pallets and not leaning over on one side; if this is the case one pallet may foul the pallet cock in a place where it is difficult to observe. On the other hand, if the endshake of the pallet staff is full the wheel teeth may not be free in one position, which may be with the dial either up or down. The result may be a watch which will stop and go on again at the slightest disturbance.

The 'Scape Pinion

When writing about an escapement a few remarks must be made about the 'scape pinion. This is a very important unit, and whatever the type of lever escapement to which it is set, it must be right. There is very slight recoil in a chronometer, but this is not enough to affect the 'scape pinion. With a lever there is appreciable recoil.

If the 'scape pinion is proportionately too large the power arrives in fits and starts as the fourth wheel teeth engage or disengage the leaves of the pinion. If the pinion is proportionately too small, then as the wheel recoils off the draw the pinion will move backwards and change from a follower to a driver, and the pinion leaf may butt on the tooth of the fourth wheel, thus creating another 'nasty stopper'.

Another point is that the 'scape wheel must be firmly mounted on its pinion. One often comes across wheels which cannot make a full turn but which will move just a little on the pinion, and this can happen whether the wheel is mounted on a collet or directly on the pinion leaves. The 'scape pinion should have as high a number of leaves as possible, so that the engaging friction of the fourth wheel is as little as possible. The usual number of leaves is 6, 7 or 8, but in some very high-class watches there may be as many as 10 leaves. Some idea of the sequence of events has now been arrived at.

Ratchet-tooth Wheel and Pallets

The pallets of the ratchet-tooth escapement contain all of the impulse, and there is none at all on the wheel teeth, therefore any thickness of tooth is loss. Again, there must be locking, and although in theory 2° is sufficient, in practice this is risky, because with the necessary freedoms there is a chance of the wheel mislocking or jumping off the locking. 3° is therefore the necessary locking, and in a ratchet-tooth escapement this means that there must be extra drop, which again means loss.

Freedom in Unlocking—As stated earlier, the locking face is cut back to form draw, and so as the wheel unlocks it must be forced backwards, or to recoil. Now owing to the shape of the teeth, which become thicker towards their roots, the back or dropping-off corner is very near to the back of the tooth as the wheel recoils, and as it continues to recoil so the pallet goes into the wheel circle, or nearer to the tooth, and at the same time the wheel is turning backwards and approaching closer to the pallet. Thus, as there is 3° locking there must be at least 2° drop owing to the wheel recoiling, and a further 1° to allow the pallet to clear the backs of the wheel teeth, so there is 3° locking and 3° drop.

It has already been stated that the two pallets together equal the distance between two consecutive teeth, *i.e.* in a 15-tooth wheel 24°, or each pallet has a width of 12° less loss.

The Impulse Plane—On this width, which is 9°, *i.e.* 12° less 3° drop, a lifting or turning of 10° is required, or the lever has to be moved 10° from one side to the other. There is 3° locking, which leaves a total of 7° as the maximum lift which can be got on 10° pallets. Thus, on a plane 9° in length 7° impulse is required. If this amount could be used it would be necessary to have a weaker mainspring or less motive power, but there are other factors to contend with.

The Inertia of the Wheel—Draw has already been mentioned, and also the fact that as the pallets are moved off the locking the wheel must recoil or go backwards until the pallet reaches the point where the tip of the tooth runs over the corner. Now it is known that if a wheel is moved backwards it must pause or stand still before it can change direction to move forwards. During this pause the pallets are still moving away from the wheel teeth, and by the time the wheel catches up with the pallets a few degrees of impulse are lost or the first section of the impulse plane is missed altogether. This can often be seen on a pair of pallets which have been in action for some time; if they are examined it will be seen that there is a small pit where the wheel teeth actually hit the impulse plane. This loss depends on many factors, the speed of the balance playing a large part

The Train—Thus with a 21,600 train the loss is likely to be more, whereas with a 14,400 train the loss is less. The terms 21,600 and 14,400 trains mean that the balance has 21,600 or 14,400 vibrations per hour, and the train of wheels driving the balance is calculated accordingly. The most common or popular train is an 18,000. With a 21,600 train the balance completes 1 vibration in one-sixth of a second, whilst a 18,000 train completes it in one-fifth of a second and a 14,400 in one-quarter of a second. Another train which is often seen is a 16,200, which has 4½ beats per second.

The extent of the vibration is another item. With a watch in good condition the vibration will consist of 1½ turns, or the balance will turn ¾ of a turn in each direction, or in degrees a total of 540° in all, *i.e.* 270° in each direction. It will be appreciated that the balance is travelling very fast, and when it reaches the dead point or the centre of its vibration it is travelling at its maximum speed. The balance engages the escapement during a period of 30°, or 15° each side of the dead point. The 'scape wheel is stationary, added to which is the fact that it is pushed back and then has to stop and change direction; it is not difficult therefore to understand this loss of impulse. In a good escapement this loss may be only 2°, but with a poor escapement it can be 3° to 4°. The maximum impulse is therefore about 5°.

This stresses the point that the 'scape wheel must be as light in weight as possible, and yet of sufficient strength to ensure that it is not easily damaged.

The Balance Arc—This term is not generally understood, but what it means is the amount the balance, or perhaps it would be better to say the roller which is fitted to the balance staff, is in contact with the escapement. As the aim is to have the balance disturbed in its vibration as little as possible, the balance arc must be kept to a minimum, or the balance must be detached for as long a period as possible. Now if the pallets are 10° and the proportion of the lever and roller is 3 : 1 the balance arc would be 30°, but a 30° balance arc cannot be obtained with what is called a single-roller escapement, the reason being that there must be some arrangement to prevent the lever getting out of position if it receives a jar or a shake of any sort.

The Single Roller

A single roller must be considered as two rollers in one, the impulse-pin circle being taken as one roller and the metal outside this circle as the guard roller. The impulse pin engages the lever in its notch, whilst directly behind this notch is a perpendicular pin known as the guard pin, which is fitted tightly into the solid part of the lever and as close to the bottom of the notch as safety will permit. When the impulse pin is clear of the lever notch the guard pin rests close to the edge of the roller and prevents the lever passing from one side of the roller to the other, or it holds the lever in position so that the impulse pin on its return will correctly engage the notch. Without this guard the lever could pass across to the other side, and the impulse pin would bank against the outside of the lever, thus stopping the watch. This condition is called ' overbanked '.

Proportion of Lever and Roller—With a single roller the proportion between the lever and roller must be at least $3\frac{1}{2}$: 1, because if it is less the intersection of the guard pin into the roller is too little and the guard pin will wedge on the roller edge to stop the balance, or will be forced across and will overbank, thus stopping the watch in any case. This can mean a balance arc of 35°.

Lever with Solid Guard—The guard pin in some single-roller escapements of Continental make is solid, *i.e.* the guard is formed by the notch being in a lower plane or stepped down on one solid piece of steel. There is a certain advantage in this, because the guard can, and is, more forward than a pin, and also allows a certain amount of scope in the manufacture, but its advantages are outweighed by its disadvantages. If this type of guard happens to wedge, the result is a bent pivot or even a broken pallet or balance staff.

177

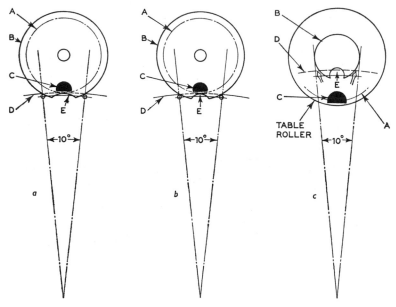

Figure 102. Showing guard or safety action. Comparison between 3 : 1 and 3½ : 1 single roller and illustrating the advantage of a double roller. *a* single roller, lever and roller proportions 3 : 1. A = pin circle; B = roller edge or guard circle; C = impulse pin; D = dotted line showing intersection; E = roller crescent. The guard is unsafe. *b* single roller, 3½ : 1 showing a greater and safe intersection; *c* double roller, 3 : 1. A = pin circle; B = guard circle; C = impulse pin; D = line showing intersection; E = roller crescent.

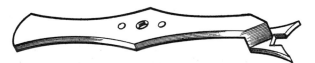

Figure 103. Single roller lever with solid guard.

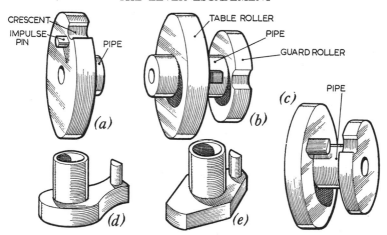

Figure 104. Lever escapement rollers: *a* ordinary single roller;
b English double roller comprising separate table and guard rollers;
c Swiss double roller all in one piece; *d* and *e* types of table roller.
Type *d* is used when guard roller is situated above table roller, to
enable balance to be removed.

The Double Roller

Although the single roller is an extremely good type of lever
escapement and is easier to make by hand in block production, it is
more difficult to make by mass-production methods.   It is a cheaper
escapement to make than the double roller, and its performance is
really very good, as has been proved at the National Physical Labora-
tory.   The type termed the double roller has, however, many
advantages, and is now universally adopted.

The double roller was invented by Thomas Mudge and was incor-
porated into the first detached-lever watch ever made.   The next
detached-lever watch was made by Josiah Emery; this may have
been made with the permission or co-operation of Mudge, and it also
used the double roller.

Types of Double Roller

In a single roller the edge acts as the guard roller, but with a
double roller the guard roller is a separate unit.   There is, first, the
table roller or impulse roller as it is often called, into which is fitted
the impulse pin, and secondly, a small separate roller whose sole
function is to act as the guard, this being called the guard roller.
The guard roller can be above or below the table roller, depending
on the layout of the watch.   The rollers can be separate or they can
be joined together by a pipe made from one piece of metal rod.   In

179

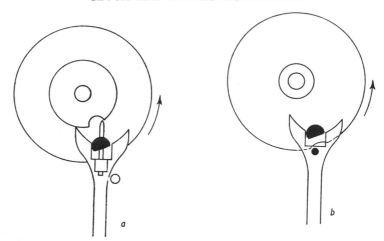

Figure 105. Showing position of impulse pin, dart and guard pin as wheel tooth is dropped when all actions are correct; *a* double roller, 3 : 1; *b* single roller, $3\frac{1}{2}$: 1.

another method the guard roller has a pipe solid with it, the table roller being fitted friction tight on this pipe.

Advantage of Modern Double Roller

The modern mass-produced watch has the two rollers as one unit made from metal rod, the advantage of this being that there is only one fitting required or one arbor on the balance staff, whereas two separate rollers very often entail two fittings.

The main idea of the double roller is to reduce the balance arc, not the vibration. As has been pointed out, a safe single-roller action has about 33° balance arc, or if great care has been taken in the making, 30°. With a double roller the arc can be as low as 24°. In order to obtain this the pallets have, of course, to be 8° instead of 10°, and the lever and roller proportion has to be 3 : 1. This means that a balance can vibrate unmolested for 496° of its 540° vibration. There are very few double-roller escapements made with this type of low-angled pallets because of the extra cost involved in manufacture, and of course motive power adjustments have to be made to suit these requirements. The advantages when using the universal 10° pallets are still there, however, because the balance arc can be reduced to 30° with absolute safety.

The Passing Crescent—Guard action has been considered both with regard to single and double rollers, and the other point to be considered now is when the lever passes from one side to the other.

The single roller is provided with a crescent cut in the roller edge

180

immediately in front and equidistant to each side of the impulse pin, this crescent providing the clearance in the roller for the guard pin to pass when the impulse pin is in the lever notch, and only then. Likewise, with the double roller the guard roller is provided with this passing crescent, to permit the dart, which is another type of guard pin, to pass when the impulse pin is in the lever notch. There is quite a distinction between the single and double rollers which is not often understood, and this concerns the lever horns.

The Lever Horns—With the single roller the guard pin is all that is required for a safe guard action, the horns of a single-roller lever being unnecessary and purely ornamental. These horns do not

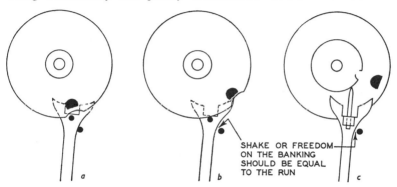

Figure 106. Showing position of guards and banking pins, also position when wheel tooth is dropped: *a* single roller, showing the run to the banking; *b* single roller, showing shake on the banking (horns are unnecessary), *c* double roller, showing lever horns as part of the guard action.

come into action at all, and the escapement will function in a correct manner without them.

It is, however, a different story in the case of the double roller, because the lever horns are an essential part of the escapement. With some of the small watches made today a partial compromise is effected, and horns of this type of double roller are almost non-existent or else are very short. The function of the horns in this case is taken over by the impulse pin, which is very wide, and the guard roller has an almost square passing hollow which cannot really be called a crescent. However, in spite of this, the lever still has horns.

In the ordinary type the horns are curved and not flat. To be correct they should be formed by the path of the impulse pin, thus the horns are not on the same circle as each other. They are marked with the lever in two different positions, *i.e.* first on one side for the one horn and then with the lever on the other side for the second horn. Thus, if the impulse pin is resting on the lever horn and is moved from one end of the horn to the other the lever will not move.

181

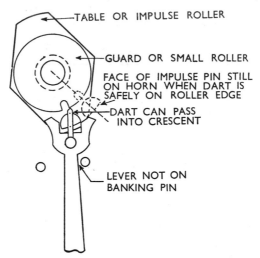

TABLE OR IMPULSE ROLLER

GUARD OR SMALL ROLLER

FACE OF IMPULSE PIN STILL
ON HORN WHEN DART IS
SAFELY ON ROLLER EDGE

DART CAN PASS
INTO CRESCENT

LEVER NOT ON
BANKING PIN

Figure 107. Double roller escapement. Lever
in position as wheel tooth drops. The short
horns are on Tavannes movements. The impulse pin forms supplementing horns.

Figure 108. The action of
the horns in a double roller
lever and roller ratio 3 : 1,
showing position of lever as
wheel tooth drops.

The Horns as Part of the Guard—If a double roller escapement is closely examined it will be noticed that as the lever is moved from

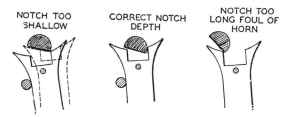

Figure 109. Correct and incorrect notch action, single roller.

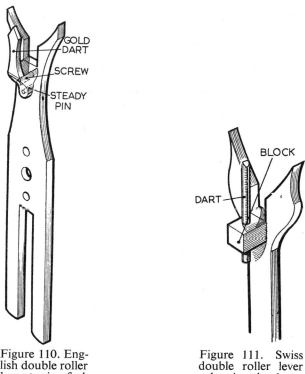

Figure 110. English double roller lever tuning fork type.

Figure 111. Swiss double roller lever showing the dart.

one side to the other the pallets will drop one tooth of the 'scape wheel. If close observation is made of the position of the dart immediately this tooth drops it will be seen that the dart is still in the

183

passing crescent; as the balance continues to be moved, and of course the roller with it, the impulse pin is resting on the lever horn, and just before the pin reaches the end of the horn the dart is safely on the guard roller edge. Now if it were not for the horns, as soon

Figure 112. Waltham type guard pin for single roller lever.

as the wheel tooth is dropped and the impulse pin clears the then outside corner of the notch, the lever would be free to pass to the other side, and the watch would overbank. So, although the guard roller is small and its intersection by the dart is greater, its safety must occupy a greater amount of the balance arc.

THE CLUB-TOOTH ESCAPEMENT

Before proceeding with further details the club-tooth escapement will be considered. The ratchet and club tooth are identical in principle, but the execution is different. With the ratchet tooth there is no impulse on the wheel teeth, it is all on the pallets or pallet faces. With the club tooth the impulse is divided between the two. The proportions vary more in the older watches than in the modern ones, and in fact it can be said that the impulse is equally divided between the wheel teeth and the pallets in all modern mass-produced watches, and also in any that are hand-finished or hand-made.

Advantage of the Club Tooth

There is the same draw on the pallets as the ratchet tooth and the same amount of locking, but the club tooth scores by virtue of the fact that the drop can be reduced to very small limits. In fact, the drop in a club-tooth escapement can be reduced to such an extent that a strong eyeglass is needed to see it, and the escapement is then almost silent.

The disadvantage, of course, lies in the fact that the pallet nibs have to be longer so that the heel of the tooth does not foul the belly of the pallets. The impulse plane of the pallets and the impulse plane of the wheel tooth must on no account become coincident, because if this does happen the impulse on the wheel tooth will be completely lost, and it will work like a ratchet-tooth escapement with very thin pallets and a very thick wheel. Usually this fault is obvious because the vibration of the balance is small and looks laboured and sluggish;

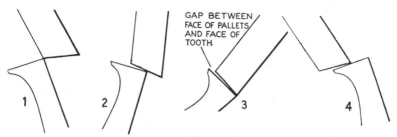

Figure 113. Showing how impulse is given. 1, 2 and 3, Corner of tooth pushing pallet stone. 4, Impulse plane of tooth continuing the push.

it is generally caused by bad pitching in the manufacture or mismatching, the pallet faces having been altered to permit the wheel to pass.

Correcting Mismatching—The easiest way to remedy this fault is to fit a new wheel and pallets properly matched to the existing distance of centres. It can, however, be put right by using a slightly larger wheel if there is room in the belly of the pallets, and altering the pallet faces to suit the wheel. This fault is usually an indication that the impulse angle of the pallets is too low, and by putting a larger wheel which will lock more heavily the impulse angle on the pallets can be raised to both correct the locking and raise the impulse angle.

It is always well to make sure that the wheel teeth are correct; sometimes a wheel has been fitted which has too high an impulse angle on the teeth, and this would also cause the same fault. The correctness of the teeth can be judged by comparing them with another wheel which is known to be correct.

The Heel of the Club-tooth Wheel—Another point which is often forgotten is the heel or dropping-off corner of the wheel tooth: for the club tooth to have any advantage over the ratchet tooth the dropping-off corner must be almost razor sharp and not cut with a flat heel as are quite a number of wheels. If the heel is sharp the pallet can move behind the heel when it recoils owing to the draw, but if it is not sharp there must of necessity be more drop to allow the pallet to clear, and this takes away any advantage possessed by this type of escapement.

The action of the lever and roller, the guard action and all other parts applies equally to both the ratchet tooth and the club-tooth escapement, and as these were all fully described when the ratchet tooth was dealt with, there is no need to go into this again.

The Pallet Jewelling

The jewelling of the pallet faces has undergone a big change, and has now become universal. At one time all pallets were made with

185

covered stones, *i.e.* the pallets were made in solid steel and were called ' pallet steels ', but nowadays the nibs or protuberances are the jewels themselves.   This will be dealt with again later in the book.

The hand-made pallets or steels as they are called are slotted horizontally, and slips of jewel, either ruby or garnet, are secured in the slots.   In the best-quality pallets sapphires are used.   The stone is then ground to be all but flush with the steels, and is finally polished to be quite flush (Figure 184).

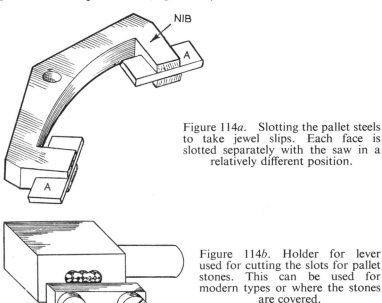

Figure 114*a*.   Slotting the pallet steels to take jewel slips.   Each face is slotted separately with the saw in a relatively different position.

Figure 114*b*.   Holder for lever used for cutting the slots for pallet stones.   This can be used for modern types or where the stones are covered.

The cheap pallets were jewelled with garnet, but the objection to this stone is that, being softer, there is considerable wear.   Some makers also object to the ruby because, being porous, it causes wear on the wheel teeth, whereas with the sapphire, being a much harder stone, the pallets do not become worn and it also takes a long time for the wheel teeth to become worn.

The ratchet-tooth 'scape wheel is mostly made in brass, although quite a number have been made in steel, but it is difficult to say whether this is advantageous or not.   In the case of the club-tooth 'scape wheel one is inclined to believe that more steel wheels were made than brass, but in the mass-produced watches the wheels seem to be mostly brass, the reason presumably being because of the ease of their manufacture.   The high-class club-tooth escapements, whether English or Continental, are always supplied with steel wheels, but where a watch is of the non-magnetic type is is often found that both wheel and pallets are made with phosphor bronze or gold. The Germans in their Glashütte watches always use gold-coloured wheels and pallets, and make a very beautiful job of them; they have the banking pin fitted into one of the pallet nibs, and this works or banks in a hole cut in the plate.

A New Pair of Pallets

If it is necessary to replace a pair of pallets or a lever and pallets in one piece it is often easier to make the pallets with the covered stones. To make the more modern or popular type of lever and pallets is a long job and requires more tools, and it is often easier to replace these by a separate lever if there is room for this in the watch. As the pallets are usually of ample thickness, they can often be made thinner to get the extra room (see *Watch and Clock Making and Repairing*).

The Banking Pins

The lever has to have some arrangement to keep it in the correct position so that the impulse pin can engage the notch correctly; the term for this is ' the bankings '.

There are many forms of bankings, but the most common and the most efficient consists of banking pins which are fitted into the plate at such a distance that the guard, whether dart or guard pin, is properly free of the roller edge, at the same time holding the lever in such a position that the impulse pin passes freely and yet correctly into the lever notch. These pins must be so placed that the lever can move far enough to allow the 'scape wheel tooth to drop or be free.

Banked to Drop—When a watch is being examined the term ' banked to drop ' is often used. This means that the banking pins are so arranged that the lever can move only just enough to let the wheel tooth drop with no movement afterwards, or, directly the lever reaches the banking pin the wheel tooth is dropped. This is a very fine test to ascertain if a 'scape wheel is true and divided equally. The difference between ' banked to drop ' and ' correct ' is the run, or the run to the banking, *i.e.* the amount that the lever moves after the wheel tooth is dropped. This run is wrong theoretically because it is another loss or extra friction, but it is essential because of the necessary freedoms in the escapement. Another factor which must not be forgotten is change of temperature. If a watch is left without run it is likely to stop as the temperature rises owing to the expansion of the metals, including the 'scape wheel.

Run, or Run to the Bankings—In a good escapement the run supplies the freedom for the dart or guard pin from the roller edge, thus the run should be equal to the ' shake ' on the bankings as it is called, the shake being the amount of freedom between the guard pin or dart and the edge of the roller. Although the two terms shake and run seem to be the same, they can actually be very different; there can be ample shake on the roller and yet no run, or there can be ample or excessive run and yet the guard can still be too tight on the roller edge.

Bankings—Other factors come into the picture, as will be seen. Sometimes the bankings are what is termed solid, *i.e.* they are formed by the junction of two sinks, or a channel cut between two sunk-out parts of the plate. Others are formed on the pallet bridge or cock, whilst in some cases, such as the Glashütte, they consist of a pin passing through a hole in the plate. One type of mass-produced watch has a pin standing perpendicular from the lever in a manner very similar to the guard pin of a single roller lever, this acting on the pallet cock. The American watchmakers use a screw with a pin planted eccentrically, and thus the pins are adjustable; banking pins must always be perfectly upright, and this principle makes it easy for them to be so.

If it is necessary to alter banking pins they must have a double bend so that the pin is perfectly upright where the action takes place, as if this is not the case the banking will vary with the endshake. If the pin is bent like a V there will be more shake when the endshake is up because the distance between the pins will be greater than when the endshake is down.

RESILIENT LEVERS (OR LEVERS WITH RESILIENT BANKINGS)

The resilient lever as it is called was introduced because of the damage caused to watches when they were subjected to a great deal of jolting, as would occur if they were worn during horse riding. The continual jolting would cause the balance to increase its vibration until it rapped or struck the bankings in a furious manner, broke the impulse pin or pallet staff, and, at the very least, generally upset the rate of the watch. A lever was therefore made which would give way and return to its correct position with the least disturbance to the watch.

The best principle was produced by E. Dent and Co., who made a lever escapement which was absolutely the same as usual except for two points, the horns of the lever being filed away to form inclined planes and the back half of the lever being filed down to form a very thin spring about as thick as the spring of a chronometer detent. Thus as the vibrations increased the impulse pin reached the outside of the lever, ran up the inclined plane and passed on. On its return it again passed into the notch and carried on. Now in this condition in the ordinary way, the escapement would be overbanked, but as the impulse pin reached the lever it was pushed over and the pin passed on. As it returned the action was corrected; the impulse pin had passed through the notch twice and could keep on doing so. The whole action was made possible by the spring tail, which bent against the banking pin, thus allowing considerable scope to the fork end of the lever.

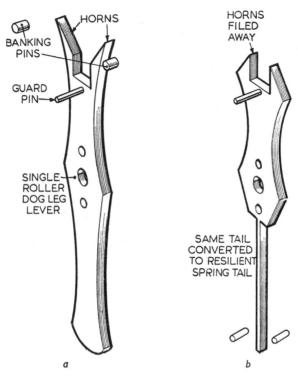

Figure 115. English single roller lever showing E. Dent and Co.'s conversion: *a* original lever banked at fork end; *b* lever tail thinned to a spring and banked at the tail.

Another type of escapement for the same purpose was made by Nicole Neilson, a fine firm now out of business. In this the resilient banking was used and was carried out on steps on the 'scape wheel teeth, the pallets being banked on the steps. Thus, as the balance passed the notch for the second time the wheel was pushed back and the lever was able to move past its bankings and to restore its position on a later passing.

With the ordinary lever escapement the maximum vibration is a full turn each side, or two turns, whereas with a resilient the balance can vibrate any number of turns. If the balance is put in place without its hairspring it can be turned continuously in one direction any number of times. The balance will pass through at whatever position the lever occupies. J. F. Cole made another type of escapement which had a semblance to a club-tooth wheel, in this type the

BANKING FOR PALLETS

Figure 116. Resilient lever wheel and pallets by Nicole Neilson. There are no banking pins for the lever.

wheel itself acted as the resilient bankings. Taylor made another type where the sides of the notch were parts of a spring. These gave way in a similar manner. They were all good ideas, but the only one which was a real success was the one made by E. Dent and Co.

Care must be taken with the clearance of the 'scape wheel teeth from the belly of the pallets. These pallets must be thinned at the belly if necessary in order to obtain the extra freedom.

SAVAGE'S TWO-PIN LEVER ESCAPEMENT

This escapement was designed so that the engaging of the impulse pin was on the line of centres; if this were so there would be no engaging friction. This type of escapement must not be confused with the one sometimes used in cheap clocks, in which two pins are used instead of the usual impulse pin.

With the Savage escapement the two pins were the unlocking pins, and this was their only function. The impulse was given by the perpendicular guard pin in this way. The single roller had a square notch instead of a passing crescent, and the guard pin engaged this notch to give impulse. The pallets were very highly angled, and the impulse planes were often as high as $15°$ to $17\frac{1}{2}°$. The vibration of the balance was usually very good, and the escapement gave an exceedingly good performance. In some of these escapements the two pins were replaced by a very broad jewel, but it was an unnecessary expense.

The objection to this type of escapement was the need for extreme accuracy in manufacture, for if it were not correct it would prove a nuisance.

The square notch in the roller becomes worn on the sides, but this is easily repaired by polishing; the sides, however, are better if slightly rounded. The guard pin or impulse pin does not fit the notch like an impulse pin in the ordinary escapement because the function is not the same. The position of the side of the notch is controlled by the unlocking, and there is no relationship between the two sides of the notch, the relationship being between the side of the lever notch

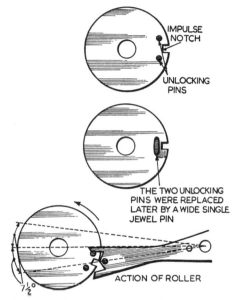

Figure 117. Savage's two-pin escapement.

on the far side of the lever and the side of the notch. In other words, the left-hand side of the lever notch controls the action of the right-hand side of the roller notch.

The size of the roller was the same as the old pattern lever, *i.e.* 4 : 1 in relation to the lever, this, of course, making a balance arc of about 60°. The Savage two-pin escapement gave a very good performance, but its popularity waned owing to the high cost of manufacture.

THE RACK LEVER

There is nothing complicated about a rack lever. It was invented by Litherland, but although many were made, mostly in the North of England, they soon faded out.

The balance staff was an ordinary pinion, usually of 6 leaves, and the lever was a rack, usually of 12 teeth. There was no guard pin because it was unnecessary, as the pinion which was the balance staff was never out of gear with the lever. The lever had banking pins, but only to prevent the balance coming out of gear with the lever when the watch had a severe jolt. The pallet faces had no draw, but were like the Graham dead-beat, *i.e.* they were part of an arc struck from the pallet hole.

PINION FOR
BALANCE
STAFF

RACK LEVER

Figure 118.   Rack lever escapement.

This is an interesting escapement, but it has many disadvantages, of which friction is the worst. The balance is never detached, and both pinion and rack become considerably worn.

Some of these escapements were made with the usual 15-tooth 'scape wheel and a usual train, but others were made with a 3-wheel train and a 'scape wheel of 30 teeth. Whilst some were very nicely made, others were extremely poor.

CLUB ROLLER ESCAPEMENT

Another interesting escapement is the Club Roller. This has many disadvantages because it is only partly detached; it is very similar to the Maltese Cross type of stop-work. The pallets are circular on the locking face like the Graham, and there is no draw.

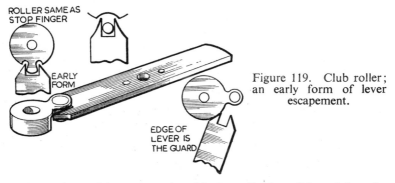

ROLLER SAME AS
STOP FINGER

EARLY
FORM

EDGE OF
LEVER IS
THE GUARD

Figure 119.   Club roller; an early form of lever escapement.

The early models were made with the roller in solid steel, but the later ones had a jewel impulse pin. The lever and roller depth was easy to adjust, but the wheel and pallet action was as critical as any other. The roller looks formidable, but this was quite easy to make with a milling cutter.

The performance of this escapement was in keeping with the requirements of its time, but it was soon superseded by the modern escapement.

THE SINGLE-PIN ESCAPEMENT

This escapement was made by E. Dent and Co. as a counterpart to McDowal's single-pin escapement for clocks, and all of those made were of the double-roller type. Their only fault was in the lubricating, otherwise they gave a good performance.

Instead of the usual 'scape wheel a roller with a jewel pin was mounted on the 'scape pinion, the pin being so arranged that it ran round inside the tail of the lever. The impulse planes were formed inside the tail, thus there was locking and impulse all on the tail instead of in the centre of the lever as is usual.

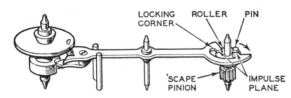

Figure 120. Single-pin lever escapement. Impulse is delivered by a roller and pin to the tail of the lever.

There are other types of lever escapement, but if the escapement as such is understood they will present no difficulties. There are two types of combination levers which are dealt with in the chapter on chronometer escapements.

THE PIN-PALLET ESCAPEMENT

This is a cheap form of lever escapement, and although the principle is good, the difficulty in keeping it lubricated is much in evidence.

The impulse is all on the wheel teeth, and the pallets consist of pins correctly placed. The lever and pallets are usually all in one piece except in the case of clocks, where they are often separate pieces. Unfortunately this type of escapement is generally very poorly made, and as a result it is a real source of trouble. As stated earlier, the wheel teeth contain all the impulse and also the locking face, which should be back cut or undercut to provide draw. The draw is one of the main troubles in this escapement, because so many of the wheels have little draw or none at all. Another fault is that the wheel teeth become worn and not only fail to lock but also work in reverse, throwing the pallet out, and as a result the guard pin catches the corner of the crescent and stops the watch.

Correcting the Locking—In the ordinary way the 'scape and pallet action can be deepened and the locking can be corrected, but with a pin-pallet this often does not work out. Very often these escapements are without banking pins to the lever and the band of the wheel is the only banking. This is a multiple fault, because it provides a path for the oil to run away, and it also makes it impossible for the escapement action to be deepened in the case of mislocking. This fault can sometimes be improved by putting a flat in the side of the pallet engaged by the locking face of the wheel tooth. It will often effect a cure if this flat is polished and arranged so that only the outer corner is engaged; another way would be to replace the pins with smaller ones. Often the pallets are drilled with larger holes than the pins themselves.

Replacing the Pallet Pins—There is no difficulty in replacing these pins for smaller ones, or in fitting replacements for worn pins. They need not be glass hard but can be made from hardened and tempered steel, providing they are polished, for the polishing will increase their resistance to wear. They can be either turned in a lathe or turns.

A piece of steel which is a little full in size is chosen, this being hardened and tempered and left as hard as possible so that it can just be turned. It is turned until it fits the hole in the pallets closely and the part which fits into the pallets will pass about halfway through, then the pin is turned on the rod in the same way as one would turn a pivot. It is essential that the whole should be dead true, otherwise the shakes will be altered and the wheel may not pass, or many other troubles may arise. In no circumstances should the acting pins be left any larger, in fact it would be far better if they were smaller. When to size the pin is polished to a high degree.

Next, the back is partly cut through so that when pushed home the back of the pin will be flush with the pallets. When this has been done the pin is tightly pushed in place and then snapped off at the partly cut through section. This is another job which is much easier if carried out in the turns.

The Guard Action—The roller in quite a number of the more modern pin-pallet escapements is a double one, and this saves a lot of trouble. They are also provided with banking pins to the lever, and these are a further trouble saver.

With some of the others, in which the banking is the band of the wheel, and a brass pin fitted into the lever and bent over at right angles is the dart, there is a lot of trouble. One fault is where the pin becomes loose enough to move: when this happens there is no freedom on the roller on one side and too much on the other. The remedy for this is to fix the pin and to position it so that the freedom or shake is equal on each side.

Some have a guard roller which is part of the balance staff, and often the crescent is too wide, with the result that the guard pin gets jammed against the corner. This is a difficult fault to correct, but if it must be put right the only way to do it is to reduce the roller by turning it to a smaller diameter and to push the guard pin forward or to fit a new guard pin or dart.

Steel Impulse Pin—Some of these escapements have a steel impulse pin, and this is often a source of trouble. In the ordinary way an impulse pin should never be oiled, but where steel is working in brass there must be oil, otherwise rust will form and the watch will stop. Thus whilst one must grease the pin, only the minimum amount of lubrication should be used because oil picks up dust and dirt.

The pivot holes must be a good fit, although it must be admitted that in some cases one would be in dire trouble if an attempt were made to make them correct. In fact, they depend upon plenty of freedom to make them go at all, and some are so bad that they should never have been manufactured.

It is not worth while attempting a repair when the wheels are worn unless the correct replacement can be obtained. There is nothing formidable about the operation of cutting a wheel, but it is a lot of trouble, and the setting up of the cutters is very critical, especially if the band of the wheel is the banking.

Two Pins Instead of Impulse Pin—Some small clocks have this escapement fitted with a single roller and often have two thin steel pins instead of a large pin. This must not be confused with the two-pin escapement, and there is no connection between the two. One of the troubles with this type is overbanking. The trouble can be overcome by reducing the diameter of the roller and deepening the guard action.

Sometimes the passing crescent is just a flat face and is often too wide, so the lever will pass. A new roller is the only cure for this, with a smaller crescent. The crescent in any escapement of the lever type should not be any wider than one and a half times the diameter of the impulse pin.

Making a Lever Escapement

The method used in making pallets and 'scape wheels was described in the author's book *Watch and Clock Making and Repairing*; the position of the balance has already been determined, and also the position of the fourth wheel and pinion. The method used in making an escapement to a new movement in the rough will now be described.

The first escapement to be dealt with will be the right-angled escapement, *i.e.* the one in which the lever is at right angles or where the 'scape hole, the pallet-staff hole and the balance-staff hole are forming a right angle. The movement is a 12 size, or in Swiss sizes about 18 ligne, whilst the escapement is a 4 size, or would have a 'scape wheel of 0·245 in. diameter.

Pitching the 'Scape Pinion—The first thing to do is to find the position of the 'scape pivot hole. The fourth wheel and 'scape pinion are put in a depth tool which is adjusted until the gearing is correct, making sure at the same time that the pinion is correct for size with the wheel. When this is correct, using the depth tool as a compass one

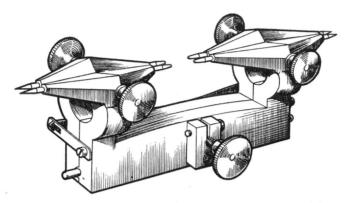

Figure 121. Depth tool used for planting wheels and pinions, escapements, *etc.* The tool is also useful for examining separate actions.

leg is placed in the fourth pivot hole and the tool adjusted until it will stand perfectly upright, with one leg in the fourth hole and the other resting on top of the 'scape cock.

Using the Depth Tool—Daylight must be used when testing for uprightness because artificial light is deceptive. The depth tool is held in position against the light so that the reflection of the legs of the tool is clearly reflected on the 'scape cock and the watch plate; if upright the reflection and the legs will be perfectly straight lines, and any error, however slight, will be very obvious.

To adjust the tool one leg is fixed and then the other pushed in or out, whichever is required, until correct. When the tool is correctly adjusted an arc is scribed across the 'scape cock, then the depth tool is left set and care is taken not to alter it.

The 'scape wheel is 0·245 in., and its radius will be 0·1225 in. This would make the distance of centres of the pallets and wheel using a club-tooth 'scape wheel 0·15 in. To be sure of getting a right angle the sides will be in the relationship of 3 : 4 : 5. Taking the pallet and wheel distance of centre as 3, the shortest distance or root as it may be called is 0·15 ÷ 3 = 0·05. The greatest distance will be from the balance-staff hole to the 'scape hole, and this is taken as 5, therefore by multiplying this by the root 0·05 the figure of 0·25 is obtained. A point is marked off on the 'scape cock which is 0·25 in. from the staff hole, and a mark is made on the arc scribed earlier to denote the fourth and 'scape pinion depth. If this comes either in or near the middle of the 'scape cock the next operation can be carried out.

The steady pins are put in the 'scape cock to fix it permanently in

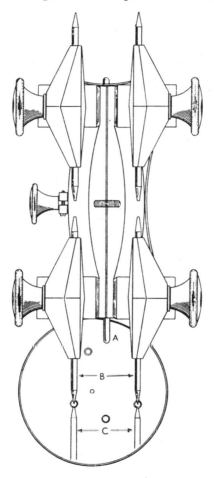

Figure 122. Pitching a depth. The depth tool is uprighted by reflection in a smooth watch plate. A = joint pin ; B = legs of tool ; C = reflection.

this position if it is not already steady-pinned in place. After the cock is fixed the fourth and 'scape depth, which is already set in the depth tool, is re-marked, and a check made to see that the mark of 0·25 in. from the balance staff is still correct, if so a hole is drilled

197

where the marks coincide. Care must be taken to avoid drift when drilling, and the hole must be drilled perfectly upright.

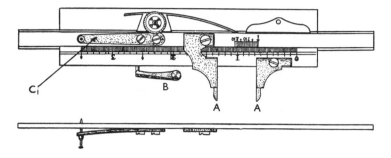

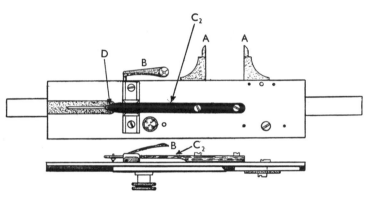

Figure 123. Vernier Gauge for accurately marking length of lever and position of impulse pin on roller, measures to 0·001 in. $A =$ fine pointed jaws to enable distance of centres to be accurately measured; $B =$ lever which lifts C_2 to enable lever or roller to be inserted on cone centre at D; $C_1 =$ spring ending with true centre punch; $C_2 =$ strong spring ending with cone centre; $D =$ cone centre of C_2.

It must be noted that some escapement makers plant their holes on the pillar plates and upright on to the 'scape cock. Either way is quite sound.

Uprighting in the Mandrel—The next operation is to drill the hole in the plate. The plate and 'scape cock are placed in the mandrel and set so that the hole in the 'scape cock is running perfectly true. To check this a point is cut on a length of pegwood and a flat cut on the side about $\frac{1}{2}$–1 in. away from the point. The point is rested in the hole and the T-rest is placed in position so that the flat of the peg is resting on it, then the T-rest is put at such a height that the pegwood lies nearly parallel to the lathe bed. The lathe is now slowly revolved, at the same time watching the end of the pegwood; if this does not move the hole must be true, but if there is any circular movement the hole is out, and the plate should be tapped on its edge with a small wooden mallet until it is correct.

When the pegwood moves nearer to the lathe bed the top of the plate is lightly tapped to move it down, and this is carried out until there is no movement of the pegwood. After making sure that the plate is securely held, the 'scape cock can be removed. A true pip is turned in the plate and then a hole is drilled which will be the lower 'scape hole. If one is jewelling the watch oneself the operation can be carried out at this stage whilst the plate is still true in the mandrel: after the holes are drilled the watch jeweller will jewel both the balance and 'scape holes.

The balance is uprighted from the balance cock whether it is being jewelled by oneself or by the watch jeweller, after which the balance staff is made and finished. It is a good idea to make the roller arbor and the hairspring collet arbor 0·025 in. in diameter, but this is not imperative. The 'scape pinion is turned in and the wheel tightly mounted on the collet, but not riveted on.

Distance of Centres—The distance from the centre of the balance to the 'scape hole is 0·25 in., and from the pallets to 'scape hole 0·15 in., so the distance from the lever or pallet hole to the balance hole is made 0·2 in., which is 0·05 × 4. This makes up the 3:4:5 ratio which is the right angle. The lever and roller proportion will be $3\frac{1}{2}$:1 as it is a single roller, which means that the pitch line of the lever and roller would entail a lever 0·155 in. long and a roller of 0·045 in. radius. After allowing 0·005 in. on each for intersection the lever is 0·16 in. long and the roller has a 0·05-in. radius.

Radius of the Lever and Roller—One must not lose sight of the fact that the dimensions of the lever and roller are measured from the centre and as such are radii. If a roller has a radius of 0·05 in. the full diameter would be 0·1 in., plus the necessary metal outside the pin circle to enable the guard edge to be formed and for a crescent of sufficient depth to allow the pin hole to be quite sound. Also the measurement of the lever is from the pallet-staff hole to the mouth of the notch, and if it is a right-angled escapement with a poised lever the length of the lever would be more than twice that length. This would not apply in the case of a straight-line lever unless one with an artistic or plain tail was being made or replaced.

Pitching the Lever and Roller—The next move is to make the lever and the roller in the rough, and this operation has been described previously. The roller is fitted on to an arbor with clean true centres, and the lever and the pallets are also mounted on a true arbor ending in large pivots with cone shoulders. The pair are then put in the depth tool, which is adjusted until the guard action is as shallow as possible, but perfectly sound,

The notch and impulse-pin action are checked, and if they are in order the depth tool is used as previously, but this time the balance hole is used as the centre, taking care not to break the jewel hole, and also making sure that the depth tool is upright. An arc is scribed across the 'scape cock, then the 'scape wheel is put in the depth tool with the pallets and the depth tool set so that the action is perfectly correct.

Checking the Size of the Wheel—The locking must be checked to see that it is correct, also the inside and outside shakes must be equal

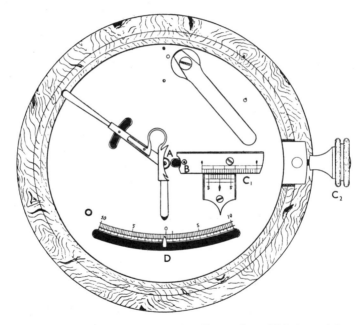

Figure 124. Tool for measuring pallet angles. This is used for both club tooth and ratchet tooth escapements. The action is tripled thus each degree shows three. A = centre for pallet or lever and pallets; B = centre for 'scape wheel; C_1 = gauge for distance of centres; C_2 = thumb nut for adjusting slide of C_1; D = gauge which shows three per degree.

and the wheel teeth free of the belly of the pallets, *etc.* If the shakes are unequal when the locking is correct the wheel must be changed;

if the outside shake is closer it means that the wheel is too small, and if the inside shake is too close, then the wheel is too large.

Marking the Centre—When satisfied that all is in order, the depth tool is set upright, and with one leg in the 'scape hole an arc is scribed which will cross the arc marked for the lever and roller depth. A centre pip is now made for the drill to follow, using a sharp-pointed graver or a three-cornered chamfer. The sharp point is rested on either line or arc, and is then moved along the line towards the junction. As the point reaches the junction the intersection will be felt, and immediately this occurs the point is pressed in with a slight twist, and there will be an accurate centre. If the junction is overrun one should go on to the other arc and try again, as it is essential that the centre pip should be correct. The hole is then drilled, and needless to say this must be upright. It is not necessary to use a very small drill unless the lever is to run in brass holes. When the hole is drilled it is transferred to the plate or 'scape cock whichever is required.

The lever and pallets are put into the frame, and if they are free in the holes the next stage can be commenced, but if they are not they must be freed to allow them to move stiffly between the cock and the plate. This is done by chamfering the holes from the inside, after which the roller is put on the balance staff and then all the parts are put in place in the frame.

The roller must be just free of the lever, and should be close to it but not touching, then with the aid of a piece of thinned pegwood the 'scape wheel is moved in its correct direction, usually clockwise, and at the same time the balance is moved so that the impulse pin is acting in the notch. The movement of the balance is continued until the wheel tooth drops, then the balance is reversed and the amount of locking or the position of the balance when the wheel tooth drops is noted, and on the reverse move the position of the balance when the tooth leaves the locking is noticed; this unlocking can be felt even if it cannot be seen.

Checking for Correct Pitching—The distance that the balance has moved is the amount of locking. Taking a balance as a circle of 360°, and also as a single bar as most balances are, a half turn will be 180° and a quarter will be 90°. If it is a balance with screws the quarter can easily be divided to give the number of degrees. It must not be forgotten, however, that the lever and roller ratio is $3\frac{1}{2}$: 1, which means that the locking will be multiplied by $3\frac{1}{2}$. Thus, 3° locking will show about 10° or one-ninth of the quarter turn of the balance. The screws of the average balance are a good guide, inasmuch as the head is about 10° of the balance rim.

After being satisfied that the locking is in order one can test for inside and outside freedom. Starting from where the wheel tooth is resting on the locking face of the pallet, say on the entry pallet, the balance is moved until it all but unlocks the wheel, *i.e.* with the tooth just resting on the locking corner. The wheel is then moved backwards and forwards, and the shake will be felt or maybe seen. Whatever freedom there is at this point is the outside shake.

The balance is now moved round until the tooth drops inside the pallets and the next but one tooth is resting on the exit-pallet locking face. The balance is moved as previously until the tooth on the locking face reaches the locking corner. The amount of movement of the wheel or freedom is the inside shake. If the locking is correct and the shakes are equal the wheel and pallet depth is correct.

Lever and Roller Action—Now for the lever and roller action. The wheel and pallet action must still be used, however, because they are all dependent on one another. In order to examine the lever and roller the balance is moved again until the wheel tooth is released or just drops, then the lever is pushed or pressed with the pegwood, against the direction of movement and of course against the impulse pin, and as the balance continues to turn the impulse pin will continue to move the lever until the pin comes out of the lever notch, and the lever will then drop back a certain distance. The action should be tried first one side and then the other.

This extra lift shown by the drop back will mean that the lever notch is too long. In order to test the horns the guard pin is rested against the roller and held there lightly with the peg, then the balance is moved and the amount that the lever drops back after release until the guard pin rests again on the roller edge is noticed. This lift is now reduced to a minimum by shortening the notch by filing back the horns.

When there is a very slight lift and fall with the lever on either side, and when they are equal, the action can be rechecked against the wheel and pallet action. The wheel is moved by the pegwood and the balance is turned until the wheel tooth drops, then the peg is changed to the lever as before, seeing if the lever is moved or lifted by the impulse pin.

Lever Out of Angle—It may be found that there is lift on one side and fall on the other, and this will mean that the lever is ' out of angle ' or that it is incorrectly placed in relation to the pallets; this fault must be corrected at this stage. First, the side is taken where the lever has fall but no lift. This means that the lever is carried too far in relation to the pallets, so the lever must be moved in the direction of the fall, or brought nearer to the roller in relation to the pallets.

Looking down on the escapement with the notch on the far side, *i.e.* away from the body of the repairer, if the fall of the lever is on the left-hand side the lever must be moved to the right or twisted clockwise on the pallet staff. Before proceeding further it must be ascertained that these actions are correct and equal. It may be found that when they are equal without the wheel and pallet action there is a different result when the wheel and pallet is brought into the combination. Thus when the wheel tooth is dropped the lever may still be moved by the roller as the balance is moved, holding the lever against the impulse pin.

Correcting a Deep Guard Action—If this does happen it means that the guard or safety action is too deep, and this may either mean that the lever and roller have been pitched too deeply or that the outside diameter of the roller is too large. If the latter is the case the roller can be removed and its full diameter reduced by turning an appropriate amount off the edge, providing, of course, that there is sufficient metal to allow this to be done. This will put the action right. If there is insufficient metal it can only be assumed that the lever and roller have been pitched too deeply, and this means that the pitching must be altered As there are brass holes these can be drawn a little so that the pallet staff is a little farther away from the balance staff.

Altering the Depth—Both the top and bottom holes are drawn, making them slightly oval, then with the aid of a small round-nosed punch they are closed from the inside, placing the punch to that part of the hole nearest to the balance staff. A sharp blow on the punch with a hammer will force the metal towards the hole and close it. The hole is then broached quite round until the rough pallet-staff pivots fit close, then the actions are tried all over again. It will almost certainly be found that the lever is out of angle again through the wheel and pallet action being interfered with, but if all is in order the next stage can be proceeded with.

There is an alternative method of carrying out the correction which has just been described, and that is by working on the actual lever. If a highly finished escapement is being made the hole for the pallet staff can be drawn in the lever itself. The hole is filed slightly oval, and the front closed in the same manner as the brass pivot holes. When correct the lever is countersunk and the punch mark is eliminated, then when finishing up the countersink is polished. There is no way of altering the guard pin itself, and bending it one way or the other only means trouble.

Drilling the Holes in Lever and Pallets—The next operation is to drill the holes in the lever to correspond exactly with the holes in the pallets. These can be called steady pins or holding pins because they hold the lever and pallets together. When the holes are drilled the lever and pallets must be held in a pair of soft metal tongs to prevent any movement. After drilling the holes are broached from the lever side to give them a slight taper. They are also chamfered where they come together between the lever and pallets so that there are no sharp edges, the idea being that if any angle adjustment becomes necessary the pins will not shear off. This will be dealt with later.

203

The hole for the pallet staff is now broached so that it is an easy fit on the pallet staff. The pallets fit the pallet staff, but when finished the lever does not. If the lever is a steel one it can now be hardened and tempered, the tempering colour being purple. It is unnecessary to harden the pallets, because only the stones or jewels are in action.

Making and Fitting the Holding Pins—The next step is to make the pins for the guard pin and holding pins. Hard-drawn brass wire is used for these, and is filed quite round and very slightly tapered. The pins are fitted through the lever and into the pallets, making sure that the pins fit both. They are then shortened until the part fitting the pallets is about three-quarters of the length required to pass right through the pallets, and then left standing proud on the lever side by the amount they are short on the pallet side, *i.e.* about one-quarter of the thickness of the pallets.

The guard pin is now made, leaving it nicely burnished on the sides. The pin is pushed through to the height of the roller edge, with a part about the thickness of the lever remaining to be pushed in. The ends of the pins are now rounded up, making sure that the pins do not become mixed up, because each pin only fits the hole for which it was made. A good idea is to draw circles on the board paper and put the pins in them; they will be easy to find and will not get mixed up.

Polishing and Finishing up the Escapement—The lever and pallets are now polished (see p. 277), and after the holes have been jewelled, or, if brass holes, have been correctly finished, the permanent pallet staff is made. The lever is pinned up to the pallets and the pins are given a final push with an ivory punch; if the pins have been shortened correctly they will be flush both sides. The guard pin is now pushed in, making sure that it is quite tight, then first the roller edge is polished, then the crescent and finally the flat face. The wheel is finished up, and the rivet rubbed over but not riveted with a punch and hammer, as this may cause distortion however carefully it is carried out.

Banking the Escapement—The whole escapement is now put into place and rechecked to see that all is in order and that nothing has altered in the finishing. The banking pins are now fitted. A marker of some sort must be used to do this, and it must be so shaped that it can be easily held upright and yet be able to follow the profile of the side of the lever. The guard pin must be rested against the roller edge, the tool held quite upright and a line marked coincident with the lever edge. The banking pin must always be put at the fork end of the lever except in the case of resilient-lever escapements. The idea is to save the pallet staff should the watch receive a violent jerk and the impulse pin hit the back of the banked lever.

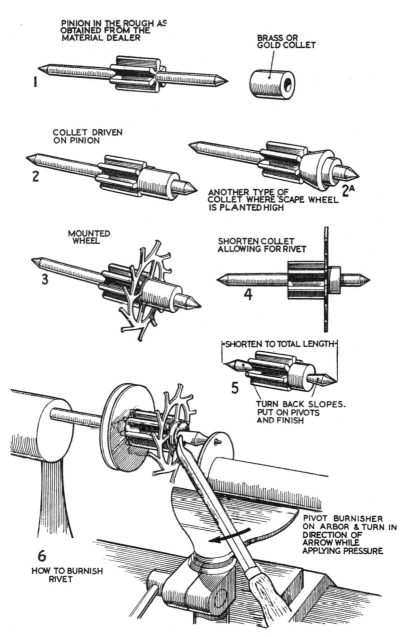

Figure 125. Turning in an English 'scape pinion and mounting the
'scape wheel by burnishing the collet over the wheel.

205

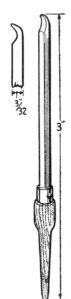

Figure 126. Burnisher for wheel mounting
or rubbing over the collets.

Figure 127. Blueing pan for tempering small steel pieces
as levers, detents, *etc.*

Position of the Banking Pins—The holes are drilled where the lines
have been scribed for the lever edge, allowing for the necessary freedom, *i.e.* the holes should be drilled about 0·002 in. outside the line
instead of on the line. The holes are well chamfered, using a deep
chamfer where the banking pins protrude through the plate on the
active side. If the position has been misjudged and the holes have
been chamfered, the pins can be moved one way or the other and yet
they can still be kept straight and upright. It is essential that they
should be upright so that the action is the same whether the endshakes are up or down.

Making a Double Roller

The manner of making a single roller has already been described,
and the double roller will now be dealt with. As the main points
are the same, it is only necessary to deal with those ways in which the
double roller differs from the single roller.

The first difference concerns the lever and roller. With a single
roller the proportion is $3\frac{1}{2}$: 1, but with a double roller the proportion
is 3 : 1 using 10° pallets and a 30° balance arc. The distance of centres
is 0·2 in., which means 0·15 in. as the length of the lever and 0·05 in.
for the radius of the roller. Adding 0·005 in. to each for intersection, the lever length becomes 0·155 in. and the roller radius 0·055 in.

Pitching the Escapement—The wheel and pallets are pitched as usual,
but before the lever is pitched the horns must be shaped as near as

possible to the circle of the impulse pin. First one horn is filed with the lever on one side until the pin does not move the lever when run along its length, then the lever is moved over to the other side and the action is repeated on the other horn. This can all be carried out in a depth tool. When all is correct the lever and roller can be pitched. After checking up in the frame to see that all is in order the small or guard roller and the dart on the lever are made. When pitching a double-roller lever it must be remembered that there is no guard in place. The horns are used in the same capacity as the guard pin on a single roller.

Making the Dart—If a gold piece as it is called is being made the whole operation is carried out while on the lever, which is, of course, in the rough. The small roller should be of such a size that if it were laid on top of the impulse or table roller its edge would just reach the inside of the impulse-pin circle. The crescent should be the same width as the diameter of the impulse pin and almost as deep. The final finishing of the small roller and the dart or guard is carried out at the very last because both are adjustable. This gives a distinct advantage over the single roller, in which there is very little scope for adjustments.

Crank Roller for Thin Watches—In some watches where flatness is required the impulse roller can be cranked and put below the guard roller instead of above as is usual, thus reducing the thickness by the thickness of the pallets, because the lever and roller are then in the same plane instead of one above the other.

Swiss Type of Dart—In most Swiss watches the lever is made leaving a block behind the notch underneath the lever, and the dart is a pin fitted through a hole drilled in this block. In Swiss hand-finished watches, however, the dart is usually the same as in the English watch, with the exception that the Swiss make a steel guard piece and

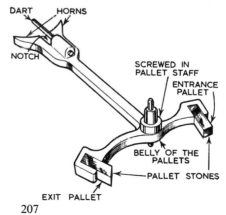

Figure 128. Lever and pallets in one piece.

the English a gold one. This type of dart or guard piece is screwed and steady-pinned to the lever.

The procedure is identical whether a club-tooth wheel and pallets or a ratchet tooth is being used, and the principles are exactly the same.

Older Pattern Lever Escapements

In passing, it would not be amiss to make a few remarks about some of the early lever escapements. Quite a number were provided with round impulse pins, and with a $3\frac{1}{2}$: 1 lever and roller proportion the balance arc was about 40°. It was necessary to have a lot of run so that the pin could clear the corner of the notch.

Flattened Impulse Pin—If any of these come to hand they can be improved by fitting a flatted impulse pin which will increase the

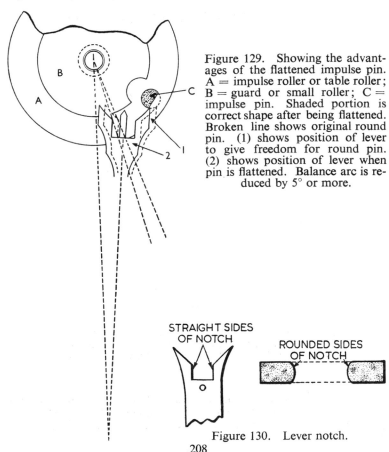

Figure 129. Showing the advantages of the flattened impulse pin. A = impulse roller or table roller; B = guard or small roller; C = impulse pin. Shaded portion is correct shape after being flattened. Broken line shows original round pin. (1) shows position of lever to give freedom for round pin. (2) shows position of lever when pin is flattened. Balance arc is reduced by 5° or more.

STRAIGHT SIDES
OF NOTCH

ROUNDED SIDES
OF NOTCH

Figure 130. Lever notch.

208

vibration. It is, however, a mistake to use a completely half-round pin, because this would tend to cut hollows in the notch; the pin should be two-thirds of a circle, or one-third should be ground away flat. In cases where the sides of the notch have been left flat there

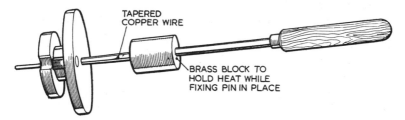

Figure 131. Tool for fixing impulse or ruby pins.

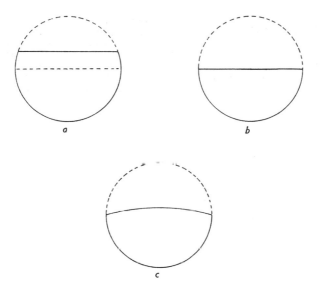

Figure 132. Correct shape of impulse pin: *a* correct shape of pin ⅓ polished away flat; *b* incorrect and very bad; it is half round and acts as a cutter; *c* incorrect, has the same errors as *b*.

will be a much better performance if these are well rounded; this does not decrease the friction, but there will then be no question of the pin binding in the notch should there be anything out of upright or not quite square.

Fitting a Gold Impulse Pin—A further point is that one should not replace a jewel pin with a steel one; if a jewel pin cannot be obtained a common gold one should be used. This will act quite well, although it obviously will not be so good as a jewel pin, but it will do the lever no harm. A steel pin would badly cut the lever notch whether the lever was brass or steel and, of course, it would be necessary to oil a pin made of this metal, whereas a gold one must not be oiled and does not need it.

Making a Straight-line Lever Escapement

Now that the actual making of an escapement has been described, that of the modern style must be dealt with. This is the popular straight-line escapement instead of the well-known right-angle type.

In the straight-line escapement the 'scape pallet and balance-staff pivot holes are in a straight line. This escapement would have to be made to depth if a single roller escapement were used, so a double roller is used, especially if the watch is a small one. This gives plenty of scope and considerably eases the work.

It will be taken for granted that the 'scape-pinion pivot holes and the balance-staff pivot holes are already fixed, therefore there is only the pallet-staff hole to be considered. The most important depth is, of course, the wheel and pallets. Again a watch will be taken of a size which will be called 18 ligne, or rather an 18-ligne movement.

Checking the Distance of Centres—The distance between the balance and 'scape-pivot holes must be measured, and it can then be decided what size escapement to use. The distance of centres of the 'scape and pallet holes will work out almost the same as that of their counterparts dealt with previously. The distance between the 'scape and balance holes will be about 0·42 in., which means that the radius of the wheel, the length of the lever and the radius of the roller are all contained in this distance. There is no need to be particular about exact detail, but if the balance is used as a guide the largest diameter of the 'scape wheel can be gauged.

Size of 'Scape Wheel—As was stated earlier, the recognised size of a balance is such that it will rest in the sink or groove which has been cut and into which the barrel cover snaps. In other words, it should be the same size as the barrel cover; in this case the balance will be 0·72 in. in diameter. As the 'scape wheel is reckoned to be three-sevenths of the diameter of the balance, the 'scape wheel will be 0·3 in. in diameter, or 0·15 in. radius.

Matching Wheel and Pallets—To proceed, the wheel will be this size with the pallets to match. A matched pair are put in the depth tool and are checked for inside and outside shake, *etc.* It must be seen that when they are pitched and correctly locking the wheel teeth are quite clear of the belly of the pallets. If all is in order a line is scribed from the 'scape hole with the depth tool as before, making sure that the line runs across a centre line between the balance and 'scape holes.   A line must next be drawn with a small straight-edge, to join the balance and 'scape holes.   The hole for the lower pallet-staff pivot is drilled where the arc struck with the depth tool crosses the straight line joining the 'scape and staff holes.

The Lever and Roller—If the distance from the remaining pallet hole to the balance hole is measured the length of the lever and the radius of the roller will be discovered.   The distance of centres of the 'scape and pallets will be 0·168 in., so if this distance is subtracted from 0·42 in. the remainder will give the length that is required, *i.e.* 0·252 in. This is divided between the lever and the roller in the proportions 3 : 1 as stated earlier.   This will give a roller-pin circle with a radius of 0·063 in. and a lever of 0·189 in. from pallet-staff hole to the notch. Allowing an additional 0·003 in. to each for intersection, the lever will be 0·192 in. in length and the roller 0·066 in. in radius.

Depth Tool as Gauge—The depth tool is set at this distance, and, is, of course, checked against the frame to see that all is in order and that the depth tool coincides with the movement, *i.e.* the pallet and balance holes.   The depth tool can be set using an ordinary micrometer, measuring across the legs of the depth tool and allowing, of course, for the thickness of the legs.   These legs or runners are usually all the same size, so if the full diameter of one leg is allowed the result should be accurate.

The next stage is to rough out the lever and roller, not forgetting the horns of the lever, which are an arc from the pin circle.   When the roughing out is complete the lever and roller are placed in the depth tool and checked to see if the pin is free in the notch, *etc.*, and that the horns are correctly curved.   If all is in order the next step will be to upright the top pallet hole on to the pallet cock.   When the pallet cock is drilled a rough pallet staff must be made as before, and then the whole escapement is tried in together.   Any necessary adjustments are carried out, and if all is correct the lever is put in angle, *etc.*, and the pin holes for holding the lever and pallets together are drilled.

The next operation is the making of the dart and guard roller. The guard roller is made first, and the diameter of the roller will be decided by the position of the impulse pin.   When the guard roller is on the staff with the impulse roller the edge of the guard roller should run through the centre of the impulse pin.   If the guard roller is smaller in diameter, which it can be, it means that the dart must be broader at the nose, otherwise there will be too much shake and the pallets may jerk off the locking when in wear.

Size of Guard Roller—Another point is that if the guard roller is too small the passing crescent must be proportionately deeper, which in a small watch means that there would be very little metal between the bottom of the crescent and the hole which fits the staff. Because of this these rollers are often found to be split across the hole and crescent.

If a gold dart is being made screwed on and steady-pinned to the lever the making is carried out on the lever when in the rough, thus using the lever as a holder. The polishing is carried out by using a special tool made for the job which has holes corresponding to the steady pin and screw holes of the lever. This means that the darts for one size of watch have these holes standard, thus making the work easier. A steel dart is made in the same way.

The lever in a modern watch is machined, leaving a block through which a hole is drilled. The hole is drilled parallel with the lever notch and has a brass pin fitted friction tight through it which functions in just the same way as the fitted dart.

When the roller and dart are finished the dart is reduced to length, this operation being carried out with all of the parts assembled in the frame. The balance is then turned, whilst at the same time a little power is put on the 'scape wheel, and as the wheel tooth is dropped or released the dart should be resting on the edge of the roller, or on what would be the edge of the roller.

With a double roller in the condition just described the dart would be in the crescent, thus the balance is moved still more in the same direction. As the balance is proceeded with, there should not be any movement of the lever either one way or the other. If the lever is pushed away when it is held against the impulse pin either the dart or horns are too long; if on carrying on in the same direction until the impulse pin is disengaged from the horn of the lever the lever drops back, then the horns are too long; on the other hand, if the lever does not fall back, then both the dart and the horns are too long.

It is most important that there is no movement of the lever after the wheel tooth has dropped; the impulse pin, however, should not pass freely through the total movement at this point, but one should be able to just feel the pin resting on the horn, and then the dart resting on the roller edge. This latter condition must be aimed for, although it will not be easy to achieve.

Examining the Escapement

The final test of the escapement is carried out when the complete movement is assembled; there is then the motive power of the watch as an extra factor, and the lever and roller action can be tested much more easily. If the watch is wound for, say, a few teeth of the ratchet wheel the balance is led round as before, but a piece of thin pegwood is lightly held against the side of the lever in opposition to the movement of the balance. If while the lever is being held in this way the wheel tooth is just released and no more, then the lever and roller action is correct, but if the wheel tooth is not released, then the horns or rather the lever notch is too short. There should be very little movement or run to the banking after the wheel tooth is dropped.

Both a right-angled escapement and a straight-line escapement with the lever and pallets as two separate units have been dealt with, and these could, of course, be made as single units, as in all modern machine-made watches. The making of the ordinary straight-line lever and pallets was described by the author in a previous book (see *Watch and Clock Making and Repairing*), and need not be repeated here. The same procedure almost in its entirety can be used to produce the right-angled lever, but if it is a question of replacement it is often easier to make as two separate units.

Pallet Stones

It must be taken for granted that when a pair of pallets is made in the modern style, *i.e.* where the pallet stones are again a separate unit, the slots have been cut at the correct angle and also at the correct distance apart.

If a pair of pallet stones is wanted and cannot be obtained, they can be made, but it is not recommended that they should be made of steel, although a number of the cheaper watches are provided with steel pallet ' stones '. The best way is to make them in jewel stone, and this would seem to be easier, although of course more care is needed in handling. The two sides together with the top and bottom form a rectangular section.

Cutting or Slicing the Rough Stone—The procedure is to shellac the rough stone to a brass plate, and slice it up to near size with a skive,

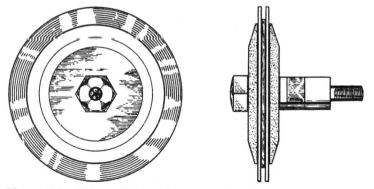

Figure 133. Skive. This tool is to cut jewel stones, all sides and edges are cut. Made of copper and charged with diamond powder it is used with water.

which is a lap consisting of two thin sheets of copper turned to identical diameters and charged with medium diamond powder. The copper sheets are mounted on an arbor and a spacing washer of the required thickness is placed between them so that they are a certain distance apart. The rough stone is presented to the skive, which is kept wet, preferably with water, and the skive will slice the stone, leaving slips the required thickness. These will be a little thinner because of the clearances, as the skive cuts front and sides. They can then be cut again to form a square section.

The small rods as they may be called are fixed on the polishing tool with shellac, and then the sides are polished to their correct width and thickness. Several rods can be worked on at once, so that there will be several available for adaption to different jobs later on when they will require only to be shortened and to have the impulse planes ground.

The Impulse Planes—The making of the impulse planes when only single stones are being made is a case of trial and error, but if several are being made a special tool is required to ensure that the angles are correct. The angle of the entrance pallet is much less steep than

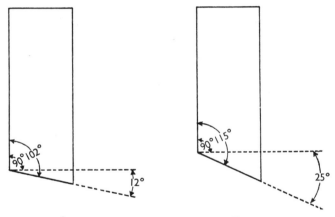

Figure 134. Lever escapement pallet stones.

the exit pallet, and whereas the angle on the former is only 12° the exit pallet has an angle of 25°, both of these being, of course, above the right angle.

Several stones can be polished together providing they are all entrance or all exit pallets. If a number are fixed together on the holder at the appropriate angle they can all be polished together in a single operation. When the impulse planes are finished the stones can be shortened from the back or inactive end until the required length is reached.

In a factory there are simple methods of fixing the stones, both for position and also for permanent fixing, but in a workshop the tools required would be too expensive for the few jobs of this nature which would be done.

Fixing and Adjusting Pallet Stones—The easiest way to fix the stones is to have an ordinary brass plate with four steel feet to keep it off the bench, and having holes drilled which are large enough for the pallet staff to pass through. This plate is heated to the necessary

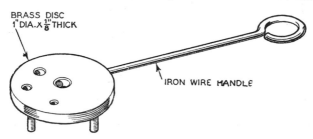

Figure 135. Simple form of pallet-warmer. A similar tool is used for blueing hands, screw-heads, *etc.*

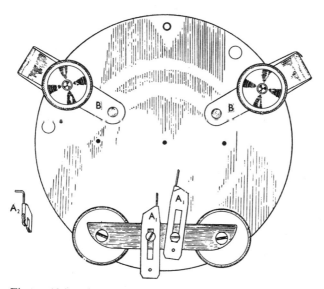

Figure 136. Tool for the location of the banking pins when inaccessible. The watch plate is fixed to the tool and the banking pins on the tool set correctly, then from their position the banking pin holes are drilled to take the permanent pins. A_1 = adjustable banking pins; A_2 = side view of A_1; B = clamps for the movement.

215

temperature, the pallets are placed on it and held in place by tweezers, the stone is placed in position and a small amount of shellac is put on the inside of the slot and allowed to melt. The stone is then moved backwards and forwards so that the shellac builds up where it is needed, after which the stone is set in its required position and lifted off the plate to cool and set.

If any adjustment is required the same procedure is adopted, but the stone is pushed forward by placing a thin wedge behind the stone, or by using a piece of pegwood or ivory to push the stone backwards. Steel tweezers should never be used to push the stone back, as they are almost certain to chip the corners off, and if this happened it would necessitate a new stone.

If and when a new pallet stone is being made a ruby or sapphire should be used; it is not worth the amount of work involved to use anything else, especially if a steel wheel is being used.

The same principle is adopted whether it is a ratchet-tooth wheel or a club tooth, the only difference being in the thickness, the ratchet tooth requiring a stone almost twice as wide.

PLATFORM ESCAPEMENTS

The details which have already been given apply in every way to most of the platform escapements which are fitted with lever escapements. The size of the escapement varies with the size of the clock, and also according to the length of time that it is required to keep going on one winding. A 30-hour clock can have a larger balance than an 8-day clock of the same size, and a slow train such as a 16,200 or a 14,400 can also carry a larger and heavier balance.

The average French carriage timepiece, which is an 8-day clock, carries a 6-size escapement, but the average French carriage repeater, which is a larger timepiece with more motive power, carries an 8-size escapement. The English clocks of a similar type usually have 10-size escapements, but they are often rather heavy and it is difficult to obtain a good vibration. Most of the later and more modern types of English platforms are now made much lighter, and this is a point in their favour.

Contrate Wheel

When a clock with a platform escapement is being dealt with it must always be ensured that the contrate wheel is correctly proportioned to the 'scape pinion of the platform, and also that the contrate wheel teeth are bevelled off about 45° and not to a knife edge, in order that there may be a constant engagement.

There are one or two types of lever escapement which are quite different from usual; in one of these the lever and pallets and the balance are on a platform but the 'scape wheel is between the frames. The pallets are the tail of the lever, and the wheel teeth engage from underneath the pallets. There is no contrate wheel. This will not be gone into fully, for if the details given have been understood there will be no difficulty experienced in handling this escapement.

In another type only the balance is vertical, but the only difference of importance is that the lever notch is at right angles to the plane of the lever. This is not a good principle, but the escapement will work if it is in good order.

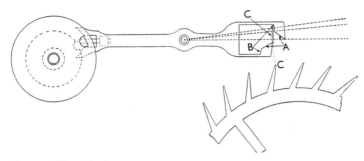

Figure 137. Platform escapement where 'scape wheel is vertical and lever and pallets horizontal. A = impulse planes in tail of lever; B = locking faces; C = 'scape wheel tooth locked: locking faces have draw as usual.

The well-known V.A.P. movement must not be forgotten. This escapement is often applied to a pendulum, but is most often seen with a lever and balance. There is no need to describe this movement in detail because it is really a large club-tooth escapement, and all that applies to a lever escapement applies in a like manner; the pallets span 7 teeth and are embraced by 8, whilst the 'scape wheel has 30 teeth, and this is really the only difference.

GENERAL REMARKS

When a lever escapement is being examined there are certain points about which one must be sure, and of these the most important is the truth of the turned parts.

Before the action can be checked the balance staff must be true so that the roller is running true. This is a point which is very much neglected. If a roller is misfitted a new staff is the only way out; it is no use bumping the roller so that it runs out of flat or truth, nor is it any good using a three-cornered punch to close the hole. Likewise a balance must fit the balance seat on the staff correctly, and that seat must be true.

Another point is that the pivots must be round and perfectly cylindrical, only the shoulder of what is termed the conical pivot is conical. The pivots must fit the jewel holes correctly, and must be long enough to pass through the hole by their own diameter but should not be any longer than this. The 'scape pinion itself must be perfectly true so that the 'scape wheel runs truly and flat. The pallet staff must be true and upright to the lever; an out-of-true pallet staff causes no end of trouble, especially if the watch is a small one which is difficult to observe.

Above all, all the parts must be turned between dead centres or by some other method which can be guaranteed trustworthy. Of course, these remarks apply to all escapements, but they must be

Figure 138. Breguet type ratchet tooth lever escapement. A = impulse pallet often solid with balance staff; B = guard roller; C = dart or guard which is often jewelled; D = impulse pins; E = pallet faces on arcs from pallet hole; F = impulse faces, curved to decrease losses. The entrance pallet is convex, the exit pallet concave; G = wheel 20 teeth; H = the lever tail which banks on 'scape pinion arbor; J = 'scape pinion arbor.

emphasised with a lever escapement, because a better performance is expected from this than from most of the others.

Before closing this chapter mention must be made of the famous horologist A. L. Breguet. It cannot be hoped to deal with all of his lever escapements, but the early ones can be analysed.

The first ones were ratchet-tooth wheels usually of 20 teeth, some having pallets spanning 3 teeth and others 4 teeth; the principle, however, was the same. The pallet faces followed the same pattern as Mudge and Emery, inasmuch as the locking faces were on circles struck from the pallet centre; thus there was no draw and nothing to prevent the dart or guard from fouling the guard roller edge.

Some of the darts, or perhaps one should say the head of the lever, were slotted and jewelled to ease the friction. The lever notch was represented by two upright pins fitted into the lever head, and the impulse roller was a triangular-shaped protuberance. In some cases this roller or pallet was also slotted and jewelled.

In the ordinary way brass pins were used if the roller was made of solid steel, but steel pins were used where the roller was jewelled. The tail of the lever was shaped to act as the banking and the 'scape-pinion arbor as a banking pin. The lever was poised by a piece of platinum riveted into the lever tail.

The Impulse Planes

The impulse planes on the pallets were curved instead of being flat, the idea being to make up the losses during the early stages of the impulse. The wheel was sunk out in the centre both sides of the wheel, thus leaving the ends of the teeth wide, the object of this being to keep the oil at the tips. The wheel teeth also had holes drilled through them to help to trap the oil. The pallet staff was often screwed into the lever, and the pallets secured to the lever by one or two pins.

Club-tooth Wheel Drilled

Breguet also made escapements with club-tooth wheels, which were also sunk out and the teeth drilled. Most Breguet lever watches had long levers and large rollers. The levers were invariably poised, and as a rule the poising was carried out by pieces of platinum

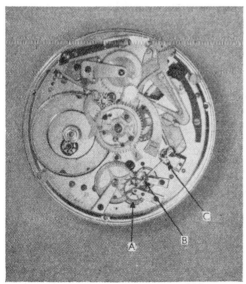

Figure 139. Breguet lever escapement. A = ratchet tooth 'scape wheel; B = lever and pallets; C = rollers.

(Reproduced by courtesy of Rt. Hon. Lord Harris.)

fitted into the tail. The later Breguet watches were very similar to the modern watch.

Another point regarding Breguet watches which must be noted is that the balance staff and rollers were very often made from one piece of steel and the balance was screwed with two screws to the table roller itself.

The impulse pin is a beautiful piece of work but is rather delicate. It is usually very wide and extremely thin, and thus has to be handled with great care. Should one of these balance staffs become broken or have to be replaced it would be a very difficult and costly job.

Breguet Parachutes

All Breguet watches were, however, provided with what were termed parachutes. These were very fine steel springs into which were fitted the balance bearings or jewelling; they are not likely to have a broken balance staff caused by a fall. This type of shock-proof mechanism is the only type one can call shockproof. The staff pivots often vary in shape, some are as usual, whilst others are pointed and back cut, somewhat resembling the profile of a spear- headed drill.

All watches by this maker must be handled with the greatest care, and not treated like the modern machine-made watch. There are, however, some watches called 'Mixed Breguet' which are in a different category. This was a cheaper type of watch.

MUDGE AND EMERY

The early lever watches by these makers were again very different from the modern watch. The 'scape wheels had 20 teeth, and in the case of Mudge were of the ratchet-tooth pattern. Those by Emery were club tooth, and had the teeth slotted to form an oil trap. A later one by Emery had 18 teeth in the 'scape wheel and the pallet faces were provided with draw. This was an improvement of great importance.

In each case almost half of the wheel was spanned by the pallets. The locking faces were circular with no draw, and thus the watches were unsuitable for pocket wear; they would, however, give a good rate if left lying flat.

The Rollers

The rollers were double rollers or on the double-roller principle. The notch was in two halves, one side being on a higher plane than the other. Each side of the notch had its own impulse pin, or in the early ones a cam instead of a pin.

The old makers were all aiming at getting the impulse to operate on or after the centre line, and some of these ideas led to complicated escapements. It must, however, be remembered that Mudge made the first detached-lever escapement and Emery followed. They had no data to work to, and had to start from scratch.

13

THE CHRONOMETER ESCAPEMENT

THE CHRONOMETER OR SPRING detent is the most accurate of all escapements, one of its greatest assets being that no oil is required except at the pivot holes.

A type of detent escapement was invented by Le Roy, but this was very different from the chronometer escapement of today, and it fell to Arnold and Earnshaw to bring the chronometer to perfection. It is difficult to say which of these two actually invented it, and it can only be assumed that they both had the idea at the same time, but Arnold's first, or what is presumed to be his first, chronometer was not a success because it was necessary to oil the wheel teeth. Arnold's escapement will be described first, and this will be followed by a description of the chronometer escapement in its present form.

THE ARNOLD SPRING DETENT ESCAPEMENT

The Arnold escapement consists of a 'scape wheel which usually has 15 teeth, although wheels of 12, 14 or 16 teeth are not uncommon, and a spring detent containing a locking stone and a passing spring. On the balance staff is an impulse roller above which is the discharging or unlocking roller. The escapement is detached and is also a single-beat; in other words, it only has impulse every alternate vibration. In considering the escapement it will be assumed that the balance is at rest, and it will therefore be examined from this position.

The 'scape wheel teeth are locked by the locking stone on the detent, which is lying against its banking screw tail. The jewel pallet in the discharging roller is just resting against the end of the passing spring, which is lying flat against and parallel with the body of the detent.

The Action of the Escapement

If the balance is moved so that the discharging pallet is moving the passing spring it will be noticed that the detent is also moving towards the centre of the 'scape wheel; as the balance continues to be moved the detent moves, carrying the locking stone out of the path of the wheel teeth, and as the detent continues to move the wheel is unlocked or released and a tooth falls or drops on to the impulse roller; as the balance continues to be moved, so the tooth is pushing on the impulse roller.

After a short period the detent will be dropped by the discharging

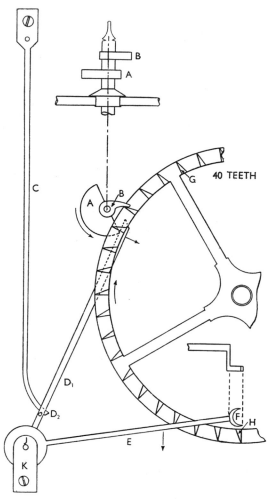

40 TEETH

Figure 140. The first detent escapement made by
Pierre Le Roy in 1752. A = roller operating the
locking; B = impulse roller or pallet; C = detent
return spring; D_1 = arm engaged by locking
roller; E = locking arm joined to D_1; F = tooth
of wheel about to be locked in crescent; G = tooth
giving impulse to roller B; H = tooth which will
be locked by F; D_2 = pin engaged by C; J =
arbor and pivots of detent; K = bar supporting
detent arbor.

222

roller, but the wheel tooth will continue to push on the impulse roller. After more movement of the balance the wheel tooth will drop off the impulse roller, and the next but one tooth in succession to the one which was previously dropped or released will be locked on the detent.

The Dummy Vibration—On its return the balance will again come against the passing spring through the discharging roller but on the opposite side. However, as the balance proceeds, instead of lifting the detent the passing spring gives way, and as the balance continues

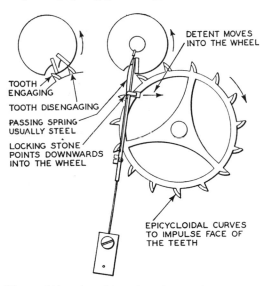

Figure 141. Arnold spring detent chronometer escapement. The detent is above the 'scape wheel and locks the root of the tooth; also the detent is moved towards the centre of the wheel to unlock. Inset shows the action of impulse.

the passing spring is released, taking up its position by the side of the detent. Thus there is no release of the wheel, and no push or impulse is given to the roller; again, on the return of the balance the sequence starts anew. It will be noticed that the detent is moved towards the centre of the 'scape wheel to unlock, also the inside or roots of the teeth are locked on the locking stone.

The Wheel Teeth—The front of the wheel teeth are curved and engage the impulse roller at the base or root of the tooth. The shape of the tooth is epicycloidal like one side of a gear-wheel tooth. This idea would be good except for the friction, and as a result of this friction

223

the teeth have to be lubricated. Another point, however, is that the method of locking the wheel has a tendency to pull on the detent, which is a distinct advantage; if, however, the unlocking was carried out the opposite way, *i.e.* by moving the detent away from the wheel, it would be unsafe, because the action would tend to throw the detent out and the wheel would be released instead of being safely locked.

Disadvantages of the Arnold Escapement

One is bound to say that the principle of the Arnold escapement is very good indeed, but the fact that it has to be lubricated outweighs the advantages that it possesses. A further disadvantage is the fact that the detent is situated between the balance and the impulse roller, and as a result the detent should be removed before the balance is removed. This may be thought to be an advantage and to make for safety, but in actual fact it increases the risk of damage; it makes certain of the 'scape wheel being released, and the wheel and detent being broken if in the hands of an inexperienced workman.

Danger to the Escapement from Inexperience—There is one golden rule which must be inflexibly applied in all instances where chrono-meters are concerned, and that is that in no circumstances should a balance be removed from a chronometer until all power is removed from the 'scape wheel, or failing this the 'scape wheel must be held by some method so that there is no possibility of it moving. If this rule is ignored the 'scape wheel will be released as the balance is removed, and as it gathers speed it will smash itself and also both the locking stone and the detent, and in all probability will run its pivots off as well. Such an accident is a costly one, and unfortu-nately is all too common.

The Locking Stone

The locking stone of an Arnold escapement is usually a rectangular slip of jewel fitted into a slot underneath the detent. The stone drops into the sunk-out centre of the wheel and must be close to the band of the wheel, but must, of course, be perfectly free when the endshake of the 'scape wheel is ' up '. That part of the stone near the body of the detent is bevelled off so that when the detent is dropped the stone cannot foul the back of the tooth it has just released. This often happens in a close escapement, and if one is unaware of it it is difficult to find such a fault.

The Passing Spring

The passing springs of most Arnold escapements are of steel and are held to the body of the detent by a rivet. The detent is banked or held in position by a banking screw, and as the passing spring often runs very close to this banking screw, care must be taken to make certain that it is perfectly free of it; also, as the detent is between the balance and the impulse roller one must make sure that the horn of the detent is perfectly clear of both.

The Draw

Another point is that the locking stone must be set so that a small amount of draw is available to make sure of a safe locking and that there is no possibility of the detent being jerked out, thus releasing the wheel at the wrong time. At the same time the draw must not be too great, because the wheel recoils as it is unlocked, and if the draw is too much the wheel teeth will be pushed on the roller edge. This fault may not be obvious, but if the action is slowly tried it will be readily seen. The offending tooth is the one resting near the far side of the roller or the last tooth which has given impulse.

The Lights

When the tooth is locked on the detent the ' lights ' must be equal, *i.e.* the two teeth spanning the roller edge must be equidistant from it. This is called the ' lights ' because the light is used to view this condition; by arranging the movement so that the light shines between the lower or pillar plate and the roller this clearance will be very obvious.

ARNOLD'S PIVOTED DETENT

There is another type of chronometer escapement also made by Arnold which has what is called a pivoted detent, and the action is different from the one already dealt with. The wheel is often of steel, and the straight side of the tooth engages the roller and gives impulse. The locking is in the reverse, *i.e.* the detent is moved away from the wheel to unlock, also instead of the detent being in one piece, as with the spring detent, it has an arbor through the centre which is pivoted between the frame. It has a separate spring to hold the detent against the banking.

The Body and the Locking Arm

The body of the detent is again a separate unit, and the locking stone or the locking arm is also separate and is adjustable for its intersection into the wheel or for depth of locking. It has no separate adjustment for positioning the detent. As with the spring detent, it has to be in such a position that when the wheel is locked the lights are equal or the wheel teeth are equidistant from the roller edge. This point does not arise where the roller is only a rectangular pallet as it is in this case, but it must be ensured that the pallet does not foul the back of the tooth on its return.

The passing spring is of steel, but is usually screwed to the body of the detent, also instead of resting along the side of the detent it lies above and banks against a pin. The pressure of the spring against this pin is the medium to unlock the detent.

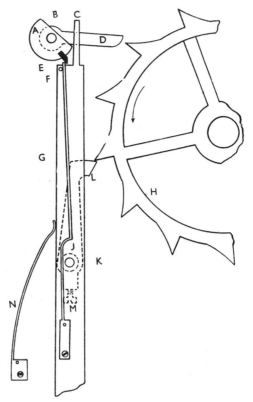

Figure 142. Early form of chronometer escapement by John Arnold with pivoted detent. A = discharging roller; B = flat side to allow horn to pass; C = horn of detent; D = impulse pallet or roller; E = discharging pallet; F = pin acted upon by passing spring; G = steel passing spring; H = wheel 15 teeth; J = locking arm; K = detent arbor; L = jewel set in arm; M = grub screw to fix locking arm when set; N = tension or return spring for detent.

It is difficult to say whether this escapement was made before the previous one, although one is inclined to believe it was; it has the disadvantage that the pivots of the detent arbor or staff have to be oiled, and also the spring returning the detent to its banking has to be oiled.

A Safety Device

There is a very interesting point regarding this escapement, and this concerns the discharging roller, which is a little more than half round and has a flat side to it. The only time that the detent can be moved to unlock the wheel is when the long horn of the detent will be in a position parallel to this flat side. At any other time the round part of the roller prevents the detent being moved either intentionally or accidentally. Thus the discharging roller acts as the safety roller. This is the only known escapement with this principle.

THE EARNSHAW ESCAPEMENT

This version of the chronometer escapement is always credited to Thomas Earnshaw, but there is some doubt as to whether Arnold or Earnshaw first invented it. There is no doubt that the two types already described went a long way towards the Earnshaw, as it will be called. However, the chronometer escapement as it is today is fundamentally the same as the Earnshaw. There are variations, just as there are different numbers of teeth in the 'scape wheels.

As with an Arnold the escapement consists of the 'scape wheel, the spring detent, the impulse roller and the discharging roller. The wheel differs from the Arnold in the shape of its teeth, the Arnold having teeth with a curved face, whereas the teeth in the Earnshaw have a straight face cut back 24° from the radial so that only the point of the tooth is in action. Another point is that whilst the wheel being locked on the detent of the Arnold tends to stretch the detent, the reverse is the case with the Earnshaw, and the locking tends to compress the detent. This is considered to be a disadvantage by some people, but if the detent is proportional there is no possible risk of buckling the detent spring.

Strength of the Spring—The spring part, which is, of course, solid with the rest of the detent, must be of such strength that the minimum amount of resistance is given to the balance, and yet strong enough to withstand the force of the wheel when it is locked on the locking stone. A good test is to place the balance with the balance spring in place into position in the frame, arranging it so that when the balance is at rest the detent is lifted half the required amount; if in this position it balances, then the detent spring is not too strong; if, however, the detent pushes the balance back against the strength of the hairspring, then the detent is too strong.

Test for a Weak Spring

If the detent is too weak the test is in action; first, the power on the wheel will tilt the locking stone, and of course the detent will fail to return to its resting place quickly enough to lock the wheel, or will bounce off again.

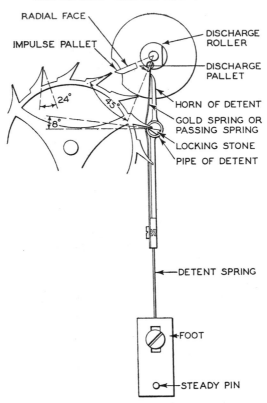

Figure 143. Spring detent chronometer escapement as invented by Thomas Earnshaw. Theoretical drawing of escapement showing the acting parts. Note detent is below the 'scape wheel.

The Draw—As with the Arnold, the locking stone must have a slight angle of draw to ensure safe locking, and about 8° is a suitable angle, as this will not recoil the wheel in unlocking sufficiently to bring the wheel tooth foul of the roller edge. The locking stone in the Earnshaw stands perpendicular to the detent, and is shaped in section like a right-angled triangle, this shape giving the maximum clearance to the back of the tooth previously released.

Half-round Locking Stones—Some Continental chronometers have half-round locking stones, but as will be seen the roller is different, although the action in regard to the release of the wheel is very similar. In the Earnshaw the passing spring is of gold and is usually screwed to the side of the body of the detent. A slot is filed in the

228

foot of the spring instead of a round hole, and this allows for adjustments to be made to the depth of the spring in the discharging roller.

Differences between the Arnold and Earnshaw

The differences between the Arnold and the Earnshaw are, first, that whereas the detent in the Arnold is moved towards the centre of the 'scape wheel to unlock the wheel, with the Earnshaw the detent is moved away from the wheel, and secondly, whereas the Arnold 'scape wheel is locked at the back of the locking stone, the Earnshaw has the locking on the front of the stone, or near the horn of the detent or the balance staff; one might almost say that the two escapements are in reverse to one another.

The Impulse

The Earnshaw scores in the impulse or in the way in which the impulse is given, and it is this which really made the chronometer escapement. Not only is oil unnecessary but it is also imperative that no oil is given in any circumstances, as any oil on any part of the escapement other than the pivot holes is detrimental to the correct action of the escapement.

In action, the impulse is given almost as a blow, and is thus: as the balance moves, the discharging pallet on the balance staff engages the passing or gold spring and moves the detent until the locking stone releases the wheel tooth; as one tooth drops the next in advance engages the impulse pallet, which is a jewel set into the impulse roller; as the balance proceeds the wheel tooth continues to push the pallet, and after a short movement the detent is released and drops back to rest ready to lock the next tooth. The wheel tooth continues to push on the pallet until the tooth drops off, and the appropriate tooth is locked on the detent. The point is the only part of the tooth in action.

As with the Arnold, when the balance returns it again lifts the passing spring, but away from the side of the detent which is not lifted. As the balance carries on the passing spring is dropped to rest beside the detent. Thus no impulse is given and no movement is given to the detent.

Action of the Passing or Gold Spring

When the escapement is being examined this latter action must be closely watched, because if the gold spring is strong and the detent is weak or not properly set on, the fact of the gold spring falling may lift the detent and unlock the wheel at the wrong time. If this does not stop the chronometer it will play havoc with its rate.

The term ' set on ' means that the detent will move to the band of the wheel if the banking screw is withdrawn.

The Locking—The amount that the detent is lifted is important, with a marine chronometer the locking should be about one-third the width of the locking stone, *i.e.* about 0·015 in. Thus the detent must be lifted far enough to release the wheel tooth. If everything was perfect and there were no freedoms anywhere this would be enough, but as there must be freedom in the bearings, *etc.*, there must be a greater lift of the detent to make sure that the wheel is released.

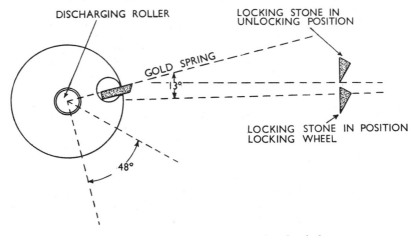

Figure 144. Chronometer escapement showing balance arc.

The general rule, and a very good one too, is that the detent should be lifted enough to release the wheel plus half as much again. Therefore if the locking is 0·015 in. the detent must be lifted 0·022 in., *i.e.* 0·015 + 0·007 in. Likewise, on the return or dummy vibration the gold spring must be lifted the same amount as when it is unlocking.

Adjustment of the Detent Horn—When the escapement is examined it is often found that this action is unequal, *i.e.* the lift for the unlocking is less than for the passing; if this is so, the action must be altered because it means that the detent is out of line or out of angle. If this is the case the horn of the detent requires alteration. As the unlocking is less than the passing, the horn must be bent towards the gold spring so that the action starts earlier or nearer the centre line. This will lessen the action of the gold spring on the passing, but will increase the lifting. If the unlocking is too great and the passing lighter, then the detent horn is bent away from the passing or gold spring.

Lift of the Detent—If when the two lifts have been equalised the detent lifts higher than required it means that the gold-spring action is too deep into the discharging roller. This means that the gold spring must be pushed back a little or it can be shortened the required amount. Of course, if the unlocking is too light the gold spring must be lengthened or pushed forward to engage deeper into the discharging roller. If this action is too deep it means that the detent may not be released from the discharging roller quickly or early enough to be in place to lock the wheel tooth after the impulse is given.

This action may be tried slowly and it will appear quite safe, but in action, where everything is happening in a short time, the chances are that it will miss the tooth. A good test for this is to try the action slowly. The balance is moved to unlock the wheel, and the wheel tooth will drop on the impulse pallet, then the balance is moved farther the same way and the point at which the detent is dropped is carefully noted. This dropping should take place as soon as the wheel has given about one-quarter of its impulse, or after the detent is dropped the wheel should be giving impulse three times as long as it took to release the detent. This nearly always works out correctly.

Altering the Drop

As the action is being tried slowly it must be particularly noticed *when* the wheel tooth drops off the locking stone. The tooth near the roller which is to give impulse will move or drop at the same time as the locked tooth is released. This tooth should drop cleanly on to the impulse pallet, not on to the roller in front or on to the roller edge behind. If the tooth drops in front it has missed the pallet, and therefore the roller must be altered to correct this fault.

The roller must be moved in the same direction as the balance will move when it is given impulse, or the drop must be increased. The easiest way to do this is to move the discharging roller the opposite way, or in other words, looking at the two rollers it will be noticed that the angle between the impulse pallet and the discharging pallet is about 90°. When more drop is being given the angle between the two must be reduced or closed up the required amount. If, on the other hand, the tooth drops on to the roller edge behind the impulse pallet there is too much drop or the impulse roller is too much in advance; in this case the angle between the two pallets is widened.

The Solid Impulse Roller

Where the impulse roller is solid and has no pallet the face of the roller which receives impulse is considered the impulse pallet. A solid roller is not detrimental to the action of the escapement, but a jewel is preferable because this does not wear and the friction is also less. A jewel pallet can be polished to a much higher degree than a steel one.

As has been noticed with all of the escapements, drop is loss, and as such must be kept to a minimum. With a chronometer the drop can be varied within limits, the main control of the drop being the intersection of the wheel into the roller. The aim is to have this intersection so that each tooth of the wheel is about 1° clear of the roller edge when at rest and with the wheel locked on the detent.

There are 24° between each two teeth if the wheel is of 15 teeth, thus if 1° clearance is allowed each side the roller intersects the

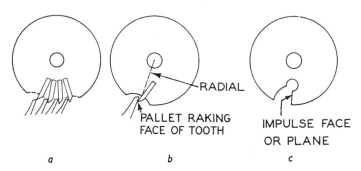

RADIAL

PALLET RAKING
FACE OF TOOTH

IMPULSE FACE
OR PLANE

a   *b*   *c*

Figure 145. Spring detent chronometer escapement: *a* stages of impulse when impulse pallet is correctly fitted; only the tips of the tooth are in action; *b* action of impulse pallet when incorrectly fitted. The pallet cuts a hollow in the side of wheel tooth, greatly increases the friction and spoils the close rate. It acts like a pinion which is too large; *c* solid roller instead of jewel pallet. Gives a good performance until worn, but can be easily repolished.

wheel 22°. In the case of a wheel of 12 teeth, where there is 30° between each two teeth, the roller will intersect 28°. In the case of a wheel of 15 teeth the diameter of the roller is made half the diameter of the 'scape wheel, and this gives an ideal intersection with the minimum amount of engaging friction.

Foreign Chronometers without Safety Edge to Roller

The Continental manufacturers do not always adopt this principle in their chronometers, and one often finds that the impulse pallet stands beyond the roller edge and that there is quite a gap between the roller edge and the wheel teeth. The advantage with the English type is that the roller edge serves as a guard and prevents the wheel running through if released at the wrong time. If, however, the circle scribed by the protruding pallet is measured it will be found that the proportions of the action are the same as the English.

English Roller Adopted Abroad—It is difficult to understand why the roller edge is made smaller, the only reason that can be seen is that a D-shaped or half-round locking stone, which is easier to manufacture, can be used. It has, however, been noticed that all the latest marine chronometers manufactured by Lange of Germany and by Ulysse Nardin of Switzerland have adopted the English type of roller, and the impulse pallet is coincident with the roller edge.

Locking Stone Foul of Back Tooth—The idea of the triangular locking stone is to enable the actions to be closer and the drop less. If a chronometer escapement has the wheel planted very close the drop off the locking stone is close, and as the detent is released it may drop on to the back of the tooth is has just released. This will spoil the rate of any chronometer because it may push the wheel or retard it, depending on the smoothness of the back of the tooth. Now if the intersection of a wheel into the roller is increased the friction can be very severe, so this is kept as small as possible.

If the wheel is one of 12 teeth the size of the roller has to be increased in proportion to the wheel in order to keep the intersection low; if, on the other hand, the wheel is one of 16 teeth, like the Ulysse Nardin or the American Hamilton, the size of the roller must be decreased in proportion to the wheel.

The Disadvantage of a 16-Tooth Wheel—The disadvantage with a wheel of 16 teeth is that the intersection is small, and this, of course,

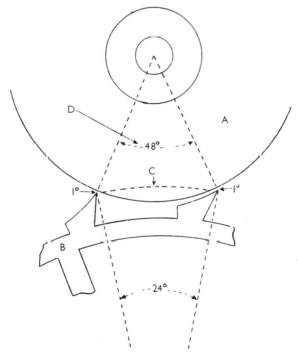

Figure 146. Wheel and roller diameters 2 : 1 showing wheel teeth 24° apart but balance arc 48°. In each of these cases there is loss of 1° each side for freedom.

means that extra motive power is required. If the wheel is one of 16 teeth there is 22·5° between the two teeth into which the roller intersects. This reduces the balance arc in the case of a 2 : 1 proportion of the wheel and roller, but it also makes the arc of intersection more shallow or flat, which means that there must be more drop to secure a safe impulse or that a proportionately smaller roller must be used. If a smaller roller has to be used extra motive power is required.

Experiments by English Makers

As a result of experiments carried out over a number of years by English makers, such as Johannsen and Kullberg, both of whom were Scandinavians who came over to England and made English chronometers, and E. Dent & Co. and Frodsham, both well-known firms, the conclusion was reached that a wheel of 15 teeth with a 2 : 1 proportion of wheel to roller was the best combination. It must be admitted that these four firms stood alone in the production of the chronometer as it is today. The German chronometers mentioned earlier all adopted this same principle.

It is an interesting point that a 2-day marine chronometer requires more motive power than an 8-day regulator, and the motive power required for an 8-day chronometer will be even greater.

The Impulse Pallet

Another point of major importance is the way in which the impulse is given to the impulse roller. The action with a solid roller is usually correct, and if the impulse face is examined it will be seen that it is radial to the centre of the roller.

If the chronometer is an old one the wear on the face will be noticed, and this will give one an idea of the amount that the wheel tooth slides down the face as the impulse proceeds. This wear must always be polished out, because it reduces the effectiveness of the impulse. When the impulse face is radial, whether it is jewel or solid, only the point of the wheel tooth is in action, and the actual engagement of the pallet by the wheel tooth is more certain. Some chronometer makers, including A. L. Breguet, set the impulse pallet at an angle so that the point of the pallet was advanced in the direction from which it received impulse. The later types by Breguet were made with the pallet radial.

The result of this was that the point of the pallet ran down the face of the tooth until the centre of the impulse was reached, when the point of the tooth then took over the remaining part of the impulse, thus causing a small indentation to be worn in the top of the wheel tooth; after a period this tended to lock on to the pallet and could break the balance staff if it happened at the right moment and if the vibration were a large one. In order to offset this the drop of the tooth on to the impulse pallet had to be increased; again, after a period another indentation was formed, with the same result, and once more extra drop had to be given.

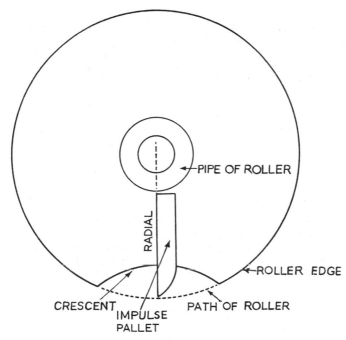

Figure 147.   Correct position of impulse pallet in a chronometer
escapement.

Impulse Pallet Placed at Angle—The idea of this angled pallet was an
endeavour to obtain the same results as with an involute gear, and
the same results that Arnold had in mind when he brought out
his escapement, in which the face of the wheel tooth was curved.

No doubt Arnold had the right idea, and all the watchmakers
were working on these lines at that time. If, however, the two
actions, or perhaps one should say the three actions, are compared
one will not fail to see the advantages of the radial impulse pallet.
The action is exactly the same where the pallet is advanced, and gives
the same result as would a very large pinion in proportion to the
wheel in a gearing train of wheels.

The Fit of the Pivots to their Holes

With any chronometer both the 'scape and balance pivots must
be very close in their holes or bearings, both for endshake and side
shake.   The intersections are all very critical, and it is often found
that although the chronometer functions well when tilted in one
direction, say with the balance towards the 'scape wheel, when it is
tilted so that the balance tends to move away from the wheel the

235

chronometer stops, although the balance continues to vibrate. More often than not this fault indicates easy fitting or wide holes in the balance staff caused by the discharging pallet missing the gold spring.

It may be thought that by increasing the action of the gold spring this trouble will be overcome, but it will be so only at the expense of the efficiency of the escapement. If this trouble is present either new pivots which fit the holes or else new and smaller jewel holes to fit the pivots must be fitted. Above all, in order to get a good rate from a chronometer the pivots must be perfectly cylindrical, and highly polished.

Tapering Pivots and Fit of Detent—Any forward tapering of the pivot must be corrected, because as the endshakes vary so do the pivot freedoms, *i.e.* when the endshake is away from the tapering pivot a smaller part of the pivot is in the hole. In the same way the detent must be firmly anchored, and if possible should be so arranged that it can be taken off and replaced without any change in position. There is no greater nuisance than that caused by a detent taking up a different position each time the chronometer is dismantled for repairs and then re-assembled.

The Locking Stone

The locking stone of a chronometer fits into either a slot cut into the body of the detent or, as in the case of most modern chronometers, into a pipe which is part of the body. The stone should be long enough to fit firmly into its seat or pipe, and be sufficiently proud to stand slightly above the top of the wheel.

Some makers intentionally tilted the stone, so that either the top or bottom only of the tooth engaged the stone, and the impulse pallet on the roller was tilted in the opposite way so that the wear on the wheel was halved. Whether this was any advantage is just a matter of opinion.

Fixing the Locking Stone—Where the seat for the stone is only a slot, as in the case of the Arnold, the stone is simply fixed in place with shellac. With a piped detent the locking stone is fitted to the pipe and a D-shaped wedge, usually of brass, is placed in the pipe with the stone, the wedge being so shaped that it does not protrude at either end of the pipe and holds the locking stone firmly but not tightly in position.

The pipe and wedge are then securely fixed with shellac; this fixing must be nicely carried out, because one does not want shellac all over the place. A pair of sliding tongs placed on the pipe of the detent or on the body of the detent near the pipe is ideal for the job, and these tongs are heated whilst holding the detent so that the heat travels from them to the pipe. A small piece of shellac just sufficient for the job is applied to the inactive end of the pipe, and as the heat reaches it the shellac melts and runs into the pipe.

Clearing Surplus Shellac—As the shellac melts it will form on the end of the pipe like a bubble, but as it cools it will run into the pipe and be flush with it. If the shellac does stand above the pipe it can be scraped off with a graver point when it is cool; if it is left standing above it may foul the thread of the banking screw, and if it stands above on the active end of the pipe it may be fouled by the 'scape wheel teeth.

If any shellac gets on to the sides of the pipe it must be cleaned away, because if the shellac is on one side it will interfere with the locking, as it will be between the banking-screw head and the pipe, and if it is on the other side it will interfere with the gold spring and prevent it occupying its correct position in relation to the horn of the detent.

TYPES OF DETENT

There are many types of detent and many ways of fixing them in position. Many of the early chronometers had the detent made with a dovetailed foot, and this was a very good idea, because it almost assured the position of the detent. There was a screw with an eccentric pivot which decided the forward but not the backward position of the detent.

The securing screw was slope headed to correspond with the slope of the side of the detent foot. This screw and the dovetailed section on the slide secured the detent in its horizontal plane. This was all in order until the detent was replaced; if the new one did not correspond it meant trouble.

The Foot Detent

The foot detent as it is called is the best answer, but it is much more difficult to make. In the case of marine chronometers the screw securing the detent is a shouldered one, and this shoulder fits the rectangular slot in the plate. A steady pin in the foot of the detent fixes the position from back to front. Now if the steady pin fits its hole closely but not tightly, and the shoulder of the screw fits the plate closely, there is a constant factor, and the detent can be taken out and put back with the assurance of the position being constant. With pocket chronometers of the three-quarter plate or half plate types the detent has the rectangular hole instead of the plate, but the advantage is the same.

The Germans fit their detents to a brass block, and there are two steady pins and a screw to secure the detent with one of the pins at the back and one at the front of the foot. The steady pins position the detent both horizontally and back and front, being made secure by the screw which is between the two steady pins. This is a very good arrangement, and the detent is easier to replace.

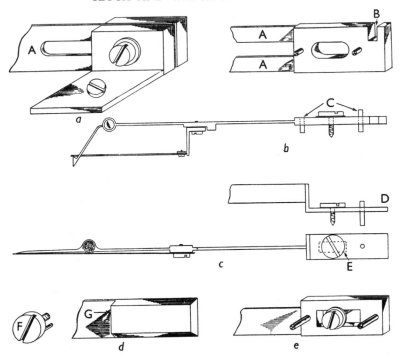

Figure 148. Types of spring detents used in a chronometer escapement: *a* Breguet type clamp for detent, A = double spring; *b* Ulysse Nardin and Hamilton detent, A = double spring, B = slot for head of adjusting screw; *c* typical English detent, D = $\frac{3}{4}$ or $\frac{1}{2}$ plate, E = $\frac{3}{4}$ or $\frac{1}{2}$ plate rectangular hole; *d* full plate or marine dovetail foot which is held against banking screw F in position indicated at G; *e* German type of detent foot. In this case the detent proper is the same as the English type.

Adjustable Detent

The Ulysse Nardin and the Hamilton have a similar arrangement but of an adjustable nature. The two steady pins are fitted tightly into the detent foot but run closely into a slot in the detent banking block, thus the detent can slide backwards and forwards. The visible end of the banking block is fitted with a square-headed screw which rests on the back of the detent foot. This allows one to push the detent nearer to the staff by screwing in the screw, but it has to be pulled back with tweezers as there is no arrangement for carrying out this operation. The Hamilton has a cut-out slot for the screw to fit into. This enables the detent to be pulled out as well. The detent is secured by a screw between the steady pins which screws into the banking block. The detent foot has an elongated hole

238

through which the securing screw passes to allow for adjustment, thus every time these are taken to pieces readjustment is necessary. An adjustable detent is at all times a nuisance.

In cases where the detent is fitted to the banking block the complete unit can be removed from the frame by removing the screw passing through from the plate.

The Pivoted Detent

The pivoted detent, of which there were many types, was favoured by the Continental manufacturers. The principle was much the same as with the solid detent, but instead of the detent body and

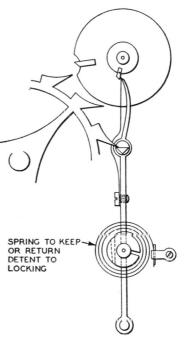

Figure 149. Pivoted detent chronometer escapement. The detent is mounted on the arbor and is pivoted between a cock and the plate. The action is the same as the Earnshaw, but the pivots of the detent arbor have to be oiled, thus spoiling the qualities of the escapement. The spring used to return the detent to locking is similar to a balance spring

SPRING TO KEEP OR RETURN DETENT TO LOCKING

spring being one piece of steel, the body had an arbor through the centre which was pivoted between the frames or between a bar and the frame.

The spring was often like a hairspring and was fitted in the same way, *i.e.* first to a collet which fitted the detent arbor and anchored to a steel stud screwed to the plate. The tension of the spring could be adjusted to the correct tension for safe locking by twisting the collet on the detent arbor. In some cases a spring was screwed to the side of the body of the detent and the tail of the spring fitted into a slot cut in the plate, whilst in another type a spring was

239

screwed to the plate, which acted on a pin fitted into the body of the detent.

The hairspring type was the lesser of the evils, because all the others had to have the springs oiled where they moved or rubbed. In any case the advantages of the detent were lost because the arbor pivots had to be oiled.

Planting the Detent

Looking from the top plate, there are two ways in which a detent can be planted, *i.e.* either on the left or right side of the wheel, whichever way the wheel turns. When viewed from the top plate the 'scape wheel of a marine chronometer turns clockwise, therefore the detent must be planted on the right-hand side of the wheel, but in the case of an Arnold the detent must be planted on the left-hand side.

The ideal arrangement is for the detent to be as near tangential to the wheel as possible, *i.e.* the whole of the detent should be on a line drawn from the balance-staff hole passing through the point where the locking takes place and through the screw hole securing the detent. By this means a straight detent and an almost straight passing or gold spring are obtained.

Ulysse Nardin and Hamilton Types of Detent

Apart from the risk involved, it is a nuisance to have to bend the horn of the detent so that the action can be correctly lined up, although the horn is always softened. The Ulysse Nardin and the Hamilton, almost identical chronometers, have their detents planted in such a way that the horn of the detent is bent about 45°. This makes it a difficult detent to replace.

Another point about these chronometers is that the gold or passing spring is mounted on an angular bracket, which is in turn screwed to the body of the detent. This is rather an elaborate arrangement for obtaining results which could be far more easily secured.

Differences are also to be found in the spring of the detent. The Nardin and Hamilton have the spring divided into two blades, very similar to the early chronometers of A. L. Breguet. It is difficult to see the object in these types, for the plain single spring always seems to be more rigid and will certainly stand handling much better, and is also easier to rectify in the case of accidental damage, whilst it is very difficult to straighten out the double spring if it becomes buckled in any way.

Thickness of Detent Spring

It is sometimes maintained that the spring should be thinner near the foot than at any other part of the spring, but again the disadvantages outweigh the advantages. If it is thin near the foot it is more easily broken, and it seems much better for the spring to bend overall rather than to have the bending concentrated in one spot. If the spring is parallel, with its thinness spread out over the whole of its length, it will be more rigid.

Planting the 'Scape Wheel

When chronometer escapements are being made the aim is to have the impulse roller as nearly as possible mid-way between the two pivots or ends of the balance staff. In order to do this the 'scape wheel must be as high as possible, *i.e.* in the case of a marine chronometer it should be as near as possible to the top plate. The Nardin and Hamilton chronometers go one better and have their wheels brought neatly through the plate, and also have a separate bridge for the top 'scape pivot, a very sound idea.

The Advantage of a Full Plate

Marine chronometers are invariably full plates, or in other words the balance is mounted over the top of the top plate and the plate is not cut out to receive it. The whole of the mechanism other than this is between the plates. This makes the overall thickness of the instrument greater, but this does not matter as much as it would in the case of a pocket chronometer.

The full plate has a great deal of advantage over the three-quarter or half plates, and there are no obstructions like a 'scape cock or fourth cock to contend with; these certainly are a factor to be considered, and they can affect the rate of a chronometer to a great extent due to barometric changes, or it may be said that they can increase any barometric error.

Most 8-day marine chronometers have a guard fitted round the balance to protect it in case of the chain or mainspring breaking. If this guard is omitted the variation from mean time is surprising. This variation is caused by the air which is disturbed by the balance heaping up against obstructions and retarding the balance. In a three-quarter-plate or half-plate pocket chronometer the 'scape cock and fourth cock have the same effect.

Jules Jurgenson, a famous Danish watchmaker, designed his watches without any obstruction to the balance, and it was evidently realised that these various cocks do cause interference with the free run of the balance.

Pitching the 'Scape Wheel and Roller

Another point when making a chronometer escapement is that the 'scape wheel and impulse roller come into the picture only when the escapement is being pitched. It is usual to plant the wheel and roller so that there is no freedom between the two teeth spanning the roller and the roller edge. The pitching is carried out while the wheel and roller are in the ' rough ' as it is called. The amount of metal taken off in finishing the roller edge is sufficient to give the necessary freedoms.

Polishing the Roller Edge

The roller edge can be polished in several ways, but the easiest is to have three rollers, one on each side of the one which is being used on an arbor, and to polish all three together. This method prevents the polisher bumping into the crescent as the roller revolves. The guide rollers can be soft, but the roller which is to be used must be made of steel and must be hardened and tempered. In order to obtain a high polish it is better if the roller is as hard as possible, or so that it can only just be turned with a graver. Another advantage about a hard roller is that it is not so easily damaged. It must be remembered that all roller edges must be smooth wherever they are likely to come into action and the impulse roller edge is the guard.

Slotting the Roller to take the Impulse Pallet

As stated earlier, some rollers are solid, but most of them have a jewel impulse pallet. When making a roller which is to have a jewelled pallet a slot has to be cut to take the pallet, and this can be carried out either in the turns or in the lathe. A circular saw is mounted between centres in the turns or on an arbor in the lathe,

Figure 150. Holder for impulse roller used to cut slot for impulse pallet. The two screws can be changed to suit the size of roller.

then the roller is held in a holder fitted to the slide rest of the lathe or to a slide on the T-rest holder; the roller is slowly presented to the saw as it revolves.

The saw cut needs to be as deep as possible in order to give the pallet plenty of holding surface. The slot is perfectly radial to the centre of the roller, and, of course, must be cut whilst the roller is soft.

Fixing the Jewel Impulse Pallet

The pallet is fitted by holding the roller on a tool similar to the arrangement used for fitting an impulse pin, and only the minimum amount of shellac is used so that a nice clean job is the result. The block on the tool is sufficiently heated to melt the shellac, but not to such a heat that it colours the roller.

The stone is placed about halfway from back to front and also halfway through the roller, and as the shellac melts the pallet is wriggled about until the part of the stone which is to go in the slot is lightly smeared with shellac, as is also the slot in the roller. The pallet is then placed in its permanent position and allowed to cool. It pays to clean the slot and the pallet in methylated spirit prior to setting the stone, as this acts like a flux and the shellac runs more easily into place.

The Roller Crescent

The roller crescent is polished in just the same way as a crescent in the roller of a lever escapement.

The Discharging Roller

The discharging roller is not difficult to make, the aim being to have it as small as possible, because the smaller it is the easier it will lift the detent, and also the intersection into the gold spring will be relatively deeper; at the same time the roller can be so small that at no time can it lift the detent far enough. The usual size for a discharging roller is about one-quarter the diameter of the impulse roller. The pallet will, of course, stand out beyond this roller edge, so the acting radius will be about three-fifths the diameter of the impulse roller, but it should be no larger than this.

The Discharging Pallet

The pallet is of triangular section with one side rounded and the other flat, the flat being the lifting side of the pallet or the side which

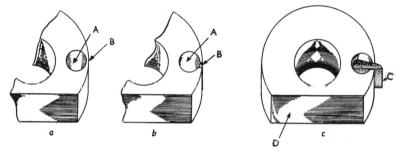

Figure 151. Making a discharging roller: *a* hole drilled safely inside edge, A — hole; B = metal left after drilling; *b* slot filed to open aperture; *c* discharging roller with jewel pallet C in position. The flat side for adjusting the position of the roller is indicated at D.

lifts the detent to unlock the wheel. In order to fit the discharging pallet the roller is made to size, and then a hole is drilled through the whole length of the roller and as near as possible to the edge, but just not breaking through. After the hole is drilled its edge is broken into with a file. Thus the discharging pallet by its shape will slide into this shaped slot, after which it is again secured with shellac. If the pallet is correct it cannot fall out at the front but can only slide out.

243

Filing Flat on the Discharging Roller—It is always advisable to file a flat side on the edge of the roller at right angles to the pallet, to help to grip when the roller is being adjusted for position during the setting up of the escapement. The method employed for fitting this roller differs from that used for fitting an impulse roller in so far as whilst this one must not be viciously tight on the balance staff, the impulse roller must be very tight, although it should not, of course, be driven on with a hammer in any circumstances; if a roller is correctly fitted to the staff it is certain to be tight when pushed home.

Sinking and Crossing out the 'Scape Wheel

The 'scape wheel of a chronometer escapement has the centre of the wheel turned or sunk out so that the main weight of the wheel is on the outside edge. The wheel is crossed out so that it is as light as possible and yet of sufficient strength to be handled, the idea being to counteract inertia. It does not matter whether there are 3 or 4 arms to the crossing, as this is just a matter of convenience or choice.

The front face of the wheel is not touched at all after cutting, but the concave part of the tooth is polished. The point of the tooth must be thin but not razor-edged, and a very slight flat is most desirable, but it must be no thicker than absolutely necessary, because any thickness is, of course, loss of impulse.

Thinning the Detent Spring

The making of a detent was described in the author's book *Watch and Clock Making and Repairing*, so there is no need to deal with this in detail again; a few comments, however, will not come amiss. The detent spring is thinned after the detent construction, planting, *etc.*, is all complete. The easiest way to thin this spring is to rest it on a piece of cork cut to about twice the width and exactly the same length as the spring, *i.e.* the length between the gold spring block and the foot of the detent.

The actual thinning is done with a soft steel polisher a little narrower than the length of the spring so that there is very little side play. The edge of the polisher is curved to avoid catching the edge of the foot or the block. The polisher is surfaced with a file and is then charged with oilstone powder and oil. It is rubbed backwards and forwards and also with a combined sideways movement on the spring to-be.

Keeping the Spring Flat and Parallel—The spring is resting on the shaped cork, and the give in the cork helps to keep the spring flat. When the spring is to the correct thickness it is thoroughly cleaned, a fresh piece of cork is cut and the polishing is completed using a zinc polisher smeared with diamantine instead of the steel polisher. The same action is used as with the steel polisher until the spring is highly polished. When it is finished one should be able to bend the spring almost to a right angle and it should still return to straight when released.

Set of the Detent

When the detent is in place and the banking screw removed the locking-stone pipe should reach the band of the wheel; it should not be hard on the band but just definitely on it. This ensures that the detent is firm against the banking screw when in action.

Strength of the Gold Spring

The gold spring or passing spring should be very much weaker than the detent spring, and if the detent is held by the foot it should be possible to move the gold spring away from the side of the detent a little more than its movement in action without moving the detent. This can, of course, be done if the detent spring is too strong, but one has to consider that the test for the detent has already been carried out.

Putting a Chronometer in Beat

Putting a chronometer in beat is quite a different operation from putting a lever in beat, because a chronometer receives impulse in only one direction, but at the same time one must aim at getting the same or a similar result.

The general rule is to lead the balance from rest, moving in the direction to unlock the wheel and receive impulse. The balance is led the full distance until the wheel tooth drops off the impulse pallet after giving impulse. Immediately the tooth drops the balance is released and the chronometer should start and carry on. Again holding the balance at rest, it is moved in the opposite direction, *i.e.* the way it receives no impulse; as the balance is moved it lifts the gold spring and after a short period drops or releases it. Immediately the gold spring is dropped the balance is released and the chronometer should start and carry on.

If, however, the chronometer fails to start after the gold spring is dropped, then the balance-spring collet must be turned in the direction in which the balance is moving when lifting the gold spring, or to put it another way the balance must be moved in relation to the hairspring and in the opposite way to which it is moving.

This action has the effect of moving the discharging pallet a little farther away from the gold spring when the balance is at rest, and thus delays the action of the discharging pallet, or the balance must be moved a little farther round before the gold spring is dropped. If it fails to start on the impulse side the reverse is, of course, the case, providing that the escapement is in good order.

Setting Heavier on the Impulse Side

There are certain things to contend with on the impulse side, *e.g.* if the detent is too strong the chronometer will have difficulty in starting.

Another point is that if the motive power is too weak the chronometer may not start on the impulse side, thus although the actions may be equal, it does not follow that the chronometer will start off.

As is already known, the chronometer sets very heavily, and unlike the lever or cylinder it will not start off on its own if it is stopped. When a chronometer is run down the balance will sometimes come to rest with the wheel tooth on the impulse pallet in a released condition, and in this state the chronometer will probably start off as soon as motive power is applied. If, however, it is at rest with the wheel locked it will not start off without a twist of the movement.

Chronometer Set out of Beat Intentionally

It has been stated that a chronometer gives a better performance if it is intentionally set off beat, *i.e.* with the balance spring so arranged that when the balance is at rest the impulse pallet will be in such a position that it has apparently received half its impulse, or in other words it is half the length of impulse out of beat. This is a mistake, because if one side of the escapement is favoured the other side is handicapped by the same amount. Another point is that this error must make any irregularity in the motive power more apparent and more effective. The idea of this arrangement is that the impulse is delivered after the dead point or neutral point in the balance spring.

Affect of Changes in Motive Power

All escapements are affected by changes in motive power, however well they are made, and the only way to combat this is by the adjustment of the terminal curves of the balance spring. In other words, the terminal curves must be so formed that any alteration in the arc of vibration will be performed in the same time. Any natural error is a constant factor and can be taken care of by the balance spring.

Ferguson Cole's Escapement

Many experiments have been carried out to overcome escapement errors. Ferguson Cole constructed a chronometer escapement on very similar lines to the method he adopted with a duplex, in which the discharging roller was mounted on an arbor pivoted in the frame instead of being mounted on the balance (see Figure 94).

The arbor was provided with a wheel, and a wheel of the same number of teeth was also mounted on the balance staff. These two wheels were geared together, and thus as the balance turned so the arbor with the discharging roller turned also, and the same unlocking action was carried out by this secondary arbor. Whatever advantages were to be found in this arrangement were outweighed by its disadvantages, which were the extra friction in the gearing and also two extra pivots which had to be oiled. The locking could be arranged so that the detent tended to be stretched rather than compressed, and any other advantages could be obtained in the usual type of escapement.

DUPLEX WHEEL CHRONOMETER

The duplex chronometer was another idea, and consisted of a 'scape wheel having two sets of teeth very much like a duplex 'scape wheel, and hence its name. The horizontal teeth were locked by the detent, and the vertical teeth engaged the impulse roller. It is difficult to see any advantage, but the wheel is difficult to cut.

DUPLEX LEVER CHRONOMETER

This was another type of duplex chronometer, which was not really a chronometer except that the impulse was given in a similar manner, and was a combination of lever duplex and chronometer.

The pallets had no locking faces, but were made so that all the drop was inside the pallets, which were mounted on a staff pivoted

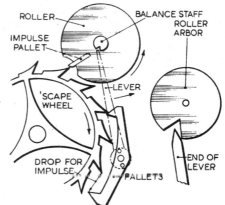

Figure 152. Single-beat escapement after duplex.

between the frames. Also mounted on the staff was an arrangement like a brass finger thinned to a point where it engaged the balance staff, the latter having had a groove cut into it like the slot in the ruby roller of a duplex. The finger rested on one side of the staff, and as the balance was turned the finger dropped into the slot; as the balance continued the finger was released, and this in turn through the pallets, released the 'scape wheel; thus the roller on the balance staff received impulse in the same manner as a chronometer.

As soon as the wheel dropped off the impulse pallet the finger was returned to the staff by the action of the wheel and pallets; as the balance returned the finger dropped into the slot and was carried across whilst the wheel was released and left ready for the next impulse. There are only disadvantages in the arrangement and no compensating advantages, and it is to be wondered whether the idea was for safety rather than for an improved performance.

LEVER CHRONOMETER

Another type of escapement very similar to this duplex type bore more similarity to the lever, and the notch action was almost identical to the old club-roller lever escapement. The impulse pin is the unlocking pin, and is as close to the balance staff as possible; in

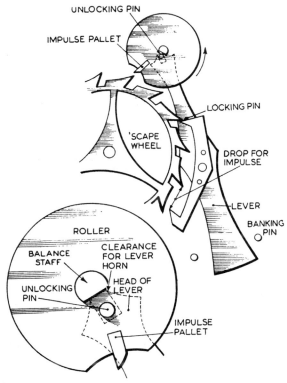

Figure 153. Single-beat escapement action with lever.

fact, the hole to receive the pin is drilled through the pipe of the roller, on which is also carried the impulse pallet.

In both of these types of single-beat escapement the impulse rollers are the same as in the usual chronometer, but they do not act as a guard, because they are smaller in proportion to allow extra clearance for the first short drop from the outside pallet where no impulse is given. The 'lights' cannot therefore be equal, because one tooth is always nearer to the roller edge than the other when the balance is at rest.

One is inclined to think that the duplex type is the lesser of the two evils and that it would certainly give a better performance. If it is provided with a jewel for the lever to act upon instead of the steel balance staff it may be quite a good idea, but the pallets and also the pallet-staff pivots must be oiled, and this would be a serious loss to a chronometer.

POCKET CHRONOMETERS

The principles already dealt with apply in the same way to pocket chronometers, and in fact most of the older watches of this type were made entirely on these principles. All of the older ones were full plates, and even in wear gave a very good account of themselves; a number of these are still in use today after many years of service. The later ones, however, were made as three-quarter and half-plate watches.

Vibrations per Hour—The marine-chronometer balance beats 14,400 vibrations per hour or 4 per second, 2 of these being dummy and 2 impulse. The pocket chronometers were provided with an 18,000 or 21,600 train. The disadvantage of an 18,000 train which was 5 beats per second was that the true second was shown only every alternate second, or in other words the beat was $2\frac{1}{2}$ per second. The 21,600, which is 6 vibrations per second or 3 beats, was preferable because it gave the true second, and also being a fast train there was less likelihood of the chronometer setting should it receive a shake when the wearer was performing any vigorous action.

The Pocket Chronometer Detent

The detents in the three-quarter or half plates were different from the marine or full plate. The latter had the screw tapped into the detent itself and the rectangular slot for setting the detent in position in the plate, but the three-quarter of half plate had the screw tapped into the plate and the rectangular hole in the detent foot.

Objections to Pocket Chronometers—The rollers vary in proportion to the wheel, consequent upon experiments carried out to help to prevent the chronometer setting in wear. This setting is one of the objections to pocket chronometers, another being that if a pocket chronometer is dropped the balance staff may be broken, and if the bottom pivot is broken the wheel may get clear and smash the escapement, thus necessitating an expensive repair.

With the improvement in the performances of the lever escapement, and the various improvements in balances and balance springs the pocket chronometer lost its popularity and is seldom made now.

CHRONOMETER TOURBILLONS

Some mention must now be made of the chronometer tourbillon. Although this is not a different escapement, it works on a different principle. With a tourbillon the escapement is mounted on a carriage which revolves at a predetermined speed.

[*Reproduced by courtesy of Colonel H. Quill.*

Figure 154. Pocket chronometer by Bridgeman and Brindle. This has two balance springs each fitted to resilient studs. 1 = resilient studs; 2 = spring detent; 3 = two balance springs.

One version of this escapement is the 1-minute tourbillon, which performs one complete revolution per minute, the seconds hand in this case being mounted on the pivot of the carriage itself. Another type is the 4-minute tourbillon, and there are also 5- or 6-minute types, the carriages of these performing one revolution in 4, 5 or 6 minutes respectively.

Types of Chronometer Tourbillon

The tourbillon was the invention of Abraham Louis Breguet, one of the world's most famous horologists, whose watches were second to none.   There are a number of Breguet chronometer tourbillons, two of which are illustrated in Figures 155 and 156.

Figure 155 is fitted with an Arnold-type escapement, and was made about the year 1797.   The passing spring in this is fitted to the detent

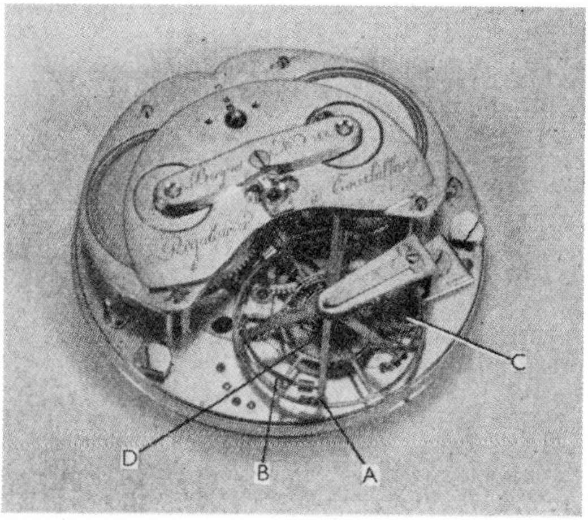

Figure 155.   Breguet chronometer tour-billon.   A = Tour-billon carriage;   B = balance;   C = 'scape wheel;   D = fixed fourth wheel.

Figure 156.   Back view of Breguet chronometer move-ment.   The jumper spring on the clutch lever is seen above the intermediate train wheel on which the cannon pinion is fitted.

in an almost identical manner to the Ulysse Nardin and Hamilton marine chronometers.   In Figure 156 the detent and passing spring are anchored on opposite sides of the carriage.   The detent proper has what may be called the horn extended and passing right round the roller to engage the passing spring on the other side.   In this case the action is the Earnshaw with extras.

Chronometer Tourbillon Receiving Impulse in both Directions

The third one of the group which is illustrated in Figure 158 is, one would say, unique, inasmuch as impulse is given in both directions. It is a complicated piece of mechanism, and consists of two wheels geared together but on opposite sides of the balance staff.

Figure 157. *Left*, 100-toothed wheel on carriage showing passing spring at top, then intermediate wheel, 'scape wheel and detent proper; *right*, base plate for carriage with fixed wheel at the other end.

Each wheel is locked in turn by a sort of pivoted detent combined with a lever, the head of the lever being almost identical to the head of the usual double roller, *i.e.* it has a notch, and above the notch is the guard or dart, which is screwed and steady-pinned to the lever.

The action is almost identical except that no impulse is given by the lever. Screwed flat to the lever is a small arm, and this carries the locking stone, which is situated under the lever just behind the head. Each wheel is locked in turn by this locking stone.

Action of the Double Chronometer—When the balance is moving anti-clockwise if viewed from the tail of the lever, the small wheel on the left is unlocked to give impulse, and as the lever is moved across, the locking stone is moved into the path of the wheel on the right and locks it. As the balance reverses, this wheel is unlocked, so giving impulse and locking the small wheel.

Assembling the Unit—These two wheels have to be carefully meshed together in the correct way, otherwise neither is locked and neither can give impulse. Each wheel also has two sets of teeth, the impulse teeth and the locking teeth, and of course the teeth connecting the two wheels. The impulse roller has two impulse pallets set at about 90° to each other, whilst the unlocking pin, which is again triangular, is mounted on a separate roller. The guard roller is a small roller into which a hole is drilled to allow the lever to pass instead of the usual crescent.

The balance is beautifully made and has 3 arms and, of course, 3 compensation arms, which are bimetallic. Both the mean time screws and the compensation adjustment screws are of gold. This

Figure 158.   Breguet tourbillon with double action chronometer.

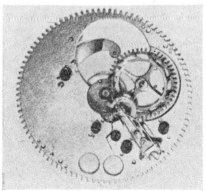

Figure 159.   Carriage unit Figure 158 showing two 'scape wheels and lever detent.

escapement has a 21,600 train and has a typical Breguet overcoil balance spring. If the chronometer escapement is fully understood there will be no difficulty experienced in repairing this fine piece of work.

REMONTOIRES OR CONSTANT-FORCE CHRONOMETERS

Remontoires as such do not generally come into the category of escapements, as they are based on a system to ensure constant motive power to the escapement. A. L. Breguet introduced an escapement, however, which gave constant impulse to the balance. It was a complicated escapement but worthy of consideration.

The Impulse Arm

The impulse was given by a detent or spring arm, and the action of the escapement was the lifting and releasing of this impulse arm at the correct moment. The arm was also provided with a supplementary spring to enable the force of the impulse to be increased, and thus to increase the vibration of the balance.

Likeness to Gravity Escapement

One naturally thinks of a gravity escapement as one having impulse one way only. The action is that as the balance is at rest the impulse arm is lifted and locked on the locking stone of the detent.

The Main Detent

This detent is the one which is engaged by the balance or rather the discharging pallet on the balance staff or the main detent. The action of the balance that as usual with a chronometer: as the balance is moved one way the passing spring is lifted and dropped and no impulse is given; on the return vibration the detent is lifted and the impulse arm is released, thus giving impulse to the balance; as this arm falls the end of the arm engages a detent and releases the setting-up section.

Setting up the Impulse Arm—The setting-up section is activated by the motive power and consists of a double wheel and a pinion and fly, *etc*. The one wheel is the usual gear-wheel, but the other one mounted on the same pinion has teeth of an epicycloidal shape or curved back.

The gear-wheel gears into a pinion on which is mounted on one end a fly to slow up its action and on the other end a semicircular arm, this arm being locked on a secondary detent which is engaged by the impulse arm as it falls after having given impulse to the balance.

As has already been observed, the balance has been given impulse and the impulse arm has fallen, engaged the secondary detent and moved it away from the semicircular arm; the train at once runs, and the curved teeth of the lifting wheel engage and lift the impulse arm; as the impulse arm is lifted the secondary detent is released,

254

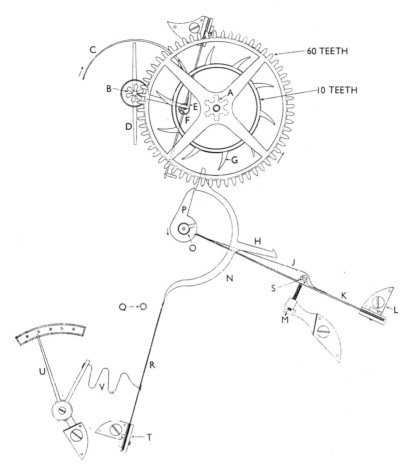

Figure 160.   Breguet constant force remontoire escapement. A = pinion from main motive power; B = pinion of six leaves; C = semi-circular loop safety device; D = fly to slow up hoop; F = locking stone on detent holding hoop; G = tooth to lift impulse arm; H = hook of impulse arm which is locked on main detent; J = passing spring; K = spring 0·002 in. thick; L = detent foot clamp; M = banking screw; N = impulse arm; O = discharging roller; P = impulse pallet; Q = banking pin for impulse arm; R = spring 0·002 in. thick; S = locking stone of detent on which impulse arm is locked; T = impulse arm foot clamp; U = impulse adjusting; V = spring to adjust amount of impulse.

255

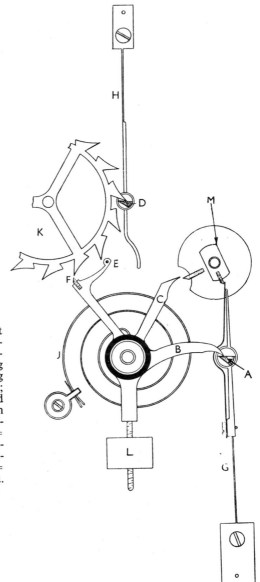

Figure 161. Constant force chronometer escapement. A = main detent; B = detent holding main train; C = locking arm; D = impulse arm; E = pallet engaged and lifted by main train wheel; F = releasing pallet for main train; G = impulse spring; H = impulse roller; J = discharging roller; K = weight to vary the inertia.

and as the arm is lifted farther it is locked in position by the main detent.

Locking the Impulse Arm—The lifting carries on a little farther until the semicircular arm is coincident with the secondary detent and is locked by it. The curved teeth are thus just clear of the impulse arm when the semicircular arm is locked. The start of the sequence of events has now been reached again, with the balance ready to receive impulse.

As can be seen, it is a complicated escapement to set up. The lifting wheel and the fly pinion and arm must be correctly set up, *i.e.* the mesh of the wheel and pinion is critical. The lifting wheel must be locked so that it has lifted the impulse arm to the locking and dropped off with its teeth clear of the arm and not in a position to obstruct its fall.

The impulse arm must also be lifted a very little higher than required in order to make sure that it is locked on the main detent locking stone. The impulse, release, *etc.*, are identical to an ordinary chronometer, only the method of their use is different.

The Disadvantages of Lubricating

The disadvantages are the necessary oiling of the pivot holes and also of the lifting-wheel teeth. This latter is the greatest disadvantage, because although one would put only the absolute minimum of oil, it would be almost certain to spread to places where it was not wanted.

The advantage is that one can, of course, increase at will, or vary the extent of, the vibration, and this can be a help in rating the instrument. The impulse is, of course, very nearly a constant factor if it is not completely constant. It is, however, hardly a portable

Figure 162. A type of remontoire chronometer escapement: (1) Wheel driven by train which returns wheel (2) to its original position; (2) wheel which gives impulse; (3) motive power for impulse wheel can be adjusted by altering the setting of the collet on the arbor. A = tooth which releases secondary detent; B = tooth which is engaged when wheel 1 is released.

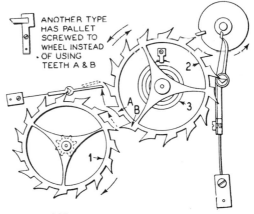

escapement, and is not meant to be so. The impulse arm is a comparitively heavy piece, and if it is held sideways it may not give impulse at all, owing to its weight, whilst if it is held upside down it will drop away from its acting position.

Robins Remontoire

Two other types of remontoire follow something of the same principle. One of these was invented by Robin and had a pivoted arm which was set up in position by the train, released by the

Figure 163. Chronometer platform escapement. A = 'scape wheel; B = the detent; C = banking block; D = balance staff jewelling; E = balance.

balance as usual and, after giving its impulse to the balance, was set up again by the train. The other type had two 'scape wheels, one of which was mounted on the 'scape pinion whilst the other pivoted in the plate. The action was again like an ordinary chronometer, but as the impulse was given, so the wheel was returned to its original position by the second wheel on the 'scape pinion. In each case two detents were used, one detent as usual and the other one locking the motive power.

Impulse by Coiled Spring—In each case the impulse was also given by a coiled spring like a hairspring, the strength of which could be varied by setting up or letting out the spring by turning the collet. Both have the disadvantage that unless a fly is provided to slow the resetting mechanism there is a great tendency to trip and so allow more teeth to pass, thus causing the instrument to have a wide gaining rate.

All these ideas were tried because it was realised that a chronometer needed a constant arc of vibration to give a good or a very close rate. As stated earlier, however, the manipulation of the terminal curves of the balance render most of these ideas more or less unproductive.

14

THE DEPTH TOOL

THE DEPTH OR DEPTHING tool is primarily used for measuring the distance of centres, and any two pieces which operate or work together can be put between its centres and the tool so adjusted that the actions are correct. This setting of the tool can then be marked off on a clock or watch plate.

The tool consists of two halves which are accurately jointed at the base; the top half is made into two heads, each of which is drilled to take runners. Thus with the two halves there are four heads and four runners, whilst each runner has a draw-in block and a thumb-nut to enable the runner to be secured. The runners are carefully turned between centres, one end of each being a clean tapering point and the other a clean female centre (see Figure 123).

The two halves are pressed together by a strong spring, and a setting screw with a thumb-nut is fitted at the base of one half, enabling the two halves to be held at a required distance apart.

Each piece is put between the centres and held quite firmly but not on strain, then the thumb-screw is turned until the action between the two is correct (it must be taken for granted that the tool is accurate here). The pieces are then removed, making sure that the thumb-nut is not disturbed.

One end of the tool is now to be used as a pair of compasses, and care must be used in the operation. First, the tool must be perfectly upright in relation to the plates on which the pieces are being planted; to make sure of this, daylight and shadow are used. Artificial light can be deceptive, and should be avoided if at all possible. The plate is given a little shine, but should not be elaborately cleaned up, then one leg or runner is placed in the hole from which it is being marked off; if an escapement it will be the 'scape pivot hole. It is as well to secure one runner by its thumb-nut. The plate is held to the light and the other runner set until the legs proper and their reflection in the plate make a perfectly straight line or are as one continuous piece. This will be found to be an extremely accurate method.

To check up, again position the depth tool until the protruding joint pin joining the two halves is reflected midway between the reflection of the two runners. If still showing upright the marking off can be done. If ordinary compasses were being used they would be rotated on stationary paper, but when marking off with a depth tool, this is held firm and the plate turned against it. There is no need to scribe a full circle but only an arc where required; in any case, these marks have to be removed later. If an escapement is being pitched or marked off there is a centre line on the plate, so all that needs to be done is to mark in a way to just cross the centre line.

To be certain of marking in the right place for drilling a sharp-pointed tool like a three-cornered chamfer should be used. The point is lightly rested in the score lines and moved towards the junction of the arc and centre line. As soon as the junction is reached the tool will click, although not in an audible manner, but sufficiently for it to be felt. Immediately this happens the point of the tool must be pressed and given a twist; this will make a dot which can be centre punched suitably for drilling. This, of course, will all be wasted effort unless the hole is drilled perfectly upright, as any drift in the drilling will seriously alter the position.

If it is preferred to do the pitching by measurement it can be done by carefully measuring the distance apart of the two runners with a micrometer and noting the result, then measuring the diameter of the runner and subtracting this from the first measurement. This means, of course, half a runner each side.

The depth-tool marking is the best course if an individual job is being done, as there is less chance of error. A depth tool is always best if it is accurate, but some tools have an error which is known by the craftsman and automatically allowed for in his working. To check a depth tool it is set at any distance, stood upright and then used to mark off an on old plate.

It is tried at both ends to see if each end coincides in its marking, then the runners are reversed so that the points are inside, and the plate is marked off again, using both sides. If all four sets of lines coincide the tool is accurate.

If the points become worn they should not be merely touched up with an oilstone slip, but the runner should be put in the lathe and turned. In no circumstances must the runner be put in a split chuck; instead the female centre is put in a male centre at one end and the other end is put partly through a hole in a lantern runner so that the best part of the taper stands out. It is then turned with a sharp graver, or if a lap is available it is lapped until quite true. If there is any doubt about the female centre the procedure should be reversed and the male centre or pointed end put in a female centre and the female centred end put through a hole. The runner is invariably slightly tapered at the ends.

The female centre can now be cleaned up with a sharp-pointed graver. It must be ascertained that there is no root at the bottom of the V, and this is done by testing it with a sharp-pointed needle; any movement of the needle will show a root.

Great care should always be taken of a depth tool, and it should not be knocked about or left to get damp and rusty; it is a very good friend and has many uses apart from pitching a depth. If one is doubtful of a wheel-and-pinion action and it is difficult to view when in position in the instrument the depth tool can be set to the distance of centres (using the procedure for uprighting), the wheel and pinion put in it and examined quite easily. If a wheel and pinion is missing the depth tool makes the replacement job easy, and for making pallets to depth it is a godsend. Even an old worn-out or damaged depth tool can be used for polishing, snailing and many other uses. In fact, a depth tool should be found in every workshop.

15

POLISHING

IT IS GENERALLY CONSIDERED unnecessary to polish the various parts of an escapement these days, but the necessity of it will be clear if the matter is looked into closely. It will be seen that very little power, or an extremely small proportion of the original motive power, arrives at the escapement, and that polishing will keep this loss to a minimum.

In some clocks which are provided with a recoil escapement the pallet faces are often left rough or finished with an emery finish, and as an experiment, if the vibration was noted while the faces were roughly finished and then noted again after polishing, the increase in vibration would be surprising.

Polished Pallet Faces

Another point in favour of polishing the pallet faces is that a polished face will not show signs of wear for an appreciable time, the reason being that a polished surface does not so readily hold fragments of foreign matter with which the wheel may be charged, or there are not so many cavities in which foreign matter can lodge. This also applies to surfaces which do not come into frictional action.

A polished surface will resist the effects of the atmosphere much better than will a grained one, whilst the face of a pinion, although not coming into action itself, may if left rough cause trouble. It is almost impossible to detect any inaccuracies in its divisions or in the shape of the leaves if these are left rough. Upon examination it may be found that the wheel teeth gear into the extreme ends of the leaves, and polishing the face of the pinion will remove any burrs which may have been a source of trouble.

Polished Lever Notch

Although in many modern watches the lever notch is left in the state in which it came from the cutter, their performance would be improved if the notch was polished. The horns of a double-roller lever escapement also benefit by being polished; these do not come into action in the ordinary way, but if the watch should receive a jolt the horns often jump against the impulse pin; if they are polished the interference is very little, but if they are left rough a jolt may temporarily hold up the watch, whilst if the impulse pin is sharp cornered the watch can stop.

The polishing of all parts is easily carried out on a semi-mass-production scale, but a repairer or maker of single watches or parts has to adopt the methods accordingly.

Speed of Polishing

One rule to bear in mind is that a piece must be polished in as short a time as possible, and the longer the time spent on polishing, the less chance there is of a successful job. Thus the foundations must be right and correct.

If a surface is rounded it will take a long time to polish it flat, so before attempting the polishing it must be ensured that the surface is flat. The surface must also be smooth, otherwise by the time all the marks have been polished out a colossal amount of time will have been wasted.

Faults Shown up by Polishing

Polishing shows up all the faults in a piece of work. If a roller is being fitted to a balance staff a firm, tight fit can be obtained on a polished arbor without the need to drive it on, and in fact a roller can often be pushed on to a polished roller arbor with the fingers, but cannot be pulled off in the same way because of a better fitting. Another point is that oil will not spread as readily over a polished surface as it would over a rough surface.

Use of Oilstone Dust

With clockwork and heavy work it is advisable to prepare the surface with a coarser abrasive before polishing. Powdered oilstone powder, or oilstone dust as it is termed, thinly mixed with oil is a good medium, and is used on a suitable soft steel polisher which is smeared with the mixture and then rubbed against the surface until the deep marks are removed. This same procedure is adopted when it is required to polish large pieces of steelwork like keyless wheels, bridges, *etc.*

Overhand and Underhand Polishing

There are two methods of preparation and polishing, and these are called overhand and underhand, *i.e.* when the polisher is held in the hand and the work is resting on a block of some sort the method is termed overhand. Polishing an arbor or polishing a pivot in the lathe or turns is overhand, but where the work is held in the hand or in a tool of some sort with the polisher or polishing block stationary the method is underhand. Many pieces can be polished either way, as will be seen.

Polishing by Laps

There is also polishing by lapping, *i.e.* by holding pieces in a tool against a revolving lap which is held in a lathe or on an arbor held in the turns. This is a very convenient way to polish odd shapes.

There are various powders which can be used for polishing, most of which are unobtainable because the demand is too small. There is, however, a powder which in the trade is called diamantine, and this is still obtainable, although the quality is rather uncertain, and therefore a new supply must be tested to find its quality.

Diamantine has no connection whatsoever with diamond powder, the latter being made from diamonds crushed to dust and graded according to requirements. These two powders will be considered in turn.

Using Diamantine Powder

This is an oxide of aluminium and is mixed with a suitable oil to the consistency of well-worked putty. It is used sparingly, not on the grounds of economy but because if too much is used on the polisher it will take a long time for the surface of the work to become polished. Diamantine cuts while it is wettish, but polishes as it dries and gives the final bloom to the surface when completely dry.

The whole process is rather difficult to explain because one must really experience its use, or perhaps it may be said that one must acquire experience by practice to be able to achieve the high finish possible.

When a piece is being polished a small quantity of diamantine is smeared on to the polishing medium and the work is rubbed on the medium. As one proceeds the diamantine turns black and at that stage starts to cut, and as the operation proceeds the diamantine gets drier and drier until the polishing medium and the diamantine assume a shiny surface. When this stage is reached the work should be highly polished.

When to Stop Polishing—The vital point to bear in mind is that the rubbing should be stopped as soon as the shiny effect is obtained, and this is the whole secret, because the precise moment which is chosen to cease the rubbing will decide the quality of the finish.

If the rubbing is stopped too soon the surface will be only shiny, whilst if it is prolonged the surface will be foxy or will be covered with a brown smear. If the former is the case the polisher must be recleaned, the diamantine renewed and the piece polished again. If, however, the surface is foxy the polisher should not be cleaned, but just the minimum of diamantine put on the section which has been polished and a few rubs of the work on this will often give the required finish.

Cleanliness When Using Diamantine

The use of diamantine demands absolute cleanliness, and any dust or dirt on the diamantine will cause scratches to appear on the work, thus the polisher must be resurfaced after use or when first brought into use.

Some difficulty other than dust or dirt is often experienced in polishing, and the oil which is mixed with the diamantine can play an important part. Sometimes, however one tries, the work will have a brown smear even before the diamantine is dry, or there may be streaks across it, especially if a flat piece with a hole in it is being polished. This is a sign that the oil is unsuitable.

Ragosine Oil for Mixing with Diamantine

Smiths Ragosine oil is a splendid medium for mixing diamantine, although rather an expensive one. Another oil is the common '3-IN-ONE', but it is always as well to keep a fresh supply of this for some time to allow any fragments of grit or dirt to settle before it is put into use. The usual watch or clock oils are not always suitable. The two oils mentioned are suggested because of the author's personal experience of them.

Mixing Diamantine

Another point to be borne in mind is that when diamantine is being mixed one must be sure that it is really well done. The best way is to mix a small quantity of diamantine with the oil and beat it well until the mixture is quite fluid. When this stage is reached a little more diamantine is added and the mixture is again well beaten. The process is repeated until it will not become at all liquid when beaten but will retain its putty-like consistency. If it is required to be wetter a small portion can be put on one side, and after a little oil has been added this can again be beaten until suitable.

Hard Steel as Mixing Plate

Diamantine is best mixed with a narrow knife blade on a hard steel plate, and when not in use should be kept in an air-tight container. These containers are purchased from material dealers, and usually consist of three separate compartments in tiers, but the best ones are single units. It is often convenient to have two or three types of diamantine on one plate but in separate heaps, the reason for this being that if one is blueing screws they are first polished with dryish diamantine and then finished with a wettish mixture.

Polishing and Blueing Screw-heads

A zinc polisher is used to polish screw-heads, and this is followed by a boxwood polisher with the wettish diamantine. A better and richer blue will be obtained by this method. When screw-heads have to be polished flat a screw-head tool which is provided with laps can be used, or the polishing can be done in a tool in which the tail of the screw is gripped at one end whilst the other end has two legs which are adjusted until the screw-head and legs are all in one plane.

Using a Bolt Tool

The whole is rubbed on a flat zinc block smeared with diamantine until the head is polished to perfection. If the screw-head is not flat when it is first placed on the block the appropriate leg, or perhaps both of the legs, is adjusted accordingly. The first few rubs on

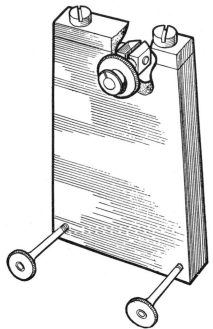

Figure 164. The bolt tool.

the block will show where the screw is resting. This same tool can be used for numerous purposes, and sub-tools may be added to the main tool for special jobs. This type of polishing is termed underhand.

Polishing Bosses of Hands

The polishing of a minute- or hour-hand boss is also executed on a zinc block, but there is no need for a special tool because if a piece of pointed pegwood is held in the hole the hand boss can then be rubbed on the zinc block until polished. The flat face of a roller is polished in the same way.

Polishing Using Metal Block as Tool

If a lever of a chronograph or repeater which is large but thin is being polished, a piece of plate brass about $\frac{1}{8}$ in. thick and just a little larger than the overall size of the piece is used as a holder. The piece is fixed to the block with shellac and polished on a zinc block. In such a case a heavier tool than pegwood is used, and this consists of a piece of rod steel fixed in a small file handle.

267

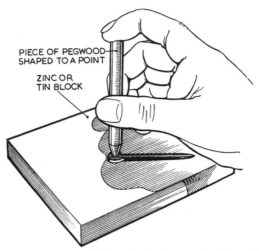

PIECE OF PEGWOOD
SHAPED TO A POINT

ZINC OR
TIN BLOCK

Figure 165. Polishing hand bosses, flat face of
rollers, steel collars, collets and similar pieces.

Tool for Adding Pressure to Block

The steel is hardened and tempered and ends in a point which is
placed in a suitable part of the plate, then the plate with the piece
fixed to it is pressed against the diamantine on the zinc block. If
one part is found to be polishing more than another the point of the
tool is moved on to a different part of the plate until all the piece
is being polished.

The flat face of an index is polished in the same way, but the brass
plate has a hole drilled into it so that the index pins can pass through.
The work must, of course, be fixed centrally on the plate. When
polishing in this way either a round-and-round motion or, alternatively, a backwards-and-forwards motion may be used, and if
one method does not succeed the other will.

Polishing Bi-metallic Balance

The visible part of a compensation balance can be polished in the
same way, but a grain tin block is used instead of a zinc block. If
the balance staff is in the balance the procedure is reversed, *i.e.* the
balance is rested on a piece of cork which has a small hole in it into
which the lower half of the staff passes. A small tin block, also with
a hole in it and smeared with diamantine, is rubbed on the rim of
the balance until it is polished. This again is underhand polishing.

Polishing 'Scape Wheel

A brass 'scape wheel is polished in the same way, but a small tin
block without a hole in it is, of course, used. A brass 'scape wheel

can be burnished, and the procedure is similar to that with the tin block, but it is advisable to place a piece of thin tissue paper between the wheel and the cork. The burnisher must be carefully prepared and used absolutely dry, as any dampness, either oil or water, on the burnisher will cause serious scoring or scratching.

Preparing the Burnisher—If the burnisher is first rubbed on a No. 2 emery buff, and then has the extreme sharpness taken off with a No. 0 emery buff it will be ready for use, but it must always be rubbed with a clean, dry rag before use.

The wheel is placed on the cork, which is so cut as to be slightly larger than the wheel, after which a piece of tissue paper is wrapped round the cork and the wheel is rested on this, then the burnisher is rubbed on the wheel for a short period. The wheel is then moved round on the cork about half a turn and is again rubbed with the burnisher. When the wheel is quite burnished it is reversed and the other side treated in the same way.

The precaution of brushing the tissue on the cork must always be taken, as if any dust has landed it will scratch the side already polished.

Polishing Steel Wheels

A flat steel wheel can be polished on a cork in the same way, but a zinc polisher must be used instead of a tin one. Steel endpieces are polished in this way, as are any other small pieces of steel which are flat on both sides. It must not be forgotten, however, that a zinc polisher is used for steel and a tin polisher for brass or gold.

Polishing Brass or Gold Train Wheels

Train wheels of watches and chronometers are polished while mounted on their pinions, although some people polish the wheels before the pinion is finished, whilst others polish afterwards, but this is just a matter of choice. There is always the risk of spoiling the polish of the wheels while finishing the pinion and pivoting, *etc.*

Cupping and Balling the Wheels—The preparation for this operation is very important. The centre of the wheel is cupped and balled,

Figure 166. Various sections of an English fourth wheel and pinion.

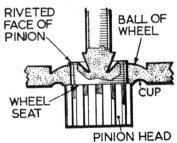

269

i.e. the centre is turned ball-shaped or convex on the riveting side of the centre and cupped or concave on the arbor side. The turning is done with a polished graver and finished with a shaped piece of willow wood smeared with diamantine.

Polisher for Wheels—The polisher for the main part of the wheel is tin backed with a steel plate for strengthening. The polisher is a little wider than the radius of the wheel, and as long as twice the diameter of the wheel. A slot is filed at the back of the polisher to enable a finger- or thumb-nail to be inserted with safety, in order that the polisher may be firmly held. The slot is about central to enable the polisher to be balanced. A backwards-and-forwards motion is essential, and this is where a bow scores.

The wheel and pinion are between dead centres, and if the pinion is a pivoted one the pivots are held in safety centres so that the pressure is on the pivot shoulders. The direction of the wheel is in opposition to the polisher, thus as the bow is pulled down the polisher is moved up, and vice-versa. The polisher is smeared with diamantine and at first goes black, then turns to brass colour; at the same time the resistance increases until the work starts to squeak.

If the wheel is flat and everything is clean, *etc.*, it should be highly polished and dead flat, with the corners of the crossings quite sharp and not broken. If the wheel is not crossed out, or is a solid wheel, it is best for it to be polished before mounting, but this is not essential.

Polishing Solid Wheels

The wheel is polished on a piece of wood which has two steel centres let in on opposite sides, whilst a small pin in the centre of the

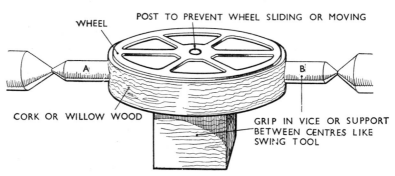

Figure 167. Tool for polishing solid wheels. This can be used as a swing tool as shown or held in the vice. Cross-out wheels can be polished in the same way providing they are fairly large.

flat side prevents the wheel moving about. The block is held in dead centres and a tin polisher is used which has been smeared with diamantine. The wheel should be turned round every so often whilst it is being polished to ensure flatness all ways. The idea of the two centres is that they keep the wheel flat back and front and act like a swing tool; they also take care of the wobble of the hands as one polishes.

Polishing Pivots and Arbors

Pivots and arbors are easier to polish between centres using a backwards-and-forwards motion as is obtained with the aid of a

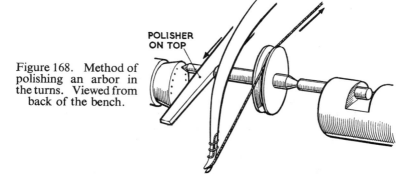

POLISHER ON TOP

Figure 168. Method of polishing an arbor in the turns. Viewed from back of the bench.

bow. Iron or steel polishers can be used, and both will give quite good results, but silver steel polishers are better, because the shoulders are not so easily rounded and the edge of the steel polisher remains sharp for a longer period.

Bell-metal Polishers—The ideal metal for polishing pivots of any size is, of course, bell metal. It cannot be called a hard metal, even though it is difficult to file and resurface, but it certainly holds its sharp corner for a considerable time. The only drawback is that it is difficult to obtain this metal these days in suitable shapes.

Balancing the Polisher—The polisher must be balanced evenly over the whole length of the pivot, because unless it is so balanced it may become tapered one way or the other during polishing. As pivots are best polished underhand, one must be able to feel how the polisher is lying on the pivot. As the polisher is moved across the pivot a round-and-round motion must also be given to it, and the shoulder should be touched only now and then. The polisher should be narrower than the length of the pivot, and also, in order to keep the shoulder square an equal amount of daylight must be seen between the polisher and the shoulder at the back and front.

The edge of the polisher should be cut back about 30° and should be slightly curved over its length, the idea again being to adjust for

271

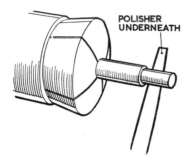

Figure 169. Method of polishing
arbors or pivots in the lathe.

the wobble of the hands. After a pivot has been nicely polished a few rubs with a hard steel burnisher of the same shape as the polisher will give an added ' bloom '.

Facing Pinion Leaves

Although many people feel that the polishing of the ends of pinion leaves or faces is unnecessary, it is really an advantage to the watch to have them polished, whatever the conditions. Where the fourth

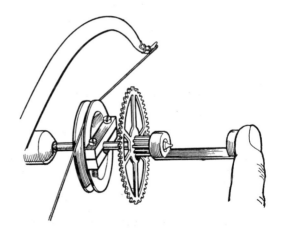

Figure 170. Method
of facing or polishing
pinion face.

wheel teeth gear into the ends of the leaves, as in a 'scape pinion, it is imperative for the pinion leaves to be quite clear of burrs, *etc.*

In the case of pinions where the gearing takes place centrally the gearing is not affected if the leaves are burred up at the ends, but the burrs do provide a likely resting place for dust and dirt, or for deposits left from cleaning solutions which can start up rust. It is also difficult to peg out the leaves because the burrs scrape off fragments of the wood and the leaves are left just as dirty as before.

Clearing Burrs from Pinion Leaves—The best way to clear all of the burrs is to ' face ' the pinion. This is carried out by means of a piece of round steel or iron rod, the size of which varies according to the diameter of the pinion. The rod should be only very slightly larger than the pinion, but must not in any case be smaller. If the tool as it is called is too large difficulty will be experienced in balancing it on the pinion face, and the results will be disappointing.

A hole is drilled in the rod, and this should not fit the pinion arbor, but should be about 10 per cent larger to allow for play. It must be long enough to withstand some usage but not be too long, or it will interfere with the balancing of the tool.

Use of a Bow when Facing Pinions—The use of a bow is essential to give a backwards-and-forwards motion, otherwise the work will be

Figure 171. Tool for polishing undercut between pinion face and pinion arbor.

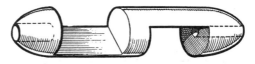

' racy ' or marked with circular lines, and will be out of flat. The only other way of doing the operation is by lapping.

In order to use the facing tool the face of the pinion needs to be smoothly turned, and a deep undercut is necessary at the centre so that the polishing will not form a root and thus force the face out of flat.

Oilstone Dust to Prepare Pinion Face—It is difficult to turn the leaves as smooth as one would like because there is always a tendency for the graver to jump in and out between the leaves. It is therefore advisable to bring the face up smooth by first using oilstone dust and oil on the tool. The operation is carried out by fixing a ferrule on the opposite end of the pinion and as near to the end as possible. This will help to make the pinion run across the face, a most important requirement, as it revolves backwards and forwards.

The end on which the brass ferrule is fixed is placed in a dead centre held in the vice, or by the tailstock in the lathe or turns. The facing tool is placed on the other or free end and held or balanced in position by the tip of the finger. Now as the bow is moved up and down the pinion revolves, and at the same time moves across the face of the tool, first one way and then the other, as the direction changes.

The face will be smoothed up with the facing tool smeared with oilstone dust, and if everything is in order will be brought up quite flat. To polish the face all traces of oilstone must be cleared away, and any traces left, however, small, will cause scratches and ruts in the face. The procedure is the same except that diamantine is now smeared on the facing tool. The polishing is continued until the work squeaks and one can judge when to stop work. The first

273

squeak does not necessarily mean that the face has achieved a polished state, but a continuance of the squeaking does mean that it is time to stop.

Selecting Polisher to Suit Type of Steel

The work should by this time be highly polished, but if this is not so a little more of the treatment must be given.   If the surface is scratchy the facing tool and the pinion must be recleaned and a little fresh diamantine put on the tool, but if the surface is foxy a slight smear of diamantine on the tool is all that is required, and a few strokes with the bow or a few turns of the pinion will remove the foxiness.   If after further treatment the face continues to be scratchy the facing tool must be changed to one made of iron and then again to one made of bell metal.   Some steel requires different polishers to get results.

When the pinion is faced there should be just a thin ring at the bottom of the pinion leaves before it merges into the undercut section.   This is not always possible on the riveted end of the pinion, especially if it is a centre pinion where one endeavours to have as large a shoulder for the pivot as possible.

Undercut where Shoulder is Large—In cases where the pivot shoulder is very close to the pinion face it is often policy to have a wide undercut to prevent the oil creeping on to the pinion leaves.   This often happens with Swiss 'scape pinions and third pinions, and also with some English third pinions, as well as with the 'scape pinion of a three-quarter-plate pocket chronometer.

Polishing the Roller Edge

The roller edge is a simple part to polish.   This thin edge is polished flat with a runner adapted for the job (Figure 172) which is

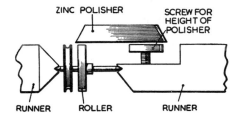

Figure 172.   Runner for polishing roller edge flat.

filed flat on one side to almost reach the centre.   A large-headed screw is then fitted through this flat face and the runner is drilled at right angles to this to take another screw which acts as a grub screw.

Using the Runner to Polish the Edge Flat—The roller is mounted on an arbor and the first screw is adjusted to the correct height, then the grub screw fixes it in place so that it does not move.   The screw is adjusted so that when the polisher is rested on both the roller and the screw-head it is at dead right angles to the face of the roller. As the roller is revolved, so the polisher is rubbed on the screw and the edge, and by virtue of the flat screw the edge will be dead flat. In the case of a roller for a single-roller escapement one does not, of course, bump up and down into the crescent.

A marine chronometer roller edge can be polished in the same way, but owing to its size this is best carried out using two extra rollers with no crescents, mounted one on each side of an arbor. A wide zinc polisher is used for the roller edges. As mentioned earlier, the flat faces of the rollers are polished underhand on a zinc block.

Polishing the Roller Crescent

The polishing of a roller crescent presents no difficulty, the usual way being to use a roller-crescent tool. The polisher is a round rod of steel of a size to fit the shape of the crescent, a large or wide crescent requiring a rod of a larger diameter than a smaller one.

Roller Crescent Tool—In the type of tool used by the author the roller is gripped between two jaws. If the roller has a pipe to it this is placed towards the inside of the tool and the flat face towards

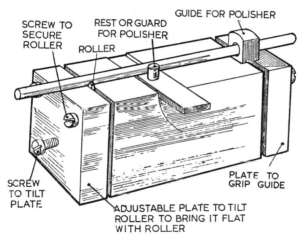

Figure 173. Tool for polishing roller crescent of single rollers.

the outside. The inside of the tool is faced with steel to minimise wear, and the outside jaw is a flat plate supplied with two screws at the top and a single screw tapped into the plate itself at the bottom and central, the object of this being to enable the roller to be tilted should the crescent be out of square with the polisher.

275

Adjusting the Tool—If the polisher is taking too much off the back the screw is screwed in, and this tilts the plate, and thus the roller and the error is easily adjusted. The rest at the back of the polisher is also adjustable; by raising the rest the front of the roller crescent is favoured, and vice-versa.

The post is also a rest or guard for the polisher; sometimes two posts are used, but only one is required and one's finger-nail will act much better as the other one. This post keeps the polisher to the centre of the crescent and also prevents it slipping off and marking the roller edge. As before, the finger-nail placed on the opposite side prevents the polisher from slipping that way.

Polisher for the Roller Crescent—The polisher is smeared with dia-mantine and rubbed backwards and forwards across the crescent, or from back to front of the roller. At first the roller may cut the polisher, but as soon as the burr is removed from the crescent the polisher will run quite smoothly. The roller-crescent tool can be used for many other purposes of a similar nature, and not only for roller crescents.

Polishing Lever Edges

Lever edges are polished flat in what is called a swing tool. This is a tool provided with jaws to grip the work as required, and also

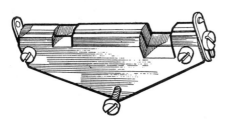

Figure 174. Swing tool for polishing the foot of a chrono-meter detent or for polishing lever edges flat.

provided with male or female centres, the idea being that the tool with the work can be put between dead centres.

The Swing Tool—The centres on the tool are adjustable to enable the parts to be polished to be brought true with the supporting centres, and thus polished dead flat. This is again difficult to explain, but if, when polishing, the far side of the work is being polished and not the front the centres on the tool must be moved forward until the whole work is being touched by the polisher.

If, as sometimes happens, the work will not stay put, *i.e.* as one polishes so the work rolls backwards and forwards, it means that the work is too high in relation to the centres. If this is the case the centres on the tool must be raised. This also happens if the work is too low in relation to the centres of the tool.

Principle of Swing Applied to Squares

This same principle applies in the case of squares of a winding stem, or centre or fusee squares. If the winding stem is put between dead centres the sides of the square can be polished dead flat very easily by just resting the polisher on each side in succession. As one rubs it will be noticed how the square will follow the movements of the polisher.

Polishing Rounded Edges

In the same way if one wishes to polish the edges of a lever with a rounded surface a swing tool can be used, but will be moved back-

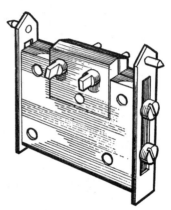

Figure 175. Swing tool for polishing edges of levers, *etc.*

wards and forwards with the fingers as the polishing proceeds instead of letting the tool find its own level. The polisher in this case is made of bell metal shaped to suit, if the lever is hardened steel.

Polishing the Lever Notch

Lever notches can be polished with a very thin bell-metal polisher with the side of the lever resting on a piece of willow wood. They

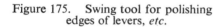

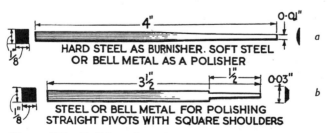

Figure 176. Polishers for arbors and pivots: *a* burnisher for conical pivots; *b* polisher for pivots with shoulders.

277

can also be polished by using a piece of thin steel, like a saw blade only soft, stretched between a miniature saw frame. This frame must be small to enable one to have full control when a small notch is being polished.

Polishing a Double-roller Lever

Lever horns are polished by using a shaped polisher with the lever itself resting in a slot cut in a strip of brass or steel and hollowed out, leaving a step as a guard. This is to enable one horn to be polished without touching the other or the corner of the opposite notch. Single-roller horns, which are only ornamental and have no active part to play, can be polished in a similar way.

Polishing the Lever Tail

The lever tail can be polished using a special tool, or by holding the lever in the hand. If the tail is dead flat the tool must, of course, be used. The tool is double-ended, one end having clamps to hold a

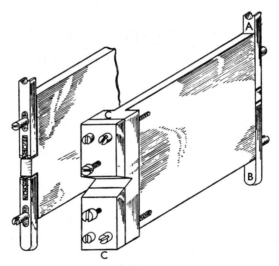

Figure 177. Lever tail polishing tool. This can be used for other purposes of a like nature. Using a suitable shaped polisher the tool is held in the hand. A = template for hollow ends; B = template for rounded ends; C = holders for work to be polished.

lever and the other having the same shape as the tail being polished. The two ends are adjusted so that the tail to be polished presents a flat surface to a flat block, and is then polished underhand on a zinc block.

Tool for Polishing the Belly of the Pallets

There is also a special tool for polishing the belly of a pair of pallets or similar pieces; this is one of the swing tools. The jaws of the tool are filed away inside to leave small triangular-shaped jaws standing

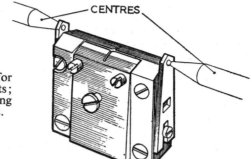

Figure 178. Tool for polishing belly of pallets; also showing how a swing tool is used in the turns.

proud which grip the body of the pallets without touching the nibs. The tool is set as usual, and a thin zinc polisher is used to polish the belly. If the pallets are of gold, brass or some other soft metal the jaws are made from ivory, or can be covered with lead solder so that there is no bruising.

Polishing and Bevelling Angular Backs

The angular backs of the pallets are polished in a tool which clamps the pallets as required, and is provided with two screws to adjust the height so that the backs are flat with the block. A zinc block is used

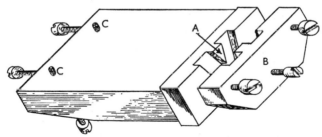

Figure 179. Tool for polishing back of pallets when lever and pallets are two units. A shows metal cut away to prevent chipping the stones; B = clamping plate for pallets; C = adjusting screws to enable one to polish flat.

with diamantine, and as one half of the back is polished, so the position of the pallets is changed and the other half polished.

This tool is also provided with grooves so that if there are bevelled edges to the pallets they can be polished at the same time. The bevels, however, are not polished on the block, but the polisher is rested in the slot or groove and the pallets adjusted to make the polisher touch the whole length equally. All four bevels can be polished flat while in the tool.

Polishing the Faces of Lever and Pallets

The flat faces of the lever and pallets are polished with a flat zinc polisher while they are rested, or pressed, into a piece of willow wood held in the vice. They are polished underhand.

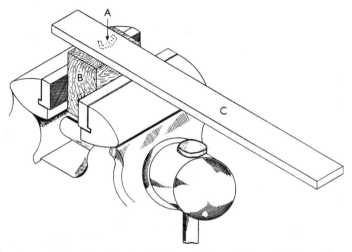

Figure 180. Overhead polishing. The polisher which is a piece of flat zinc 7 in. $\times$ $1\frac{1}{4}$ in. $\times$ $\frac{3}{16}$ in. is held in the hand and the work is supported on a willow wood block which is firmly held in a vice. A = work being polished; B = willow wood; C = zinc polisher.

When the pallets are being polished the nibs must be pointing away from the front so that the stones will not be chipped if the polisher does catch.

These various methods of polishing do not apply to one piece only, and there are many other operations on which the tools and methods can be used, most of them applying also to numerous other pieces which have to be made in watch or clock work.

Tools for Polishing Bevelled Edges

There is a tool for polishing the bevelled edges of a diamond-shaped stud, or a roller or in fact any angular piece, and also a similar tool for polishing the bevelled edges of centre arbors or

280

Figure 181. Polishing tool for stub bevels, *etc.*

winding squares. In quite a number of watches the squares are retained purely and simply for ornamental reasons, and thus are highly finished.

Polishing the Hollows

There are various methods for polishing sinks or countersinks, or hollows as they are called. If large in size a tool is shaped to suit, or

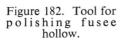
Figure 182. Tool for polishing fusee hollow.

HARDENED & TEMPERED
STEEL HOLDER OR CLAMP

a piece of plate steel shaped to suit is held in a tool and a backwards-and-forwards motion applied until the hollow is polished.

Shaping the Tool—Only by use can the tool be shaped to suit. The tool is first applied, and after finding where it is touching the hollow it is altered accordingly. In the case of small hollows an ordinary iron pin is held by the pointed end in a drill stock or in something equally suitable. The head of the pin is shaped to suit, and then the pin is revolved backwards and forwards rapidly, and moved round and round the hollow until it is perfectly polished.

Polishing Cup in Cannon Pinion—The hollow in the top of a cannon pinion is placed in one dead centre and the tip of the cannon is rested in the rounded nail. Diamantine is smeared on this end of the nail, then the cannon is revolved backwards and forwards and the nail moved with a circular motion until the hollow is brilliantly polished. The description of these operations sounds as though they are lengthy but they really occupy only a few minutes.

Brass and gold collets on 'scape pinions are all polished using tin polishers and diamantine. Large wheels, say for regulators or chronometer clocks, are often polished before mounting, especially if, as is often the case, the wheels are not riveted but screwed to the bosses or collets on the pinions.

Polishing Delicate Pieces

When delicate pieces like a chronometer detent are being polished one does not carry on in the usual way but uses guards to prevent the polisher slipping, or the delicate parts are buried out of reach to avoid any chance of damage. The detent is, of course, all finished before the spring section is thinned to its final size.

Polishing Chronometer Detent

The body, foot, shoulders and sides of the foot are all polished in swing tools, and the bevelled edges can all be carried out in the same manner. When polishing parts of the detent it is often necessary to fix the detent with shellac instead of gripping it.

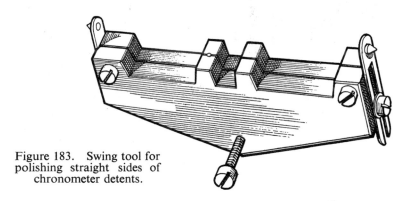

Figure 183. Swing tool for polishing straight sides of chronometer detents.

The method used for polishing a detent depends a lot on its type and size; the sides of the foot can be polished in either a swing tool or in a tool used for polishing screw-heads, with a pair of jaws screwed to the tool to hold the foot itself. Likewise the visible part of the flat section of the foot can be polished on a piece of willow wood using a zinc polisher underhand.

Polishing the Horn

The horn is polished by resting it on willow wood using a zinc or bell-metal polisher, whilst the deep bevel at the back of a marine chronometer detent foot can be polished in a tool or by resting it on willow wood. It will be seen that quite a lot depends on the individual worker.

Polishing with a Lap

If one has a lathe and a slide rest or a cross slide, polishing can be made easy. Laps can be made of ivory, tin or zinc, and they can

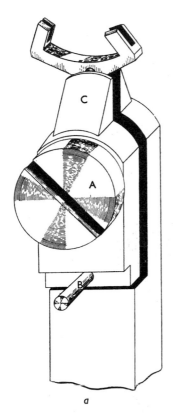

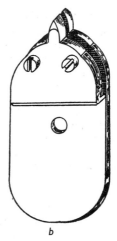

Figure 184. *a* Tool for holding pallets to grind and polish jewel stones. This can be used as a holder to fix stones. A = clamping screw; B = screw to hold jaws parallel and prevent moving; C = holding jaws which can be shaped to suit requirements. *b* Frog tool; this can be used to hold anything one wishes to polish on the revolving lap.

be smeared with diamantine or diamond powder according to requirements. A lap made of copper is charged with coarser diamond powder (it must be noted that this is not smeared on) and acts as a smooth grindstone. This can be used for steel or jewel.

Types of Lap Used—The laps are circular discs suitably shaped for the job in hand. They can be made to fit one particular arbor, or each can have its own arbor, but they must run flat and true when in the lathe. It is as well to have the arbors fitting one particular collet, so that as the change is made from one lap to another there is the minimum amount of disturbance to the set up.

Speed of the Lap—The speed at which the lap turns, or the number of revolutions per minute, depends upon the material being lapped.

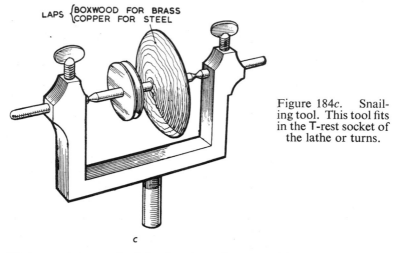

Figure 184c. Snailing tool. This tool fits in the T-rest socket of the lathe or turns.

High speed is required for jewels such as sapphire or ruby, but a lower speed is used for steel or softer stones.

Diamond Powder

At one time it was necessary to purchase diamond powder and to wash it oneself, and whereas it would have taken about 12 hours to wash a supply of powder in order to obtain the finest polishing grade, it can now be purchased ready for use in the required grade : therefore if one wants to polish steel by lapping it is not now uneconomical to use diamond powder ; it does in fact save cleaning, and thus saves time.

Presenting the Work to the Lap—The whole secret of lapping is the presentation, or the means of presentation, of the work to the lap. To be sure of accuracy one must have tools, which can be set to suit requirements and which once set will stay put. There is, however, a lot of scope, especially when polishing odd-shaped pieces. After a certain amount of experience or practice a piece can be polished on the lap and the standard of the polishing can be judged entirely by the eye.

Reflection as an Aid to the Operator—The lap has one advantage, and that is reflection, which can be used if one wishes to make the end of a piece dead square ; if the reflection of the piece and the piece itself form a straight line to each other they are absolutely square to each other. Whatever error is present will be very much amplified, and the slightest error will cause the reflection and the piece to be at angle

284

to each other. Of course, the lap must be oily or wet, otherwise there will be no reflection.

The Skive

When pallet stones are being made it is wasteful to grind one stone to the required thickness, so a double lap, or what is called a skive, is used. This consists of two thin laps of copper or tin fitted on to one arbor and spaced the required thickness apart. The stone is fixed to the tool by shellac.

The skive is charged with coarser diamond powder, *i.e.* the powder is rolled into the laps so that they remain permanently charged. The lap and the jewel are kept in water whilst they are in action.

Cutting the Stones—As the lap revolves it cuts two channels into the stone so that besides the piece in the centre between the two laps there are also two outside pieces of stone. The centre piece of stone, which is of the required thickness, is again cut up to the necessary dimensions; thus the stones can be cut to the required thickness with a minimum waste of material and time.

Altering and Making Pallet Stones—It only remains to polish the side to the finished dimensions, form the impulse angles and finally to cut to length. The impulse angles can be altered if required by fixing them with shellac on a brass tool set to the correct angle and polishing on the lap, knowing that when finished the face will be flat and square and as it is wanted.

Mixing Diamond Polishing Powder

When polishing, diamond powder is mixed with a suitable oil such as one uses for mixing diamantine. Only a smear of this is wanted on the lap, but, unlike a lap that is charged, the diamond polishing powder must be renewed each time that it is used, and it must also be kept scrupulously clean.

Adjusting the Slide Rest

The cross slide of the lathe is provided with a flat plate and is adjusted to be just lower than the centre of the lap so that anything held in a tool will be on the centre line of the lap. The plate is also provided with an upright round post or rest. In order to alter the angle of the tool which is resting against this post the slide is moved nearer to or farther from the lap as required; if it is pushed towards the lap the side nearest to the operator, *i.e.* the front, is reduced. Adjustable banking is fixed on the tool or on the plate to prevent the tool getting too close to the lap.

Using the back of the lap—Sometimes, as in the case of dead-beat clock pallets, the back of the lap is used, and as such is shaped accordingly. To put on paper the number of ways in which a lap may be useful is almost impossible, but experience of lapping will itself give the answer (see dead-beat escapements).

Lapping Using a Depth Tool

There is another type of lapping which is done with a depth tool. A polishing lap is put in one side and the work is put in the other

BELL METAL LAP FOR
POLISHING LARGE
SHOULDERS AND
ARBORS

Figure 185. Bell metal lap.

side. Two bows are required, one on the lap and the other on the work so that they revolve in opposite directions. A large barrel arbor shoulder and similar shoulders can be highly polished in this way, bell-metal laps being used for steel and tin laps for brass and gold. Diamantine used in a wettish state is the polishing medium.

Polishing Wheel Teeth

Polishing 'scape wheel teeth will not be a common practice these days, but a few hints may prove helpful should one for some reason find it imperative to carry out this operation, although it cannot, of course, be done without the necessary tools.

As 'scape wheel teeth are very delicate at the best of times, special precautions have to be taken to prevent a mishap. Most tools used for polishing wheel teeth are swing tools, or in other words tools which find their own level and stay put. It may be asked why the teeth should be polished at all, but there are plenty of reasons why, apart from beauty, one reason being that the teeth can be cleared of burrs and left thinner from a polisher than direct from a cutter, and another is that the surface is harder and resists wear.

Polishing Steel Ratchet-tooth 'Scape Wheels

Ratchet-tooth 'scape wheel teeth are not polished afterwards if they are made of brass, but are left straight from the cutting, which is done with a polished cutter, but if the teeth are of steel they are polished in a similar tool to that which is used for chronometer 'scape wheel teeth.

Although only the points of the teeth of a ratchet-tooth wheel or chronometer 'scape wheel come into action, the polishing of the teeth acts as a preservative, as well as making the wheels appear a workman-like job.

Polishing the Teeth of a Chronometer 'Scape Wheel

The wheel is held on a post or on a tapering screw either by a collar placed over it or by the screw direct to the central hole. On the

FRONT   REAR

Figure 186. Front and rear views of tool for polishing 'scape wheel teeth, showing guard and positioning click and adjustment for height.

tool is an ivory click-like piece. The height of the wheel can be changed because the post or screw is on a slide and the whole can be adjusted, thus the wheel is put in place with any one tooth resting on the click.

Adjusting the Swing Tool—The height of the wheel is adjusted until the face of the tooth which is to be polished is parallel to the tool

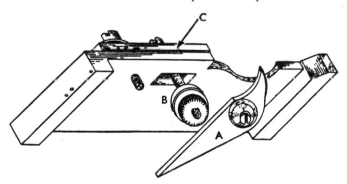

Figure 187. Tool for polishing the locking teeth of duplex 'scape wheels. It is a swing tool held between dead centres. A = ivory click to position tooth; B = holding nut for wheel; C = slide for varying sized wheels.

edge. The centres at the end of the tool, which are also adjustable, are then adjusted until the face of the tooth is central with the centres. An adjustable guard is also part of the tool, and this is positioned close to the teeth to prevent the polisher slipping and damaging them.

The tooth is now polished, and if all the adjustments have been correctly made the tooth will finish up dead flat or square, and of the correct shape. Once the tool has been set, each tooth can be polished in turn by simply moving the wheel one tooth and banking the appropriate tooth on the ivory click; each tooth will therefore take up the identical position of its predecessor.

A Polisher for the Teeth

A special polisher shaped to the teeth is used when a chronometer wheel is being polished, but for other wheels a flat polisher is used, and if the wheel is of brass the polisher is tin and the medium diamantine. The wheel teeth can be burnished by using an appropriate shape of burnisher, but polishing is often easier.

A Polishing Tool Similar to a Filing Jig

Another type of tool is something like a template or filing jig, and consists of two hard steel plates cut to the shape of the required

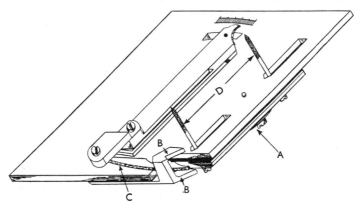

Figure 188. Polishing tool which can be used for wheels and other pieces. A = slide to move wheels or other pieces nearer or away from polisher; B = 2 shaped jaws to ensure flatness; C = adjustable click for positioning wheels; D = threaded studs to take thumb nuts for holding purposes.

tooth. The tooth is positioned in the same way as in the previous tool with a post or screw acting as the holder, and again all is adjustable. In this case the wheel is held for the teeth to coincide with the jaws and the click is adjustable as well as the jaws. Again, one setting will do for all the teeth.

The tool is held in the hand with the polisher resting on the parallel jaws which are the limit that the tooth can be reduced. Awkward-shaped teeth can be constructed or altered after use with the aid of this same tool, and provided that they are accur-

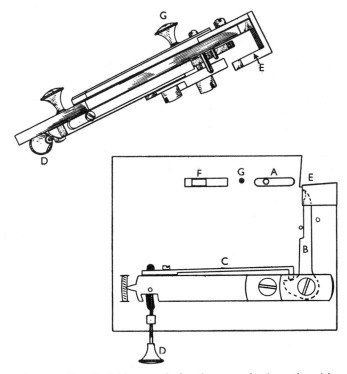

Figure 189. Polishing tool for 'scape wheel teeth with multiple-shaped jaws. A = stud on which wheels are fixed; B = click-shaped piece to place tooth in correct position for polishing; C = spring controlling B but allowing movement when changing the teeth; D = thumb nut to adjust B for height; E = shaped jaws to suit type of wheel; F = slide to move wheel horizontally to enable different size wheels to be polished; G = fixing thumb nut for slide F.

ately divided will remain accurate during shaping or finishing. The parallel jaws, however, have first to be made to suit, and the wheel must, of course, be cut approximately to the required shape.

Although one cannot hope to deal with every type of polishing, it will be possible to tackle most operations by the various methods which have been described, both for old watches and for good modern watches. Although the modern watches have reached the all but completely interchangeable stage, the day has not yet arrived when all material for their repair can be obtained from a box

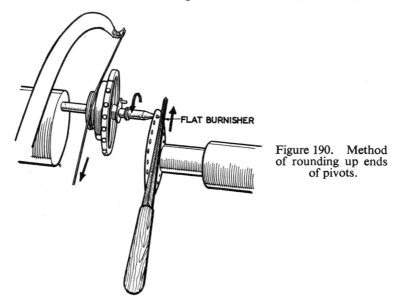

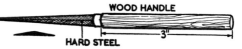

Figure 190. Method of rounding up ends of pivots.

Figure 191. Burnisher for rounding up or repairing the ends of pivots.

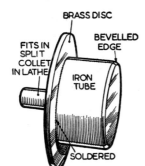

Figure 192. Lap for polishing bevel on the circle of an index. Bevelled edge is smeared with diamantine.

already finished, and quite a number of people retain a good-class machine or mass-produced watch and will have it repaired. The cheap variety of machine-made watch need not be worried about.

INDEX